END TIMES

The Death of the Fourth Estate

Alexander Cockburn
Jeffrey St. Clair

CounterPunch

END TIMES

The Death of the Fourth Estate

Alexander Cockburn
Jeffrey St. Clair

CounterPunch
PETROLIA

AK PRESS

First published by
CounterPunch and AK Press 2007
© *CounterPunch* 2007
All rights reserved

CounterPunch
PO Box 228 Petrolia, California, 95558

AK Press
674A 23rd St, Oakland, California 94612-1163

ISBN 978-1-904859376

A catalog record for this book is available from the Library of Congress
Library of Congress Control Number: 2006924195

Typeset in *Tyfa*, designed by František Štorm for The Storm Type Foundry,
and *Stainless*, Designed by Cyrus Highsmith for The Font Bureau, Inc. Cover
and Title Page also use East Bloc Closed designed by Grant Hutchinson for
Image Club.

Printed and bound in Canada.

Index by Jeffrey St. Clair.
Editing by Alevtina Rea.
Cover Design by Tiffany Wardle.
Design and typography by Tiffany Wardle.

Contents

Part 3

White on Black in Black and White

Part 4

The Dogs of War

Part 5

Faking It: Why Does the Press
Mostly Believe Prosecutors?

Part 6

CounterPunch's Side of the Story

Introduction

THESE DAYS HALF THE TEENAGERS ALIVE IN AMERICA WILL apparently live to be 100 (presumably working till they drop to pay for the other half, jobless and dying from diabetes). It seems a dubious statistic. Since 98 per cent of all teenagers spend 70 per cent of their waking hours on the Internet, are their bodies tuned for the long-distance haul? Around New Year, 2005, three very old leftists passed on: Sanora Babb died on December 31, aged 98. Harry Magdoff died on New Year's Day, at 92. Frank Wilkinson died a day later, at 91. Our line has always been that to get really old it pays to have been a Commie or at least a fellow traveler. In younger years they tended to walk a lot, selling the party paper, handing out leaflets. In the 1950s, a lot of them redeployed into the Audubon Society and walked even more. Being radical spirits, their minds kept on working and their tongues kept on wagging.

That was the old world of a mass, semi-organized left in America: of pamphlets and mimeographed leaflets; of last minute rushes to the print shop; of inky proofs and galleys; all now as distant as a hot-metal linotype machine. Back in the dawn of the nuclear disarmament movement in the Fifties and Sixties, it was thought to be a good day's work if you stood outside a U.S. air base handing out leaflets and got maybe 50 service people to take one, as they drove in and out. These days, at the end of each month here, at *CounterPunch*, we can look at the daily breakdown of our 3 million or so hits, 300,000 page views and 100,000 unique visitors and see that we've had some 15,000 regular readers on U.S. military bases around the world.

For the time being, the old David vs. Goliath struggle of the left pamphleteers battling the vast print combines of the news barons has equaled up. On a laptop's twelve-inch screen we stand as high as Punch Sulzberger, or Rupert Murdoch, who shelled out $580 million for MySpace.com in 2006 when he realized the world had changed. So, are the old newspaper empires dying or dead? Indeed they are. Twenty years ago the *Los Angeles Times* was a mighty power. The owners of the Knight Ridder chain complacently counted on a 20 per cent-plus rate of return on their properties. Today the *L.A. Times* totters from one cost-cut and forced employee retirement to the next, and David Geffen ponders whether to plunk down two or three billion for it. Knight Ridder's papers of high reputation go on the auction block. Will the broadsheets and tabloids vanish? Not in the foreseeable future, any more than trains disappeared at the end of the railway age. A mature industry will yield income and attract investors interested in money or power long after its glory days are over. But it's a world in decline, and a propaganda system in decline.

In the mid-1970s the great news empires—the ones by dint of their dominance in Washington, D.C., and New York setting the pace for national coverage—were at the zenith of their power. It's the moment at which we open our first section of the book, when the elites felt it is necessary to try to restore order after the disorder consequent upon a lost war, an evicted president, and discredited corporate leadership. The publishers and their enforcers duly restored order, and shaped the cowed press, led by the *New York Times* (the topic of our second section) as well as the *Washington Post*, that has played the right's tunes ever since. Any disturbing challenge to this compliance is malevolently denounced, never more venomously or disingenuously than in the onslaughts on Gary Webb, dealt with in our third section. The state proposes and the press clicks its heels—in the first crucial hours, days or months, as the pieces on the Iraq war and the Patriot Act in our fourth section attest, as do those in the fifth section on the press and the prosecutorial state.

Afterthoughts and confessions of error come much later, if at all. See our piece on the "gun that finally smoked" in section 6.

The left is so used to being underdogged that it is often incapable of greeting good fortune when it knocks on the door. Our final, sixth section is called "*CounterPunch*'s Side of the Story". Thirty years ago, many of these pieces, challenging the official nonsense peddled in the mass-market press, would have been mostly doomed to small-circulation magazines, or 30-second *précis* on Pacifica radio. Thirty years ago, to find out what was happening in Gaza, you would have to have had a decent shortwave radio, a fax machine, or access to those great newsstands in Times Square and North Hollywood that carried the world's press. Not any more. We can get a news story from a CounterPuncher in Gaza or Ramallah or Oaxaca or Vidharba and have it out to a world audience in a matter of hours.

Yes, of course the state doesn't like the loosening of control; of course it could start policing the Net more heavily and subsequently take sites down more often. Costs of access could shoot up. All of these could happen and, absent resistance, may well happen. But right now, as so often amid "end times," there are new opportunities to be explored and turned to the advantage of radicals.

AC/JSC
CounterPunch Editors
December 31, 2006

Part 1

Whipping the Press Back Into Line

When Tedium was Totalizing: The Political Function of PBS

Alexander Cockburn

EARS AGO, WHEN THE NIGHTLY PROGRAM WAS MANDATORY viewing in every liberal home from Montauk to Santa Monica, I wrote a parody of the *McNeil-Lehrer Report*, as it was then called before McNeil hauled down his colors and moved on. The piece ran in *Harpers*, and though it prompted a good deal of laughter, there were a surprising number of letters from outraged PBS viewers, wailing about my lack of respect. It was as though I had publicly kicked a respected greybeard.

The other night, glancing at the *Lehrer News Hour*, I shook my head yet again at the precision of my gibes. This particular show was about the efforts of Ken Tomlinson, formerly of *Readers' Digest* and Voice of America, to purge PBS of all liberal taint. From the right there was a nutcase from the *American Spectator* called George Neumayr, and from the left…. But of course there was no one from the left. There never is. There was a "moderate" from the center right called Bill Reed.

> JEFFREY BROWN (moderator): Welcome to both of you. Mr. Neumayr, do you see a liberal bias in public broadcasting?
>
> GEORGE NEUMAYR: I do. I see a pervasive bias. I applaud Ken Tomlinson for making an attempt to correct it.
>
> JEFFREY BROWN: Mr. Reed, do you see a liberal bias?
>
> BILL REED: I think this is really nonsense. You know, for over 30 years, William F. Buckley was on public television,

and I carried him proudly in the stations that I've managed in my career. He's a fine journalist, and so is Bill Moyers.

JEFFREY BROWN: So, Mr. Reed, what do you believe is causing Mr. Tomlinson to raise these questions?

BILL REED: You know, I don't know. I don't know.

Feel yourself dozing off?

Now, there were important historical reasons for the rise of this narcotic show. So, without further ado, I give my parody, as it appeared nearly 25 years ago, in August 1982, under the title, "The Tedium Twins."

ROBERT MACNEIL (voice over): A Galilean preacher claims he is the Redeemer and says the poor are blessed. Should he be crucified?

(Titles)

MACNEIL: Good evening. The Roman procurator in Jerusalem is trying to decide whether a man regarded by many as a saint should be put to death. Pontius Pilate is being urged by civil libertarians to intervene in what is seen here in Rome as being basically a local dispute. Tonight, the crucifixion debate. Jim?

JIM LEHRER: Robin, the provinces of Judaea and Galilee have always been trouble spots, and this year is no exception. The problem is part religious, part political, and in many ways a mixture of both. The Jews believe in one god. Discontent in the province has been growing, with many local businessmen complaining about the tax burden. Terrorism, particularly in Galilee, has been on the increase. In recent months, a carpenter's son from the town of Nazareth has been attracting a large following with novel doctrines and faith healing. He recently entered Jerusalem amid popular acclaim, but influential Jewish leaders fear his power. Here in Alexandria the situation is seen as dangerous. Robin?

MACNEIL: Recently in Jerusalem on a fact-finding mission for the Emperor's Emergency Task Force on Provincial Disorders was Quintilius Maximus. Mr. Maximus, how do you see the situation?

MAXIMUS: Robin, I had occasion to hear one of this preacher's sermons a few months ago and talk with his aides. There is no doubt in my mind that he is a threat to peace and should be crucified.

MACNEIL: Pontius Pilate should wash his hands of the problem?

MAXIMUS: Absolutely.

MACNEIL: I see. Thank you. Jim?

LEHRER: Now for a view from Mr. Simon, otherwise known as Peter. He is a supporter of Christ and has been standing by in a Jerusalem studio. Robin?

MACNEIL: Mr. Simon Peter, why do you support Christ?

SIMON PETER: He is the Son of God and presages the Second Coming. If I may, I would like to read some relevant passages from the prophet Isaiah.

MACNEIL: Thank you, but I'm afraid we'll have to break in there. We've run out of time. Goodnight, Jim.

LEHRER: Good night, Robin.

MACNEIL: Sleep well, Jim.

LEHRER: I hope you sleep well, too, Robin.

MACNEIL: I think I will. Well, good night again, Jim.

LEHRER: Goodnight, Robin.

MACNEIL: We'll be back again tomorrow night. I'm Robert MacNeil. Good night.

Admirers of the *MacNeil/Lehrer Report*—and there are many of them—often talk about it in terms normally reserved for unpalatable but nutritious breakfast foods: unalluring, perhaps, to the frivolous news consumer, but packed full of fiber. It is commended as the sort of news analysis a serious citizen, duly weighing the pros and cons of world history, would wish to masticate before a thoughtful browse through the *Federalist Papers*, a chat with spouse about civic duties incumbent on them on the morrow, and final, blameless repose. The promotional material for the "Report" has a tone of reverence of the sort usually employed by people reading guidebooks to each other in a French cathedral: "The week-nightly newscast's unique mix of information, expert opinion, and debate has foreshadowed an industry trend toward longer and more detailed coverage, while at the same time helping to reveal a growing public appetite for informational television. Nearly 4.5 million viewers watch the *MacNeil/Lehrer Report* each night during the prime viewing season..."

"A program with meat on its bones," said the Association for Continuing Higher Education, in presenting its 1981 Leadership Award "The *MacNeil/Lehrer Report* goes beyond the commercial networks' rushed recital of news to bring us in-depth coverage of single issues.... There is a concern for ideas rather than video images and they accord us the unusual media compliment of not telling us what to think, but allowing us to draw our own conclusions after we weigh conflicting views." And the handout concludes in triumph with some findings from a 1980 Roper poll: "Three quarters of those polled said they had discovered pros and cons on issues on which they had not had opinions beforehand."

ROBERT MACNEIL (voice over): Should one man own another?

(Titles)

MACNEIL: Good evening. The problem is as old as man himself. Do property rights extend to the absolute ownership of one man by another? Tonight, the slavery problem. Jim?

LEHRER: Robin, advocates of the continuing system of slavery argue that the practice has brought unparalleled benefits to the economy. They fear that new regulations being urged by reformers would undercut America's economic effectiveness abroad. Reformers, on the other hand, call for legally binding standards and even for a phased reduction in the slave force to something like 75 per cent of its present size. Charlayne Hunter-Gault is in Charleston. Charlayne?

HUNTER-GAULT: Robin and Jim, I have here in Charleston, Mr. Ginn, head of the Cottongrowers Association. Robin?

MACNEIL: Mr. Ginn, what are the arguments for unregulated slavery?

GINN: Robin, our economic data show that attempts at regulation of working hours, slave quarters, and so forth would reduce productivity and indeed would be widely resented by the slaves themselves.

MACNEIL: You mean, the slaves would not like new regulations? They would resent them?

GINN: Exactly. Any curbing of the slave trade would offer the Tsar dangerous political opportunities in western Africa, and menace the strategic slave-ship routes.

LEHRER: Thank you, Mr. Ginn. Robin?

MACNEIL: Thank you, Mr. Ginn and Jim. The secretary of the Committee for Regulatory Reform in Slavery is Eric

Halfmeasure. Mr. Halfmeasure, give us the other side of the story.

HALFMEASURE: Robin, I would like to make one thing perfectly clear. We are wholeheartedly in favor of slavery. We just see abuses that diminish productivity and reduce incentives for free men and women to compete in the marketplace. Lynching, tarring and feathering, rape, lack of holidays, and that sort of thing. One recent study suggests that regulation could raise productivity by 15 per cent.

MACNEIL: I see. Thank you, Mr. Halfmeasure. Mr. Ginn?

GINN: Our studies show the opposite.

MACNEIL: Jim?

LEHRER: Charlayne?

HUNTER-GAULT: A few critics of slavery argue that it should be abolished outright. One of them is Mr. Garrison. Mr. Garrison, why abolish slavery?

GARRISON: It is immoral for one man...

MACNEIL: Mr. Garrison, we're running out of time, I'm afraid. Let me very quickly get some other points of view. Mr. Ginn, you think slavery is good?

GINN: Yes.

MACNEIL: And you, Mr. Halfmeasure, think it should be regulated?

HALFMEASURE: Yes.

MACNEIL: Well, I've got you to disagree, haven't I? (Laughter) That's all we've got time for tonight. Goodnight, Jim.

LEHRER: Good night, Robin.

MACNEIL: Did you sleep well last night?

LEHRER: I did, thank you.

MACNEIL: That's good. So did I. We'll be back again tomorrow night. I'm Robert MacNeil. Good night.

The *MacNeil/Lehrer Report* started in October 1975, in the aftermath of Watergate. It was a show dedicated to the proposition that there are two sides to every question, a valuable corrective in a period when the American people had finally decided that there were absolutely and definitely not two sides to every question. Nixon was a crook who had rightly been driven from office; corporations were often headed by crooks who carried hot money around in suitcases; federal officials were crooks who broke the law on the say-so of the president.

It was a dangerous moment. A citizenry suddenly imbued with the notion that there is not only a thesis and antithesis, but also a synthesis, is a citizenry capable of all manner of harm to the harmonious motions of the status quo. Thus came the *MacNeil/Lehrer Report*, sponsored by public-television funds and by the most powerful corporate forces in America, in the form of Exxon, AT&T, the Bell System, and other upstanding bodies. Back to Sunday school went the excited viewers, to be instructed that reality, as conveyed to them by television, is not an exciting affair of crooked businessmen and lying politicians, but a serious continuum in which parties may disagree but in which all involved are struggling manfully and disinterestedly for the public weal.

The narcotizing, humorless properties of the *MacNeil/Lehrer Report*, familiar to those who have felt fatigue creep over them at 7:40 p.m. Eastern time, are crucial to the show. Tedium is of the essence, since the all-but-conscious design of the program is to project vacuous dithering ("And now, for another view of Hitler...") into the mind of the viewers, until they are properly convinced that there is not one answer to "the problem," but two or even three, and that since two answers are no better than none, they might as well not bother with the problem at all.

The techniques employed by the show enhance this distancing and anesthetizing. The recipe is unvarying. MacNeil and Lehrer exchange modest gobbets of information with each other about the topic under discussion. Then, with MacNeil crouching—rather like Kermit the Frog in old age—down to the left and peering up, a huge face appears on the screen and discussion is under way. The slightest discommoding exchange, some intemperate observation on the part of the interviewee, causes MacNeil to bat the ball hastily down to Washington, where Lehrer sedately sits with his interviewee.

By fits and starts, with Jim batting back to Robin and Robin batting across to Charlayne, the program lurches along. The antagonists are rarely permitted to joust with one another and ideally are sequestered on their large screens. Sometimes, near the end of the show, the camera will reveal that these supposed antagonists are in fact sitting chummily, shoulder to shoulder, around the same table as Lehrer, thus indicating to the viewer that, while opinions may differ, all are united in general decency of purpose. Toward the very end, MacNeil's true role becomes increasingly exposed as he desperately tries to suppress debate and substantive argument, with volley after volley of "We're nearly out of time," "Congressman, in ten seconds could you" and the final, relieved, "That's all for tonight."

It's even important that MacNeil and Lehrer say good night to each other so politely every evening. In that final, sedate nocturnal exchange everything is finally resolved, even though nothing has been resolved. We can all go to bed now.

And so to bed we go. The pretense is that viewers, duly presented with both sides of the case, will spend the next segment of the evening weighing the pro against the con and coming up with the answer. It is, in fact, enormously difficult to recall anything that anyone has ever said on a *MacNeil/Lehrer Report*, because the point has been to demonstrate that since everything can be contradicted, nothing is worth remembering. The show praised above all others for content derives its attention entirely from form: the unvarying illustration that if one man can be found to argue that cannibalism is bad, another can be found to argue that it is not.

Actually, this is an overstatement. *MacNeil/Lehrer Report* hates such violent extremes, and, by careful selection of the show's participants, the show tries to make sure that the viewer will not be perturbed by any views overly critical of the political and business establishment.

> ROBERT MACNEIL (voice over): Should one man eat another?
>
> (Titles)
>
> MACNEIL: Good evening. Reports from the Donner Pass indicate that survivors fed upon their companions. Tonight, should cannibalism be regulated? Jim?
>
> LEHRER: Robin, the debate pits two diametrically opposed sides against each other: the Human Meat-eaters Association, who favor a free market in human flesh, and their regulatory opponents in Congress and the consumer movement. Robin?
>
> MACNEIL: Mr. Tooth, why eat human flesh?
>
> TOOTH: Robin, it is full of protein and delicious too. Without human meat, our pioneers would be unable to explore the West properly. This would present an inviting opportunity to the French, who menace our pioneer routes from the north.
>
> MACNEIL: Thank you. Jim?
>
> LEHRER: Now for another view of cannibalism. Bertram Brussell-Sprout is leading the fight to control the eating

of animal fats and meats. Mr. Sprout, would you include human flesh in this proposed regulation?

SPROUT: Most certainly, Jim. Our studies show that some human flesh available for sale to the public is maggot-ridden, improperly cut, and often incorrectly graded. We think the public should be protected from such abuses.

MACNEIL: Some say it is wrong to eat human flesh at all. Mr. Prodnose, give us this point of view.

PRODNOSE: Robin, eating people is wrong. We say...

MACNEIL: I'm afraid we're out of time. Good night, Jim, etc., etc.

Trudging back through the "MacNeil/Lehrer" scripts, the hardy reader will soon observe how extraordinarily narrow is the range of opinion canvassed by a show dedicated to dispassionate examination of the issues of the day. The favored blend is usually a couple of congressmen or senators, barking at each other from either side of the garden fence, corporate chieftains, government executives, ranking lobbyists, and the odd foreign statesman. The mix is ludicrously respectable, almost always heavily establishment in tone. Official spokesmen of trade and interest groups are preferred over people who only have something interesting to say.

This constriction of viewpoint is particularly conspicuous in the case of energy, an issue dear to the *MacNeil/Lehrer Report*. "Economics of Nuclear Power," for example, was screened on November 25, 1980, and purported to examine why a large number of nuclear utilities were teetering on the edge of bankruptcy. Mustered to ponder the issue we had the following rich and varied banquet: the president of the Virginia Electric and Power Company; the vice president (for nuclear operations) of Commonwealth Edison of Chicago; a vice president (responsible for scrutinizing utility investments) at Paine Webber; and the president of the Atomic Industrial Forum. The viewers of *MacNeil/Lehrer Report* did not, you may correctly surmise, hear much critical opinion about nuclear power on that particular evening.

On May 1, 1981, the "Report" examined "the problems and prospects of getting even more oil out of our ground." Participants in the discussion about oil glut included some independent oil drillers, and "experts" from Merrill Lynch, Phillips Petroleum Company, and the Rand Corporation.

At least on May 1 the viewers had more than one person saying the same thing ("regulation is bad"). On March 27, they were invited to consider the plans of the Reagan administration for a rebuilt Navy. The inquiring citizen was offered a trip around the battleship Iowa in the company of MacNeil, and an extremely meek interview, conducted by both MacNeil and Lehrer, of the Secretary of the Navy John Lehman. No dissenting views were allowed to intrude, beyond the deferential inquiries of MacNeil and Lehrer, both of whom, it should be said, are very bad interviewers, usually ignorant and always timid. By contrast, Ted Koppel of ABC's *Nightline* is a veritable tiger in interrogatory technique.

The spectrum of opinion thus offered is one that ranges from the corporate right to cautious center-liberal. One should not be misled, by the theatrical diversity of views deployed on the program, into thinking that a genuinely wide spectrum of opinion is permitted. Moldering piles of *MacNeil/Lehrer Report* transcripts before me on my desk attest to the fact.

The show would be nothing without Robert ("Robin") MacNeil. Canadian, with a layer of high seriousness so thick it sticks to the screen, MacNeil anchors the show to tedium and yanks at the hawser every time the craft shows any sign of floating off into uncharted waters. He seems to have learned—on the evidence of his recent memoir, *The Right Place at the Right Time*—the elements of his deadly craft in London, watching the BBC and writing for Reuters.

MacNeil is a man so self-righteously boring that he apparently had no qualms in setting down the truth about his disgraceful conduct in Dallas on November 22, 1963. MacNeil was there covering Kennedy's visit for NBC. The shots rang out, and he sprinted to the nearest telephone he could find. It so happens that he dashed, without knowing its significance, into the Texas Book Depository: "As I ran up the steps and through the door, a young man in shirt sleeves was coming out. In great agitation I asked him where there was a phone. He pointed inside to an open space where another man was talking on a phone situated next to a pillar and said, 'Better ask him.' I ran inside...." Later, MacNeil writes, "I heard on television that a young man called Oswald, arrested for the shooting, worked at the Texas Book Depository and had left by the front door immediately afterward. Isn't that strange, I told myself. He must have been leaving just about the time I was running in..."

Later still, William Manchester demonstrated that there was a 95 per cent certainty that MacNeil had met Oswald. Any reporter, any human, with anything other than treacle in his veins, would naturally make much of the coincidence and divert children, acquaintances, and indeed a wider public, with interesting accounts of Oswald's demeanor at this significant moment. Not MacNeil. With Pecksniffian virtuousness, he insists that the encounter was merely "possible," and that "it is titillating, but it doesn't matter very much." Such is the aversion to storytelling, the sodden addiction to the mundane, that produced *MacNeil/Lehrer*. Like an Exocet missile, MacNeil can spot a cliché, a patch of ennui, and home in on it with dreadful speed. Witness his proclamation of political belief:

> Instinctively, I find it more satisfying to belong with those people in all countries who put their trust in Man's best quality, his rational intellect and its ability to recognize and solve problems. It is distressing that the recent course of American politics has caused that trust to be ridiculed or dismissed as some sort of soft-headedness, inappropriate to a virile nation confronting

the dangerous world. It will be unfortunate if being a "liberal" remains an embarrassment, if young Americans should begin to believe that conservatives are the only realists. Each has its absurd extreme: liberalism tending to inspire foolish altruism and unwarranted optimism; conservatism leading to unbridled selfishness and paranoia. Taken in moderation, I prefer the liberal impulse: it is the impulse behind the great forces that have advanced mankind, like Christianity. I find it hard to believe that Jesus Christ was a political conservative, whatever views are espoused in his name today.

For all my instinctive liberalism, my experience of politics in many countries has not left me wedded to any particular political parties. Rather, I have found myself politically dining à la carte, on particular issues.

This is the mindset behind *MacNeil/Lehrer.* "I have my own instinctive aversion to being snowed," he writes at another point. "The more I hear everyone telling me that some public person is wonderful, the more I ask myself, Can he really be all that wonderful? Conversely [for MacNeil there is always a 'conversely' poking its head round the door], I never believe anyone can be quite as consistently terrible as his reputation."

Hitler? Attila the Hun? Pol Pot? Nixon? John D. Rockefeller? I'm afraid that's all we have time for tonight. We've run out of time. Good night.

1982

The Fall of the Washington Post

Ken Silverstein

N THE LATE FALL OF 1974 KATHARINE GRAHAM, BOSS OF THE Washington Post Company, rose to address the annual meeting of the Magazine Publishers' Association. It was a year of supreme triumph for the *Post*. After the long siege of Watergate, Richard Nixon had tumbled on August 7. The *Post*'s reporters, Bob Woodward and Carl Bernstein, were credited with bringing him down. After two years of abuse by the Nixon administration the *Post* was vindicated. Journalists across the country were casting themselves as "investigative reporters," eager to do battle with vested power, the high and the mighty.

Mrs. Graham chose this exhilarated moment to strike a note of prudence. "The press these days," she sternly told the audience, "should...be rather careful about its role. We may have acquired some tendencies about over-involvement that we had better overcome. We had better not yield to the temptation to go on refighting the next war and see conspiracy and cover-up where they do not exist."

The chairman of the Washington Post Co. was not alone among her fellow proprietors in the publishing industry in feeling that the time had come to cry halt. Watergate had encouraged the press corps to advance recklessly across traditional boundaries and probe hitherto sacrosanct aspects of the social, political and, above all, corporate landscape. Vested power, in whose ranks stands Katharine Graham, always fears moments of populist opportunity. The story of the New Deal—as the late Walter Karp showed in a brilliant book, *Indispensable Enemies*—is in large part that of Franklin Roosevelt desperately trying to contain the popular anger threatening to overwhelm the corrupt financial institutions that presided over the onset of the Great Depression. He finally distracted this anger and the militant Democratic majority of 1937 from constructive reform with his self-consciously preposterous court-packing scheme.

Thus also was it in late 1974. The people had seen institutions corrupted, politicians plying corporate leaders for the beneficence of a bribe. They were eager for change. It was the profound, urgent task of vested power to contain that urge and to deflect it.

Graham called for a return to basics. Journalists, she said, should stop trying to be sleuths, and instead master "the ability to comprehend a number of extremely arcane fields, ranging from macroeconomics to geology to antitrust. It is no mean trick to become conversant in a specialty which experts spend their whole lives mastering—especially if practitioners devote much energy to keeping their field obscure."

The press had always been terrified of accusations that it was unreasonably hounding Nixon. Even before Nixon finished himself off with the June 23 tape, *Time* had suggested that the media was overstepping its bounds, asking in a mid-summer 1974 cover story, "Has the press gone too far?" Then the "smoking gun" tape surfaced and Nixon retired to San Clemente forthwith.

Graham's demand that journalists behave with more deference towards the powerful was widely noted. It helped set the tone for the post-Watergate period. As one of her employees put it, "The feeling behind the talk was, 'We did this [Watergate], we removed the glue, so now what?' It called for a new definition of 'responsibility.'"

The early 1970s found a substantial section of America's corporate, political, and academic elites profoundly alarmed by the seeming collapse of normal controlling mechanisms and values. Vietnam externally, and Watergate internally, symbolized the crisis.

To business the press was the enemy, indecently reveling in corporate malfeasance during the Watergate affair, poisoned by the radicalism of the 1960s.

In 1974 and 1975, the Conference Board arranged a series of meetings of top corporate officials who brooded jointly about the future for business. The assembled CEOs believed that it was crucial to win over the press. Among the complaints: "Even though the press is a business, it doesn't reflect business values"; "Unless the press stops tearing down our system and begins to tell the public how it works, business leaders will not be permitted any future participation in the formation of social goals"; and, from the wife of one CEO, "It makes me sick to watch the evening news night after night and see my husband and the efforts of his industry maligned."

The idiom of the day was that of the press insurgent: Woodward & Bernstein overthrowing Nixon; Seymour Hersh evicting James Angleton from the CIA; Nader's investigators pillorying U.S. business.

Less than a decade later, Woodward was writing a book about John Belushi, and the journalists most honored by their peers included William Safire, Nixon's former speech writer, and George Will, who hosted the welcoming party for Ronald Reagan when he came to Washington, D.C. for his first term. In 1984, Dinesh D'Souza was writing (with the pomposity that only a young man with right-wing foundation dollars in his pocket can muster) in the Heritage Foundation's Policy Review that under the leadership of A.M. Rosenthal, the *New York Times*—which along with the *Post* had long been seen by conservatives as a tool of the Kremlin—was "reaffirming its greatness by retreating from the radicalism of the last two decades and once again taking up responsible journalism. It is the first liberal institution to identify the excesses of liberalism, mainly its flirtation with Communism, and to seek to correct them."

Today, the final vestiges of critical thought in the press have been all but extinguished, and mainstream journalists are as much a part of the ruling class as the political and business elite.

During Bill Clinton's first six months in office, he and his wife Hillary hosted a series of private dinner parties, "as a way to meet some of his new neighbors," explained Roxanne Roberts of the *Washington Post* when writing about these "private soirees for the elite." On her account, the Clintons' guests drank fine wines and feasted on pan-seared lamb. On one occasion, the women joined Hillary Clinton for a private screening of the film *Sleepless in Seattle* while male guests chatted with the president and watched a basketball game.

Heavily represented among the invitees—which included political leaders, business officials, and personal friends—were leading members of the Washington press corps: notorious Clinton brown-noser Sidney Blumenthal of the *New Yorker*, Rita Braver and Susan Spencer of CBS ("You have to be jaded not to admit that being at the White House is a pretty interesting experience"), Katharine Graham and three others from the *Post*, Dan Goodgame of *Time*, Evan Thomas of *Newsweek*, Jack Nelson of the *Los Angeles Times*, Charles Peters of the *Washington Monthly*, and R.W. Apple of the *New York Times*.

The latter, a swag-bellied gormandizer of international repute, was particularly moved by his evening at the White House. Apple shared Clinton's table for a dinner on June 3, 1993, the night that the president, with incomparable servility to right-wing bluster, withdrew Lani Guinier's nomination as his assistant attorney general. Two days later, Apple paid for his dinner with a front-page story about Clinton's "brutal, heartbreaking" decision to abandon Guinier, about the pain etched on his face as he arrived at the dinner when many guests were already "halfway through their beef Wellington and some...on their second glass of Jordan cabernet sauvignon".

Behind the media's violent swing was an expensive, carefully planned corporate campaign to recapture the culture. Panic among the elites in the mid-1970s was very high. This was the period when Samuel Huntington of Harvard University and Nelson Rockefeller's Trilateral Commission wrote of the need to curb the "excess of democracy" in the U.S.A., Japan and Western Europe. Comments at the Conference Board meetings indicate that CEOs believed a popular uprising could be imminent: "Can we still afford one man, one vote? We are trembling on the brink"; "We are terribly scared within this room. We are in serious trouble"; "One man, one vote has undermined the power of business in all capitalist countries since World War II."

Corporate executives also felt pressured by labor unions, then still relatively powerful, and by the rising expectations of the citizenry. "We have been hoist with our own petard," complained one business leader at the Conference Board meetings. "We have raised expectations that we can't deliver on."

Profit margins were down; corporate debt was up. The rules of the game needed to change in favor of business. *Business Week* put the matter squarely in a mid-1970s issue: "It will be a hard pill for many Americans to swallow the idea of doing with less so that business can have more…. Nothing that this nation, or any other nation, has done in modern economic history compares in difficulty with the selling job that must now be done to make people accept the new reality."

The first target of the conservative counterculture was not the press, but intellectuals. In 1970, Patrick Buchanan, then a Nixon speechwriter, complained in a memorandum to the president that conservatives desperately needed to set up a think tank to counter the malign influence of the Brookings Institution, which then reigned supreme in Washington and was considered (wrongly) to be an extremely liberal outfit.

In the war of ideas, the right had grown a little slack. The fierce post-World War II corporate campaign against labor had achieved its objective and faded. The American Enterprise Institute (AEI) was founded in 1943, but three decades later lacked prestige, and was home to but a dozen full-time "scholars." The Heritage

Foundation, born in 1973, was regarded as an institution of the lunatic fringe.

In the Watergate emergency this tranquil panorama underwent a seismic shift. In 1973, as the reputation of big business plummeted, corporate leaders formed the Business Roundtable. They reactivated the moribund U.S. Chamber of Commerce and made it a potent lobbying force. Intensive recruitment of "opinion makers" went into high gear. Led by the John M. Olin Foundation—chaired by former Treasury Secretary William Simon—corporations and wealthy individuals were soon funneling tens of millions of dollars annually to right-wing thinkers. Recipients of Olin's cash over recent years include the late Allan Bloom, author of *The Closing of the American Mind*; the neoconservatives Irving Kristol, who took in $376,000 for general support in 1988 alone; and David Brock, for support of his book *The Real Anita Hill: The Untold Story*. Joseph Coors put up the initial $250,000 in seed money to start Heritage in 1973. Since then, he has funded Paul Weyrich's Free Congress Foundation, the reclusive Council for National Policy (the far right's answer to the Council on Foreign Relations), the Hoover Institution, the American Defense Institute, and Accuracy in Media.

Another major funder of the conservative counterattack was Richard Mellon Scaife. By 1981, *Columbia Journalism Review* was reporting that through his various foundations, Scaife had, during the previous eight years, given $1 million or more to a score of right-wing institutions, making him someone who "could claim to have done more than any other individual [in recent times] to influence the way in which Americans think about their country and the world."

Among the groups receiving substantial funding from Scaife were Georgetown University's Center for Strategic and International Studies, the Committee on the Present Danger, James Watt's Mountain States Legal Foundation, and *The American Spectator* magazine. (Then asked about his support for such outfits by the *Review*'s Karen Rothmyer, Scaife gallantly replied, "You f...... Communist c..., get out of here.")

In the decade after Watergate, corporate money helped found several dozen conservative think tanks. Aside from those already cited, they include the Cato Institute, the Manhattan Institute, and the Ethics and Public Policy Center. Meanwhile, the American Enterprise Institute's budget grew from $4 million in the mid-Seventies to $12.5 million in the mid-Nineties. By 1985, twelve years after it was founded, Heritage's annual budget had reached $11.6 million; nine years later that figure had grown to $25.5 million. Both of these outfits provided the Reagan administration with dozens of staffers.

The right's think tanks know how to ventilate their views. The Heritage Foundation publishes hundreds of books, monographs and studies annually, with complimentary copies mailed to journalists across the country. Heritage's 95–96 *Guide to Public Policy Experts* lists some 1,800 policy wonks and 250 policy groups that "share our commitment to public policies based on free enterprise, limited government, individual freedom, traditional American values, and a strong national defense." The cross-referenced guide provides deadline-weary journalists with cooperative specialists in dozens of areas, ranging from "intelligence and counter-terrorism" to "wildlife management" and "bilingual education."

Think-tank scholars make money on the side by renting themselves out to public relations firms and lobbyists looking for "independent" supporters of their clients' viewpoints. One PR industry rep. describes his technique in the following way: "I call up an "expert," feign interest in his or her work, confirm that it's consistent with the industry viewpoint and then seek to strike a deal," normally for either a study or an appearance at a press event. "We don't say that we want an industry mouthpiece, but that's what it amounts to—and they know it. There are many people in this town who are willing to prostitute themselves and their work." This person recalls asking the conservative economist Murray Weidenbaum, former head of Reagan's Council of Economic Advisers, to appear at a media briefing on behalf of an industry group. Weidenbaum said he was very busy, but would try to squeeze in half a day if the PR firm would pony up $15,000—about three times the normal rate paid to industry flacks.

It's now all but impossible to keep track of the proliferating number of think tanks and pressure groups, many of them benignly named fronts for corporate chicanery. Consumer Alert, formerly headed by John Sununu and funded by such companies as Chevron, Eli Lilly, and Philip Morris, has fought mandatory air bags on the grounds that their expense is a burden to the consumers the group claims to represent; Citizens for the Sensible Control of Acid Rain is financed by major electric utilities and coal companies and battles tougher rules on air pollution; the Princeton Dental Resource Center, which once produced a study concluding that eating chocolate could be good for the teeth, is funded almost entirely by M&M/Mars candy companies.

Reporters have always nuzzled close to power. The classic example is the *New York Times'* James Reston, a man deeply involved in the struggles over the political contours of the postwar world. Along with Walter Lippmann, he helped Senator Arthur Vandenberg write his famous speech of January 10, 1945, recanting isolationism and then, like Lippmann, gave it an ecstatic review without mentioning his own role. He had, however, made a coy gesture to his insider knowledge when, in a dispatch filed the day before the speech, he wrote, "these proposals are said to have been drafted not in a partisan sense but with the purpose of making clear that the Senate is prepared to favor putting American force behind American principles in the interests of a lasting peace."

Hugh Sidey, now at *Time*, was a fawning admirer of JFK. In *President Kennedy: Profile of Power*, Richard Reeves revealed that Sidey, upon learning that the Evelyn Wood Institute estimated that JFK read 700 to 800 words per minute, called the president for confirmation. Kennedy said that the Institute's estimate was probably too low.

Sidey suggested 1,200 words, to which JFK replied, "OK." Sidey soon had a piece for *Life*—"He Eats Up News, Books at 1,200 Words a Minute." In 1994, Sidey told the *Washington Post*, "I haven't any idea how fast he read. The figure was kind of hoked up."

Today such collaborations are far more widespread, encompassing not just a handful of State Department reporters but many in the Washington press corps. When not sipping wine with the president, the *Times'* R.W. Apple consorts with such friends as the quintessential lawyer-lobbyists Robert Strauss and Lloyd Cutler. He once told the *Washington Post's* Howard Kurtz, frankly enough, that he's an "establishment" type of guy, and that "if Lawrence Eagleburger and Zbigniew Brzezinski and one or two others were to say to me, 'that's a lot of crap,' I would tend to be hesitant to put it forward."

Reflecting their increased respectability and compliance, media figures now make up roughly 10 per cent of the membership of the Council on Foreign Relations. Once a tranquil watering hole for senior mass murderers, State Department veterans, and a sprinkling of corporate and journalistic self-seekers, the Council is now headed by Leslie Gelb, whose serpentine career has shuttled him between Pentagon, State and the *New York Times*. CFR's snooze-producing *Foreign Affairs* is run by James Hoge, another ex-journalist. Hoge's media colleagues at the Council include Robert Bartley (the *Wall Street Journal*), Karen Elliott House (the *Wall Street Journal*) and her husband, Peter Kann (CEO, *Wall Street Journal*), Roone Arledge (ABC News). Tom Brokaw, David Brinkley, John Chancellor, A.M. Rosenthal (the *New York Times*), Katharine Graham (the *Washington Post*), Robert Silvers (the *New York Review of Books*), Katrina vanden Heuvel (the *Nation*), R. Emmett Tyrrell (*American Spectator*), and coffles of pundits, great and small.

Truly "responsible" reporters also gain that most cherished of all Washington commodities, "access." Some reporters of the Federal Reserve win coveted invitations to the annual Fourth of July bash held on the Fed's roof, and to the Fed's annual economics conference in Jackson Hole, Wyoming, where reporters and their spouses wander toward seminars through an athletic haze of hiking, tennis, and white-water rafting.

Another popular affair is the year-end Renaissance Weekend in Hilton Head, South Carolina. The 1993 event was attended by Bill Clinton, Supreme Court Justice Harry Blackmun, three U.S. senators, and hundreds of other powerful Beltway players. *Newsweek*'s Howard Fineman was among the journalists invited to attend on the condition that they not write about it. During the weekend, which cost roughly $1,500 per couple, Fineman attended such seminars as "Building an Inner Life," played touch football with the president, and urged Clinton to send daughter Chelsea to Washington's Sidwell Friends Academy (annual tuition, $11,000), which Fineman's own daughter attends.

Not long afterwards, Fineman appeared on *Washington World This Week* to pontificate about the political culture of Little Rock, capital of Clinton's home state of Arkansas. The problem with Little Rock, Fineman said with scant self-reflection, was that politics is controlled by a small group of insiders: "They have the money. They've got the power. They're on a first-name basis with each other... and the line between public money and private business is very fuzzy."

The Gridiron Club, a society of successful journalists, holds an annual spring dinner which the capital's leading political figures attend. In *The Power Game*, the *New York Times'* Hedrick Smith cheerfully relates such highlights from dinners past as the delightful jitterbug by Jimmy and Rosalyn Carter in 1978 and Ronald Reagan's soft-shoe routine a few years later. "But for a sheer turnaround—and a political facelift—no Gridiron guest in recent years has outdone Nancy Reagan," Smith remarks. Mrs. Reagan's immoderate spending had created a cold and unsympathetic image which the first lady managed to reshape with one hearty song-and-dance routine at the Club: "Secondhand clothes, I'm wearing secondhand clothes... Even my new trench coat with fur collar, Ronnie bought for ten cents on the dollar."

This performance earned Mrs. Reagan a standing ovation from the audience. "Only the inner core of the Washington community had seen this side of Mrs. Reagan," Smith observes. "But that community included most of the important journalists and politicians, and among this crucial audience Mrs. Reagan's image had been remade in a few short minutes. Inside the Beltway, people talked with amusement and warmth about her Gridiron performance."

The generous salaries paid to the Washington media have allowed journalists to join with the elite on its own terms. The typical correspondent in Babylon sends his kids to private school or public school in an exclusive area, drives a Volvo, and goes overseas once every few years and to Martha's Vineyard or the Hamptons every summer.

As Benjamin Bradlee, the *Post*'s executive editor at the time of Watergate, said not long ago, "Reporters are more conservative than the previous generation. And I think there's a very good reason for that. They get paid a hell of a lot better. It's hard to be conservative on $75 a week, but seventy-five grand, you begin to think of the kids and the bank account and the IRA and roll it over and all this stuff." (This comment is somewhat ironic coming from Bradlee. He retired to a seat on the board—and a newly created vice presidency—of the *Post* in August of 1991, which paid him in excess of $1.2 million, including bonuses and stock options.)

Some top correspondents make more in a single speech to industry groups than the average American takes home in a year. ABC's and National Public Radio's Cokie Roberts—sister of D.C.'s most prominent lobbyist, Tommy Boggs, of Patton, Boggs & Blow—pulled in an estimated $30,000 for a 1995 chat with the Junior League of Greater Fort Lauderdale, Florida. JM Family

Enterprises, a $4 billion firm, picked up the check. In October 1994, Roberts and her husband, reporter Steve Roberts of *U.S. News & World Report*, netted $45,000 for a joint appearance at a Chicago bank.

Other journalists who make significant income from speeches include Sam Donaldson of ABC ($30,000 a pop), Tim Russert of NBC ($10,000), and David Broder of the *Washington Post* ($7,500). Back in 1993, when health reform was one of the day's biggest topics, CBS' Lesley Stahl took home roughly $10,000 from Cigna Corp., one of the nation's largest insurance companies.

Figures such as Donaldson and Bernard Goldberg of CBS, one TV producer recalls, are such ardent players in the stock market that they become edgy when they're away from the phone for too long and can't check in with their brokers. In 1992, David Brinkley—who earns somewhere in the neighborhood of $1 million annually—told a business group that the idea of raising taxes on the rich was a "sick, stupid joke."

In 1995, some Republicans pressed for reporters with congressional press passes to disclose sources of outside income. This sensible idea was greeted with howls of protest about intrusions into free speech.

Charles Lewis, a former 60 *Minutes* producer who resigned to found the Center for Public Integrity, says, "The values of the news media are the same as those of the elite, and they badly want to be viewed by the elites as acceptable. Socially, culturally and economically they belong to the group of people who they are covering."

The quintessential elite reporter is ABC's Diane Sawyer, the former Junior Miss from Kentucky who, after a brief stint as weather girl at a Louisville station, moved to D.C. and (thanks to the influence of her father, a prominent Kentucky Republican) got a job at the Nixon White House press office in the early-Seventies. Sawyer was keenly loyal to President Nixon, and when he resigned she flew with the disgraced leader to San Clemente.

There Sawyer remained for four years, helping her then-boyfriend Frank Gannon prepare Nixon's autobiography.

In 1978, CBS hired Sawyer to join its national team. Thanks to her cultivation of network decision makers such as William Paley (she was in close contact with the media mogul as he lay dying), she netted a slot on 60 *Minutes* in 1984.

Sawyer signed a $7 million deal with ABC in 1994 to host *Prime Time Live*. While there she has become known for her hard-hitting interviews with such figures as Marla Maples ("Was it the best sex you ever had?" she asked Maples of her activities with Donald Trump) and Charles Manson.

During an episode on social spending, Sawyer berated a welfare mother who was illegally working two part-time jobs in order to supplement her $600 per month welfare benefits. "You know, people say you should not have children if you can't support them," Sawyer sternly lectured her victim. As pointed out by FAIR, the media watchdog group, Sawyer earns every day almost as much as the welfare mom earned per year: $16,700.

Sawyer has dated a number of powerful political figures, including Henry Kissinger and Clinton's Assistant Secretary of State Richard Holbrooke. (The latter's romantic career is highly reflective of the links between the media and political elites. After splitting with Sawyer, Holbrooke dated Barbara Cohen, the former wife of *Washington Post* columnist Richard Cohen. He later married the ex-Mrs. Peter Jennings. Holbrooke's second wife has described him as a relentless bore, saying his favorite activity is "watching himself being interviewed on TV.") Though now married to film director Mike Nichols, Sawyer still protects her former beaus.

Despite her hefty paycheck, Sawyer has never demonstrated any great public appeal. When she left 60 *Minutes*, there was no impact on the show's ratings. *Prime Time* was ranked No. 18 in

1993–94, but fell to No. 87 during Sawyers first four episodes. The program's popularity today remains muted.

—•—•—•—

Historically, the financial press has been one of the least dignified sectors of the trade, perhaps because business reporters feel more keenly than their colleagues the need to relay the corporate outlook. The financial press isn't perhaps as corrupt as it was a few decades ago. Back then a business wanting to place a story needed only to negotiate the proper price with the editorial staff. Today the chief function of the business press is still to relay the claims of government officials, financial speculators, bankers, and so forth.

Morton Mintz, once a very fine reporter for the *Washington Post*, has chronicled the way that "the sense of property" is still amply reflected in the media. A few years back officials from NBC News deleted three sentences critical of General Electric, NBC's owner, from a report on shoddy standards in American industry. Reporters quickly learn that to get ahead, they must toe the line. Mintz recounts the story of Ronald Kessler, a *Post* reporter who in the early 1980s investigated the insurance industry in a series of articles: "In an irrational, hellish process lasting more than three years, [Kessler] was directed to cut the series from ten parts to six, then to three.... Finally, it became a highly compressed single article, published in a typographically repellent format.... He later resigned."

By now, there aren't many Kesslers left in the newsroom. The new breed is represented by the *Post*'s Clay Chandler, a man who never met an official source he didn't like, this being broadly reflected in his uncritical reports on Babylon's power brokers. In a profile of Lloyd Bentsen in late 1994, Chandler called the then-treasury secretary "a courtly millionaire," a "stickler for order, discipline and hierarchy," and someone who "was behind many of [President] Clinton's triumphs" while having "side-stepped the failures." In one particularly timorous moment, Chandler cautioned that "if Bentsen were to retire, the administration would lose potentially valuable experience".

When Bentsen did resign a few weeks later, Chandler was equally deferential to his successor, Robert Rubin, saying that the transition at Treasury had "the air of a venerated chairman passing the reins of the firm to a trusted junior associate." He described Rubin as a "self-effacing millionaire" who regards "the hurly-burly of Washington politics with the detachment of an anthropologist engaged in field research," and as someone with a "long-standing concern... for urban America."

This view of Rubin (net worth: $155 million) as a champion of the underclass, endlessly repeated by Chandler's colleagues in the press, is laughable. Before joining the administration, Rubin headed Goldman, Sachs & Co., a Wall Street firm whose financial speculations in 1992 generated pre-tax earnings of $1.4 billion, one-fifth the entire income of the Bronx's 1.2 million people. Rubin's share of that year's haul was $26.5 million.

Over at the *New York Times*, David Sanger is only slightly less craven than Chandler. When Mexico's economy crashed in December 1994, Rubin was vacationing in the British Virgin Islands. The treasury secretary's "initial instinct was to let the Mexicans and the market sort it out, and return to the important business of casting for bonefish in the azure waters of the Caribbean," Sanger wrote. "[But Rubin] became convinced that in Mexico the administration was faced with the most modern of foreign policy crises. No nukes, no troops, just the potential for global financial apocalypse."

Sanger failed to mention Rubin's other interests in Mexico. The treasury secretary's 1993 disclosure statement lists 42 firms with which he had "significant contact" while at Goldman, Sachs, of which six were Mexican firms or state agencies, including Mexico's finance ministry. Furthermore, during the last few years, Rubin's old firm was the leading underwriter of Mexican stocks and bonds, marketing $5.17 billion in securities.

Reporting on business is in general equally reverential. A 1993 *New York Times* profile of John Purcell, managing director for emerging markets research at Salomon Brothers, called its subject a "guru on the Third World." The *Times'* Jeanne Pinder said that "Mr. Purcell's research unit has a reputation for being hot," and that no one questions "the quality of work done" by Purcell's department.

Some of Purcell's clients at Salomon Brothers might dispute that assessment. In mid-1992, guru Purcell was touting investments in Brazil and predicting that a corruption scandal threatening the regime of Fernando Collor de Mello would soon blow over. "The current situation [is] no more than a blip on the screen," he told investors at a seminar in New York. Collor was soon impeached, shaking Brazilian stock markets.

In the *Times'* profile, Purcell chided Moody's rating agency for its "fundamental error of pessimism" towards Mexico, saying the agency was taking "a highly conservative stance." Less than a year after Purcell's strictures over Moody's needless pessimism, the Chiapas uprising took place, followed at the end of 1994 by the collapse of the peso.

John Liscio, publisher of *The Liscio Report*, a business newsletter, and a former columnist for *Barron's* and *U.S. News & World Report*, describes most business reporters as little more than glorified stenographers. "Most of them are looking to get jobs in outright flackery. They take dictation when they work as reporters and they end up doing the same thing for more money when they move to handling PR for the private sector."

Indeed, not a few economics reporters have moved from the business pages to Wall Street. The most prominent example is Steven Rattner, who swapped the offices of the *New York Times* for the executive suites of Lazard Freres. Rattner is hardly alone. Many of the members of the New York Financial Writers' Association are "associates," meaning they now work outside the journalistic profession, mostly in public relations or on Wall Street.

Even worse, economics reporters rarely talk to anyone besides Wall Street brokers and other officials from the financial sector. One source financial reporters quote constantly is Stephen Roach, the chief economist at Morgan Stanley. According to an article Roach recently penned for the *Financial Times*, the past decade's "wrenching corporate restructurings," which have produced plant closings, layoffs, outsourcing and industry-wide consolidations, "offer nothing but upside for the financial markets." Roach's main concern is to see that American companies keep firing workers. He finds that during the first three months of 1995 U.S. firms fired only 97,200 employees, less than half the rate during the same period in 1994 and far fewer than the numbers laid off by Japanese and German firms. Roach spies here a disturbing trend, which might signify a "slackening of restructuring by Corporate America." Of course, Roach and other Wall Street "analysts" beloved by reporters serve as adjuncts to their firms' sales forces, and are charged with the task of keeping money flowing into the stock market.

For example, in an early 1995 story from Buenos Aires, Calvin Sims of the *New York Times*—apparently unable to find a local analyst—quoted Salomon Brothers' Larry Goodman as saying that Argentina's economy would grow by 3 per cent that year. This wildly optimistic prediction should be set alongside the fact that Goodman's firm markets Argentine securities, which sell far more briskly if investors believe that country's economy is on strong ground. "If the Yankees are in last place in August, no sports writer will say that they're going to win the pennant because the manager says so," Liscio remarks. "[Wall Street analysts] are salesmen, but the press treats them like prophets." (Incidentally, Argentina's economy sank by 2.5 per cent in 1995.)

Two decades after Watergate, the *Post* is a highly conservative outfit. Thomas Edsall Jr. was once a good journalist with a mind of his own. In the Eighties he wrote a fine account of Reaganism, *The New Politics of Inequality*. But then Edsall seemed to realize that even the barest tincture of radicalism would doom his prospects for career advancement.

By 1995, he was attributing the murderous anger of the alleged Oklahoma bomber, Timothy McVeigh, to the rise of the women's movement and the decline in status of the vaginal orgasm. Men face a poor economic future because of affirmative action, and are being laid off in greater numbers than women. Those who hold a job supposedly live in fear of being unfairly charged with sexual harassment. Hence, men have "a private sense of siege, voiced most often only in quiet tones at lunch or more angrily over beer after work."

But nowhere, Edsall went on, has the "seismic upheaval" been greater than in the area of sex: "In the same year that Timothy McVeigh was born, the pill had just started to sever the linkage between intercourse and pregnancy... The pill opened for women the same vista of sexual opportunism that had been available to men. At the same time, the 'myth of the vaginal orgasm' was replaced by the recognition of the clitoral orgasm, further freeing women seeking such autonomy from dependence on men for sexual satisfaction."

Unemployed and listless, their women locked in the bedroom in a haze of solitary pleasure, American men of the late-20th century are frustrated. They seek relief in one of the few outlets still available: mixing fuel oil with fertilizer and blowing up federal buildings. [Edsall is now out to pasture, on the faculty of the Columbia Journalism School, tutoring impressionable youth—Eds.]

The *Post*'s decline is most glaringly illuminated in the evolution of Bob Woodward. Though he carries the portentous title of investigations editor [now assistant managing editor], people rarely see Woodward at the paper. His work now largely consists of "insider" reporting, resulting in forgettable books such as *The Commanders* (on the Joint Chiefs of Staff), *The Brethren* (on the

Supreme Court), *The Agenda* (on Clinton's economic policies), and *Veil* (on the CIA), which included the famous death-bed conversation with William Casey, regarded by some as having the same relationship to physical reality as the Prince of Denmark's interview with his father in the first act of Hamlet.

Woodward's lowest moment thus far may have come with his seven-part series—later turned into a book—on that Augustus Caesar of American politics, Dan Quayle. Woodward co-wrote this series with David Broder in 1991. The two reporters heaped praise on Quayle, mostly from the veeplet's pals. One hard-pressed Quayle aide bravely described the veep's passion for golfing as an intellectual endeavor, it being "not just relaxation [but] a version of Oriental shadow-boxing."

The series produced a flood of good PR for Quayle, a spell only broken after the vice president misspelled the word "potato" at a school spelling bee. The series also showed the depth of political insight of Broder and Woodward, who appear to have concluded that Bush was a certainty for re-election in '92 and Quayle the heir apparent for '96, and thus figured their fawning series would give them an edge on the journalistic competition.

In the Nineties, Woodward's investigative skills have been deployed largely against the powerless. In early 1994, Woodward and a sidekick, Benjamin Weiser, wrote a front-page story on children's disability, a legal category created in Congress in 1972 as part of the Supplemental Security Income (SSI) program. Requirements were extremely strict. Potential recipients had to be in a hospital or a wheelchair, or possess an IQ under 60. Those with cystic fibrosis, muscular dystrophy, autism, and Down's syndrome were routinely turned down.

The *Post*'s article zoomed in on Nora Cooke Porter, a state disability review physician in Pennsylvania, "who can barely contain her frustration as she flips through some of the thousands of applications" for assistance for children who, "in her medical opinion, are not suffering from any disability." According to Woodward and Weiser, "children who curse teachers, fight with classmates, perform poorly in school or display characteristics of routine rebellion are often diagnosed with behavioral disorders and therefore qualify for the program's cash benefits."

Parents often spent their children's benefits unwisely, Woodward and Weiser proclaimed virtuously. And while government bureaucrats required an accounting of how the money was spent, they did not have "the resources to scrutinize spending on a large scale."

When the piece appeared, two Wisconsin Democrats, Senator Herb Kohl and Rep. Gerald Kleczka, instantly distributed copies to each member of Congress. A story attacking poor people in the *Post* carries twice the firepower of one in the *Washington Times*, since the former can be introduced with the conclusive words, "Even the liberal *Post* says..." And when the article bears Woodward's name, the effect is even greater.

The story set off a hue and cry against children's disability, and led to an all-important *Prime Time* report the following October. No fewer than three of the network's millionaire correspondents made haste to beat up on crippled children and steal their crutches: Chris Wallace, chief correspondent for that segment, called it a "taxpayer scam"; Diane Sawyer said it was "a program designed to help disabled children, but parents are helping themselves"; and Sam Donaldson—who receives tens of thousands of dollars of federal agriculture subsidies annually for his New Mexico sheep ranch, ranching being a notorious sump for federal subsidies—marveled at "how easy it is to get on the receiving end of what some are calling 'crazy checks.'" *Prime Time*'s piece opened with a severely retarded white child in a wheelchair, representing a "deserving" recipient in whom the public's money had been prudently invested. The show then moved to the Arkansas delta, where a variety of white politicians and white schoolteachers berated black children as frauds. Wallace grilled a poor black woman who found it hard to articulate to the massed inquisitors and technicians why her child needed assistance. Like the *Post*, ABC trotted out Dr. Porter to decry the program's abuses.

Prime Time's attack had a big impact in the capital. The show aired before a congressional subcommittee, and several members cited it in seeking to gut children's disability.

The *Post* and *Prime Time* avoided important facts: children's disability rolls have grown heavily in recent years and now carry some 800,000 children, but the cause is not an explosion of fraud. In 1990, the Rehnquist Supreme Court decreed by a 7-to-2 margin that eligibility requirements were unlawfully tight. Under the new guidelines, more children with severe mental impairments were able to qualify. The Court also ordered Congress and the Social Security Administration to publicize the program, and thus many parents heard of it for the first time.

For children to get what are, by the standards of today's medical billings, minimal benefits, a doctor must judge them to be in very poor shape indeed. About 60 per cent have mental problems ranging from the grave to the catastrophic; about 25 per cent have severe physical problems; and about 15 per cent have serious neurological or sensory ailments.

Since 1991, more than half a million children—45 per cent of all applicants—have been rejected. In tirelessly publicized Pennsylvania, where Dr. Porter's "frustration" threatens to boil over, 43 per cent of the applicants were turned down. In Arkansas, the rejection rate is 56 per cent.

The *Post*'s and *Prime Time*'s hatchet jobs on the disability program stemmed in part from their heavy reliance on Porter, portrayed in both cases as a doughty friend to the taxpayer. In fact, Porter was fired by the Pennsylvania Bureau of Disabilities Determination because of her unceasing and baseless onslaughts on colleagues. Jonathan Stein, the general counsel for Community Legal Services in Philadelphia, who argued the 1991 case before the Supreme Court, alerted Woodward and ABC to Porter's record. But they eagerly relayed her assertions without a word of caution.

Prime Time quoted Porter as saying that the families of disabled children could "buy a Mercedes" with their benefits. Maximum benefits allowed for a single parent are $446 per month, a figure that decreases as family income rises above $13,284 per year. If family income tops $1,907 in any month, the child loses all benefits. Porter also told ABC that "fewer than 30 per cent" of children awarded benefits deserve them. If true, this enormous figure would mean that roughly 600,000 children on the rolls are frauds. Wallace echoed: "If Porter's estimates are anywhere near accurate," then the program is a "massive taxpayer-funded scam." Note the strategic use of the word "if" in this context. As Stein complained bitterly, "Isn't the purpose of [*Prime Time*'s] three-month investigation and the job of such a veteran chief corre-spondent to ascertain the validity of such an assertion, and not to use the big 'if' as a crutch to buttress the by now demagogic, media cliché of 'taxpayer scam?'"

On Stein's suggestion, *Prime Time* went to Dayton, Ohio, to film Connie Guyer and her son, Nathan, who suffers from a variety of ailments including Attention Deficit Disorder, depression, hyper-activity, and thyroid deficiency. At age 12 Nathan couldn't read, thought he was stupid and was suicidal. Qualifying for benefits enabled Nathan to attend a private school where he learned to read. Now he wants to be a scientist.

Having been burned by journalists in the past, Connie Guyer had serious doubts about working with *Prime Time*. But Jude Dratt, Wallace's producer, assured her that Nathan's story was essential to give a balanced view of the program. "I'm going to be your new best friend," Guyer remembers Dratt eagerly telling her. She says Dratt promised she'd come to Dayton a day before the crew arrived so she could spend time getting to know Nathan. But Dratt never went anywhere near Dayton, and instead sent an assistant on the day of the shoot. Guyer says *Prime Time*'s crew was rude and insensitive: "All they wanted from us was tears and breakdown."

The producers had promised Guyer that they'd let her know when the program was scheduled for broadcast. In fact, the first time she knew it was scheduled was when she saw a blurb in *TV Guide*. She called Dratt, who told her that she still didn't know when the program was going to air, then waffled when Guyer told her she'd seen the *TV Guide* announcement. Sensing a hatchet job, Guyer informed Dratt that she'd never signed a release and didn't want footage of Nathan to be used. Breaking vigorous pledges, *Prime Time* never returned family photographs to the Guyers.

Stein wrote a letter to Jude Dratt in early 1995: "Due to the press of much more important matters at ABC, you and your colleagues are perhaps not aware of the aftermath of your fall *Prime Time* program in the Congress," Stein began, adding that a bill before Congress would all but eliminate the children's disability program:

"I am sure you and ABC executives must be proud of how instrumental your work has been in bringing down this program in this short span of time... Such recognition can only further your professional careers in TV news and entertainment productions, and give you encouragement to replicate your achievement elsewhere.

"I'm enclosing some narratives of disabled children your program chose to misrepresent, the great majority of children on SSI, who will not be eligible for cash benefits, including eligibility for Medical Assistance, in the future. I do not assume that the loss of necessities of life for hundreds of thousands of such children is of any consequence to you or executives at ABC; I certainly don't assume that there is any news or entertainment value for you in their plight, as there must be other issues that you've moved on to that better address the urgency of keeping *Prime Time*'s ratings up.... But, if you or Chris wish to respond so I can pass word on to all the parents of cerebral palsy, spina bifida, AIDS, cystic fibrosis, muscular dystrophy, epilepsy, hydrocephalus, mental retardation, missing limbs, blind, diabetic, and cancer children we've talked to, your courtesy of a response—not so much for us but for these parents—will be most appreciated.

Your inability to respond will also be most understandable as well.

"The best for future coups in TV journalism."

The dominant mode now at the *Post*'s upper echelons is one of self-congratulation, with endless staff missives about colleagues moving onward and upward.

When the paper's top editorial brass returned from their annual Pugwash meeting in Florida, where they mull over ways of improving excellence at the *Post* and work on their tans, the editors—glowing with sun and health—announced to a meeting of expectant reporters that they were planning to get "really well-written stories" on the front page. One reporter then asked whether the editors would share with them whatever great ideas they had dreamed up in sunny Florida. "We just did," said one editor bleakly.

CounterPunch founder Ken Silverstein is now Washington editor of Harper's. This essay was written in the mid-1990s. Since then the situation has only got worse.

1996

She Needed Fewer Friends

Alexander Cockburn

JOE PULITZER FAMOUSLY SAID, "A NEWSPAPER SHOULD HAVE no friends." Looking at the massed ranks of America's elites attending Katharine Graham's funeral in Washington on July 23, 2001, it's maybe churlish to recall that phrase, but it's true. At least in political terms, Mrs. Graham had too many friends.

The twin decisions, concerning the Pentagon Papers and Watergate that made Mrs. Graham's name as a courageous publisher, came at precisely the moment when, in biographical terms, she was best equipped to handle pressure. She'd had eight years to overcome the timidities that bore down on her after Phil Graham's suicide left her with a newspaper she resolved to run herself. The amiable but essentially conservative bipartisanship that had the notables of each incoming administration (Carter-time excepted) palavering happily in her dining room hadn't yet numbed the *Post*'s spinal nerve.

Mrs. Graham sustained her fatal fall during an annual confab of the nation's biggest media and e-billionaires, organized by the investment banker Herb Allen and held in Sun Valley, Idaho. It was a proper setting for her passing. Sun Valley was developed as a resort by the Harrimans, starting with the nineteenth century railroad bandit E.H. Harriman. That quintessential insider, Averell Harriman, was often to be seen at Mrs. Graham's house in Georgetown.

Mrs. Graham didn't strong-arm her editors and reporters, they say. But editors and reporters aren't slow to pick up hints as to the disposition of the person who pays their wages, and she sent out plenty such clues.

Mrs. Graham had many reasons, material and spiritual, to find excessive boat rocking distasteful. The family fortune, and the capital that bought and nourished the *Post*, was founded in part on Allied Chemical, the company run by her father, Eugene Meyer. I remember a hard edge in her voice when she deplored "those f--- environmentalists"—perhaps because rabble-rousers had derisively taunted her as "Kepone Kate" after a bad Allied Chemical spill in the James River. Yes, privately her language was agreeably salty.

By the early 1980s, the leftish liberal Kay Graham of the late-1930s who would, as a tyro reporter, hang out with the red longshoreman leader Harry Bridges on the Oakland docks, was long gone. For one thing, there had been the ferocious pressmen's strike in 1975, and the successful lockout. Rhetorically, at least, Mrs. Graham did not later make the gaffe of equating the sabotage of her plant by the Pressmen's Union with the disposition of the AFL-CIO, but I don't think she ever forgave labor; and that strike helped set Mrs. Graham and her newspaper on its sedately conservative course.

In the early 1980s she associated increasingly with Warren Buffett, the Nebraska investor who bought 13 per cent of the *Post*'s B stock and who was then riding high as America's most venerated stock player. Mrs. Graham simultaneously became a big-picture mogul, pickling herself in the sonorous platitudes of the Brandt Commission, on which she served.

In the early 1990s, I used to get copies of letters sent to the *Post*'s editors and ombudsman by Julian Holmes, a Maryland resident with a career in the Navy Weapons Lab, who read the *Post* diligently every day, firing off often acute and pithy criticisms. In all, Holmes told me the other day from his Maine cabin, he sent some 130 such letters to the *Post* and achieved a perfect record of zero published.

Deploring the Dan Quayle series in a letter sent to ombudsman Richard Harwood on January 22, 1992, Holmes pointed out that nowhere in the "in-depth" exam of Quayle could be found the words crime, public land, population, healthcare, oil, capital punishment, United Nations, Nicaragua, unemployment, homeless, or AIDS.

No need to labor the point. The basic mistake is to call the *Washington Post* a liberal paper, or its late proprietor a liberal in any active sense, unless you want to disfigure the word by applying it to such of Graham's friends as Robert McNamara. When it came to war criminals, she was an equal opportunity hostess. In her salons you could meet Kissinger, an old criminal on the way down, or Richard Holbrooke, a younger one on the way up. The *Post*'s basic instincts have almost always been bad.

Former Mayor Marion Barry had some *pro forma* kindly words for Katharine Graham after her death, but I always think that one decisive verdict on the *Post*'s performance in a city with a major black population came with the jury verdict acquitting Barry on the cocaine bust. Those jurors knew that the *Post*, along with the other Powers That Be, was on the other side from Barry, and I've no doubt that firmed up their assessment of the evidence. In that quarter, for sure, neither the *Post* nor Mrs. Graham had an excessive number of friends.

Editors' afternote: The Post *has steadily got worse. Its publisher, Don Graham, is a pro-business hawk, a stance which has not escaped the attention of his obedient employees.*

2001

Woodward at Court

Alexander Cockburn and Jeffrey St. Clair

I T'S BEEN A DEVASTATING FALL FOR WHAT ARE CONVENTIONALLY regarded as the nation's two premier newspapers, the *New York Times* and the *Washington Post*. The *Times'* travails and the downfall of its erstwhile star reporter, Judith Miller, have been newsprint's prime soap opera since late spring and now, just when we were taking a breather before the Libby trial, the *Washington Post* is writhing with embarrassment over the multiple conflicts of interest of its most famous staffer, Bob Woodward, best known to the world as Nixon's nemesis in the Watergate scandal.

In mid-November 2005 Woodward quietly made his way to the law office of Howard Shapiro, of the firm of Wilmer, Cutler, Pickering, Hale and Doar, and gave a two-hour deposition to Plamegate prosecutor Patrick Fitzgerald, a man he had denounced on TV the night before Scooter Libby's indictment as "a junkyard dog of a prosecutor."

Woodward's deposition had been occasioned by a call to Fitzgerald from a White House official on November 3, 2005, a week after Libby had been indicted. The official told Fitzgerald that the prosecutor had been mistaken in claiming in his press conference that Libby had been the first to disclose the fact that Joseph Wilson's wife [i.e., Valerie Plame] was in the CIA. The official informed Fitzgerald that he himself had divulged Plame's job to Woodward in a mid-June interview, about a week before Libby told Miller the same thing.

Seeing his laboriously constructed chronology collapse in ruins, and the weakening of his case against Libby, Fitzgerald called Woodward that same day, November 3. Woodward, the *Washington Post*'s assistant managing editor, no doubt found the call an unwelcome one, since he had omitted to tell anyone at the *Post*, up to and including editor Len Downie and publisher Donald Graham, that he'd been the first journalist to be on the receiving end of a leak from the White House about Plame. He'd kept his mouth shut while two of his colleagues, Walter Pincus and Glenn Kessler, had been hauled before Fitzgerald.

Shortly after the call from Fitzgerald, Woodward told Downie that he would have to testify. On Wednesday, the *Post* carried a somewhat acrid news story along with Woodward's account of his testimony. Later in the day Howard Kurtz posted a commentary on the *Post*'s website. It's clear from the news story and Kurtz's piece that his colleagues find Woodward's secretive conduct unbecoming (Downie tamely said it was a "mistake") and somewhat embarrassing, given all the huff and puff about Judith "Miss Run Amok" Miller's high-handed ways with her editors.

And just as Miller and her editors differed strongly on whether the reporter had told them what she was up to, so too did Woodward's account elicit a strenuous challenge from the *Post*'s long-time national security correspondent, Walter Pincus.

In Woodward's account of his testimony (which he took care to have vetted and later publicly approved by the *Post*'s former editor Ben Bradlee), he wrote that he told Fitzgerald that he had shared this information—Plame's employment with the CIA—with Pincus. But Pincus is adamant that Woodward did no such thing. When the *Post*'s reporters preparing Wednesday's story quizzed him about Woodward's version, Pincus answered, "Are you kidding? I certainly would have remembered that." Pincus told Joe Stroup of *Editor & Publisher* later on Tuesday that he had long suspected that Woodward was somehow entangled in the Plame affair. After Fitzgerald was appointed special prosecutor in the fall of 2003, Woodward had gone to Pincus and asked his colleague, in Pincus' words, "to keep him out of the reporting, and I agreed to do that."

Like many others, the *Washington Post*'s staff had vivid memories of Woodward's unending belittling of the whole Plame affair as something of little consequence, "laughable," "quite minimal." Woodward said it on the *Larry King Show* the night before the indictments, almost as if he was trying to send Fitzgerald a message.

For months Woodward has been working on a book about Bush's second term. The White House, ecstatic at Woodward's highly flattering treatment of Bush in *Plan of Attack* and *Bush at War* (Washington's retort to the *Harry Potter* series), has been giving Woodward extraordinary access, confident that he will put a kindly construction on their disastrous handling of the nation's affairs.

Judith Miller was savaged for accepting what she claimed to be special credentials from the Pentagon in return for confidentiality. So what are we to say about Woodward, who is given special access and then repays the favor by belittling the Plame scandal, while simultaneously concealing his own personal knowledge of the White House's schedule on the outing of Valerie Plame?

Woodward did not disclose his potential conflict of interest while he was pontificating on the airwaves about the Plame affair, but he also apparently succeeded in stifling an investigation into his own role by his colleague Pincus. He may have also placed Pincus in legal jeopardy with his testimony to Fitzgerald that he had informed Pincus in June of 2003 about Plame. Pincus had testified under oath to Fitzgerald in September of 2004 that his first knowledge of Plame's employer had come in a conversation with a White House source at a later date.

So who was Woodward's source and what was his motive in calling Prosecutor Fitzgerald the week after Libby's indictment to disclose that he had talked to Woodward before Libby began his own speed-dial leaking? Woodward says it wasn't White House chief of staff Andrew Card. He also says he went to see his source with 18 pages of questions, whose topics included yellowcake from Niger and the infamous October 2003 National Intelligence Estimate on Iraq's alleged WMD.

After this initial interview with a White House official in mid-June 2003, Woodward learned enough that when he saw two other White House staffers shortly thereafter, he had the phrase "Joe Wilson's wife" among his questions. So the first official did the leaking. He could well have been Vice President Cheney, since Woodward's interview took place exactly at the time that Cheney's office was buzzing with alarm after a call from Pincus telling them he was working on a story about Joe Wilson.

That afternoon Cheney informed Libby that Wilson's wife worked at the CIA. Libby spent the next week gathering a dossier on Plame. On June 23, Libby and Woodward talked on the phone. Woodward had the 18 pages of questions he'd already posed twice, and began to work his way through them. He says he can't recall Libby bringing up Plame's name.

It's our guess that Libby, eager to broach Plame's role to the *Post*'s renowned investigative reporter, finally wearied on the endless questions, cut Woodward off and hastened off to lunch with Miller. Woodward claims he kept no notes, and so did Miller until her famous notebook with "Flame" in it turned up at the *New York Times*. All in all it was a bad leak day for Scooter, since Woodward wasn't working as a reporter but as historian-courtier, and Miller had been taken off the story by her editors.

If Woodward's first source was Cheney, why would the latter have called Fitzgerald on November 3? The admission by Cheney that he had spoken to Woodward could derail Libby's prosecution and also undercut possible charges of a breach of the Espionage Act, by playing into the line Woodward took on the *Larry King Show* and elsewhere that this was no dreadful affront to national security but indeed "gossip" and "chatter."

So much for the fortune's wheel. From Nixon's nemesis to Cheney's savior.

2005

Part 2

New York Times: Decline and Fall

Rosenthal's Times

Alexander Cockburn

.M. ROSENTHAL DIED MAY 10, 2006, AT THE AGE OF
84. There were respectful obituaries describing how
Rosenthal "saved" the *New York Times* in the '70s by
pepping up its news coverage, introducing the supplements, and
so forth. By the same token Rosenthal sowed the seeds for the
Times' present difficulties. He was a bully with the bully's usual
penchant for favorites. A culture of favoritism always produces
servility, since the bully affirms his power by conspicuous punishment for the disloyal.

So the *Times* that nourished Judith Miller and blared her lies
across its front pages, year after year, was A.M. Rosenthal's *Times*.
The *Times* that has painted, in two decades worth of dispatches
from Latin America and Asia and the former Soviet Union, its
infantile cartoons of a world speeding towards beneficial neolib-
eral "reform" was also in large part a reflection of the cretinism of
Rosenthal's politics, hence of the reporters he favored.

One of the most ludicrous passages written to honor
Rosenthal's memory was a paragraph in the commemorative
column composed by neoliberalism's P.T. Barnum, Thomas
Friedman, an epigone of Rosenthal, who wrote last weekend:

> Many readers became aware of Abe only after he became a col-
> umnist. He was very conservative and supportive of right-wing
> parties in Israel. But let me tell you this: When he was editor, I
> reported for him from Israel and the Arab world for many years.
> I am sure I wrote things that gave him heartburn. But in all
> those years he never once complained about anything I wrote. I
> never knew his politics until he became a columnist. As editor,

he was obsessed with keeping *The Times* 'straight,' as he used to say, with no reporters' or editors' thumbs ever on the scale.

"Straight"? As CounterPuncher Chris Reed pointed out in his obituary of Rosenthal in the *Guardian*:

> In 1981–82 few American reporters realized the extent of secret but crucial U.S. involvement in the war in El Salvador, something the authorities routinely denied. One who knew was *New York Times* correspondent Raymond Bonner, who in early 1982 exposed the rightist Salvadoran government's massacre of nearly 1,000 men, women and children in the small town of El Mozote. The U.S. insisted it had not happened and pressure mounted on the *Times*.
>
> As executive editor, Rosenthal flew to El Salvador to assess the complaints against Bonner. Sympathetic to president Ronald Reagan's rhetoric about the communist threat, Rosenthal began limiting Bonner's coverage and in early 1983 recalled him to the New York business desk. He soon resigned. Today the atrocity at El Mozote is an accepted historical truth, but Bonner's name has faded.

Naïve souls often imagine that editors and, behind them, owners, issue orders and reporters click their heels and file the stories imperiously requested. That can happen, but mostly supervision is not such an explicit process. Every reporter and editor in the news business has a compass in their heads which alerts them within the fraction of a degree to the prejudices and preferences of the boss, whether it's Katharine Graham, or Ben Bradlee, or Rosenthal or Murdoch or the executive network news producer or whoever is construed as ruling the roost.

So Rosenthal hired and fostered platoons of editors and reporters who knew survival and advancement depended to an important measure on catering to his prejudices and not causing offense. Offending the executive editor, particularly for an overseas correspondent, could bring swift and disastrous retribution, as happened to Bonner, publicly disciplined and ultimately returned to overseas duties as a more or less broken soul. The *Times* that published James LeMoyne and Stephen Kinzer in the

1980s, week after week slanting the news from Central America towards the outlook of the U.S. Embassy, was the *Times* of A.M. Rosenthal.

The idea, bizarrely advanced by Friedman, that Rosenthal's politics remained obscure till his column began to appear on the *NYT*'s op-ed page is ludicrous. But it was, nonetheless, a pleasing moment to be able to point to the ravings appearing under his name as vivid confirmation of everything one had been writing about the man down the years.

2006

Why Dumping on the NYT is a Waste of Time

Alexander Cockburn

PEOPLE ON THE LEFT SPEND A LOT MORE TIME THAN THEY should complaining about the mainstream papers, most particularly the *New York Times*. They fume at the breakfast table, at the coffee shop and often in print, or on the airwaves, bitterly decrying falsities in the "newspaper of record." What do they expect? In fact, they should express measured satisfaction when the *Times* gets things wrong, which it mostly does, and take it as a singular and not altogether welcome event when it blunders into accuracy.

These days the people who write and edit the *New York Times* have obtained their eminence on this pinnacle of mainstream corporate journalism through the sorting process deployed by the ruling elites throughout all the important institutions, albeit far more thoroughly than in the legal or religious sectors, where the occasional oddball survives. In papers such as the *Times* or the *Post*, the batting average in elevating safe figures is one hundred per cent. The chances of an eccentric editor reaching the upper branches of the tree are zero, and near zero for reporters.

The winnowing process begins in the journalism schools, where the novices are instructed in the sedate arts of being mouthpieces for corporate America. The journalism students begin to build up their inventory of clips, laboring to extirpate any career threatening element of indignation, heterodoxy, or even zest. They're beaten, cowed souls before they even apply to the *Times* for an internship.

The dreariest place on any campus is the J-school, and whenever any young person comes to me to write a testimonial for them to get into journalism school I chafe at their decision, though I concede that these days a diploma from one of these feedlots for mediocrity is pretty much mandatory for anyone who wants to get in to mainstream journalism.

Now the *Times* is nursing its bruises from the Jayson Blair affair. There are so many ranker corpses in the *New York Times'* mausoleum, not to mention that larger graveyard of truth known as the American Fourth Estate, that it's hard to get too upset about what Blair did. This same Blair was a young black reporter on the *New York Times*, exposed and denounced at colossal length on May 11, 2005, by a team of reporters from his own paper. The guy is now in hiding; his career in ruins.

To be sure, Blair made up a bunch of not very important stuff, and he's embarrassed the hell out of his former colleagues and his publisher. The New York tabloids have been having a field day. But from all the editorial hand wringing you'd think he'd undermined the very foundations of the Republic.

It reminds me of a *New York Times'* editorial back in 1982, commenting on what began with my own exposé of Christopher Jones, a young man who had written an article in the *New York Times Magazine* about a visit to Cambodia during which he claimed to have seen Pol Pot through binoculars.

In this same piece Jones made the mistake of lifting an entire paragraph from André Malraux's novel *La Voie Royale*. I pointed this out in a column in the *Village Voice*, adding the obvious point that Jones' binoculars must have been extremely powerful to have allowed Jones to recognize Pol Pot, let alone describe his eyes as "dead and stony."

My item stirred the *Washington Post* to point an accusing finger (though not, to be sure, to acknowledge who prompted the finger into activity). Then the *Times* itself unleashed a huge investigation of the wretched Jones and ran a pompous editorial proclaiming that "It may not be too much to say that, ultimately, it debases democracy."

I remember thinking at the time that as a democracy-debaser Jones looked like pretty small potatoes, and it's the same way with Jayson Blair now. He made up quotes, invented scenes, and pinched the work of other reporters, and if senior *Times'* editors had not been as optimistically forgiving as, say, the Catholic hierarchy in dealing with a peccant priest, Blair would, and should, have been promptly fired after his second major screwup. (Incidentally, Jeffrey St. Clair's friend Larry Tuttle, a noted green campaigner based in Portland, Oregon, tells Jeffrey that a few years ago he was hosting a group of young aspiring journalists, imparting to them lore about western environmental issues. Even then Blair stood out as a manic hustler, a five-minute expert, discoursing ignorantly about issues about which he had zero grasp.)

But in the larger scale of things Blair's improprieties are of no great consequence. The people into whose mouths he put imaginary words, and from whose imagined front porch he pretended to see tobacco fields instead of tract homes, are not notably put out. Ordinary Americans reckon that since you shouldn't believe a word of anything you read in a newspaper or hear over the airwaves, what's so different about Jayson Blair? The biggest story Blair was involved in was the Washington sniper story. Deployed by his editors into the media feeding frenzy following Muhammad and Malvo's arrests, he invented quotes which he attributed to unnamed prosecutors and FBI officials, and which they then angrily denounced. Again, these fabrications didn't have much effect on anything.

Day after day, in the *New York Times* and other major newspapers, one comes across blind quotes, dropped by "White House sources" or "senior administration officials," relayed by reporters and columnists mostly without any warning label alerting the public that such-and-such a quote was a volley in some savage bureaucratic feud and should be regarded with extreme suspicion.

The Jayson Blair scandal comes on the heels of what was one of the most intensive bouts of botched reporting, wild speculation and straightforward disingenuous lying in the history of American journalism, a bout which prompted an invasion, many deaths and now—given the way things are currently headed—the likelihood of mass starvation. In other words, the lousy reporting really had consequences.

The invasion of Iraq was premised on the existence of weapons of mass destruction. None have yet been found and most of the U.S. detective teams are now wanly returning home. Did the *New York Times* assist in this process of deception? Very much so. Just look through the clips file of one of its better-known reporters, Judith Miller.

It was Miller who first launched the supposedly knowledgeable Iraqi nuclear scientist Khidir Hamza on the world, crucial to the U.S. government's effort to portray a nuclear-capable Saddam.

Thus far there's been no agonized reprise from the *Times* on its faulty estimate of the credibility of Hamza. And though Blair's fabrications about the homecoming of Jessica Lynch were minutely dissected, neither the *Times* nor any other U.S. paper that I've read has had anything to say about the charges made in the London *Times* that the "heroic" rescue of Lynch was from an undefended hospital in circumstances very different and less creditable than those heralded by a Pentagon desperate for good publicity during a time when the invasion seemed to have faltered amid unexpectedly stuff resistance.

In fact, some speculate that for the *Times* the Blair scandal might be a PR boost for the newspaper, proof that it is manly enough to fess up and take its punishment, that Blair was but one lone bad apple in a sound barrel, an apple furthermore that only got into the barrel because of a laudable indulgence towards an African American, forgiven his sins because he was black.

As Glen Ford, who writes an acridly brilliant web commentary in *Black Agenda Report*, remarks apropos a theme of much white punditry on Blair, that somehow it's all the fault of affirmative action: "Black people bear no onus for white incompetence in selecting Black people to carry out white corporate missions."

Then Ford contrasts the humdrum fabrications of Blair with a run-of-the-mill piece of reporting that appeared on May 5, 2005, in a report by *Times* man, Adam Nagourney. Nagourney discussed the televised Democratic primary debate in South Carolina. There was a problem, and it apparently didn't bother Nagourney's editors. He mentioned only six of the nine candidates: Lieberman, Kerry, Edwards, Gephardt, Dean, and Graham. In over 1,000 words, Nagourney failed to once note the existence of Al Sharpton, Carole Moseley-Braun, or Dennis Kucinich. The two blacks and the leftist got purged from the newspaper of record.

That's why I can't get too troubled about Jayson Blair. The *Times* has it coming, for a thousand more serious reasons that haven't ever bothered its editors or its publisher.

Though there are a few good reporters on its staff, we ceased to have much respect for the *New York Times* many years ago, and have regarded the honors heaped on it by such servile bodies as the Pulitzer Board as ludicrous. Consider those staffers who have gone to the wall for reporting too well. Jo Thomas anticipated by many years the recent disclosures of the British Army's "shoot to kill" policies in Northern Ireland. But the British government's furious protests to *New York Times'* editors had their effect and Thomas was silenced.

In his columns on the op-ed page, Sidney Schanberg had the audacity to utter some bracing truths about the politics of real estate in New York. But of course the *New York Times* is a major player in the real estate power plays of mid-town Manhattan, and Schanberg went to the wall.

Other disgraces? The *Times* was as assiduous as the *Washington Post* and *Los Angeles Times* in throwing mud at Gary Webb for his *San Jose Mercury News* series on the CIA's complicity in drug smuggling from Central America. And even though subsequent CIA admissions have vindicated Webb, the *Times*, in company with the other traducers of Webb, has never seen fit to set the record straight.

The easiest and certainly the briskest way to read the *Times* these days is through the headlines it sends one for free over the Internet. One can mentally supply the stories, without going through the exertion of trying to remember the necessary passwords to bring them up on the screen. On the supply side, Blair cut the same corners. Just like Janet Cook at the *Washington Post*, he knew what The Man wanted, and served it up at an efficient rate. It's ironic that he finally got toasted for excessive plagiarism, since the core mode of the conventional press is collective plagiarism, endlessly recycling the same banalities, with tiny modulations to ensure "originality."

2005

The Smearing of Wen Ho Lee

Alexander Cockburn and Jeffrey St. Clair

THE COLLAPSE OF THE GOVERNMENT'S CASE AGAINST WEN HO Lee on September 10, 2000, represented one of the greatest humiliations of a national newspaper in the history of journalism. One has to go back to the publication by the London *Times* of the Pigott forgeries in 1887 libeling Charles Stewart Parnell, the Irish nationalist hero, to find an equivalent debacle.

Yet to this day not a whisper of contrition, not a murmur of remorse, has ever agitated the editorial pages of the *New York Times*. At the time of the debacle all it could muster from its editorial heart was a self-righteous call for the appointment of a "politically independent person of national standing to review the entire case."

No such review is required to determine the decisive role of the *New York Times* in sparking the persecution of Wen Ho Lee, his solitary confinement under threat of execution, his denial of bail, his shackling, the loss of his job, the anguish and terror endured by this scientist and his family.

On March 6, 1999, the *Times* carried a report by James Risen and Jeff Gerth entitled "Breach at Los Alamos" charging an unnamed scientist with stealing nuclear secrets from the government lab and giving them to the Chinese Peoples' Republic. The espionage, according to a security official cited by Risen and Gerth, was "going to be just as bad as the Rosenbergs."

Two days later Wen Ho Lee, an American of Taiwanese descent, was fired from his job. Ahead of him lay months of further pillorying in a racist witch-hunt led by the *Times*, whose news columns were replete with further mendacious bulletins from Risen and Gerth, and whose op-ed page featured William Safire using their stories to launch his own calumnies against Wen Ho Lee and the Clinton administration.

Guided by Safire, the Republicans in Congress pounced upon the Wen Ho Lee case with ardor approaching ecstasy. By the spring of 1999, their effort to evict Bill Clinton from office for the Lewinsky affair had collapsed. They needed a new stick with which to beat the administration, and the *New York Times* handed it to them.

In Safire's insinuations, the Clinton White House was but an annex of the Middle Kingdom, and the transfer of U.S. nuclear secrets merely one episode in a long, dark narrative of treachery to the American flag. Former U.S. Senator Warren Rudman went on NBC's *Meet the Press* and declared flatly, "The agenda for the body politic is often set by the media. Had it not been for the *New York Times* breaking the story of Chinese espionage all over the front pages, I'm not sure I would be here this morning."

The most preposterous expression of the Republican spy crusade against the Clinton administration came with the release of the 900-page report named after California Rep. Christopher Cox, filled with one demented assertion after another, including the memorable though absolutely false claim that "the stolen information includes classified information on seven U.S. thermonuclear warheads, including every currently deployed thermonuclear warhead in the U.S. ballistic missile arsenal."

Yet Risen and Gerth's stories had been profuse with terrible errors from the outset. Their prime source had been Notra Trulock, an embittered security official in the Department of Energy, intent upon his own vendettas within the DOE. Risen and Gerth swallowed his assertions with disgraceful zeal. From him and other self-interested officials they relayed one falsehood after another: that Wen Ho Lee had failed a lie detector test; that the Los Alamos lab was the undoubted source of the security breach; that it was from Los Alamos that the Chinese had acquired the blueprint of the miniaturized W-88 nuclear warhead.

Had the *New York Times* launched its campaign of terror against Wen Ho Lee at the height of the Cold War, it is quite likely that Wen Ho Lee would have been swept to his doom, most likely with a sentence of life imprisonment amid vain efforts of his defenders to get the scientist a fair hearing. It is doubtful that U.S. District Judge James Parker in New Mexico would have had the courage to denounce the Justice Department for a shabby case and to order the release of Wen Ho Lee after harshly criticizing the 59-count government indictment and the "demeaning, unnecessarily punitive conditions" in which Wen Ho Lee had been held.

But we are no longer amidst the fevers of the Cold War. And though the Pentagon had wanly tried to foment a budget-boosting campaign to suggest that China represents a fearsome military threat, it was not been taken with any great seriousness. The exaggerations of Chinese might were simply too egregious.

So, in these post-Cold War years, Wen Ho Lee did have his sturdy defenders. Some were government officials evidently appalled by the *Times'* campaign. Some commentators, most notably the late Lars-Erik Nelson of the *New York Daily News*, were scathing about the case against Wen Ho Lee. In July of 1999, the *New York Review of Books* published a long piece by Nelson which explicitly criticized the witch-hunt and noted the malign role of the *New York Times*. Nelson pointed out how many of the supposedly filched "secrets" had been publicly available for years. By September of 1999, the *New York Times* had evidently entertained sufficient disquiet to publish a long piece by William Broad which decorously—though without any explicit finger-pointing—undermined the premises of Risen and Gerth's articles.

None of this helped Wen Ho Lee escape terrifying FBI interrogations in which an agent flourished the threat of execution. He was kept in solitary, allowed to exercise but one hour a day while shackled, kept in a constantly lit cell. (Such horrible conditions and worse, it should be noted, are the lot—year after year—of thousands of prisoners in so-called Secure Housing Units in prisons across the U.S.A.)

Even near the end, when it was plain that the government's case was falling apart, U.S. Attorney General Janet Reno's prosecutors successfully contested efforts to have Wen Ho Lee released on bail. And when Judge Parker finally threw out almost the entire case, the prosecutors continued to insist, as has Reno, that their conduct had been appropriate throughout.

With consummate effrontery, the *New York Times*, without whose agency Wen Ho Lee would never have spent a day in a prison cell, perhaps not even have lost his job, then urged an investigation of the bungled prosecution. On September 16, 2000, *New York Times'* columnist Anthony Lewis excoriated the Reno's Justice Department and proclaimed piously that "this country's security rests in good part in having judges with the character and courage, like Judge Parker, to do their duty despite prosecutorial alarms and excursions." No word from Lewis about the role of his own newspaper.

Lewis knew well enough, as did every staffer at the *Times*, the infamous role played by Risen, Gerth, Safire, and the editors who condoned their stories and columns. No doubt even if Lewis had noted the role of the *Times*, an editor would have struck the tactless phrases from his column.

In an extraordinary breach of conventional decorum, the president of the United States criticized his own attorney general for the way Wen Ho Lee has been maltreated. Yet the editors of the *New York Times* could admit no wrong. Risen and Gerth were not required to offer reflections of the outcome of the affair.

When the forgeries of Richard Pigott, described in the 1911 edition of the *Encyclopedia Britannica* as "a needy and disreputable Irish journalist," against Parnell were exposed, he fled to Madrid and there blew out his brains. The London *Times* required years to efface the shame of its gullibility. Would that the *New York Times* was required to admit equivalent error. But it was not. This was no-fault journalism, a disgrace to the Fourth Estate.

2000

Gerth's Saving Prose

Alexander Cockburn and Jeffrey St. Clair

THE RIGHT IS WHINING. CARL LIMBACHER AND HIS CREW complain on the popular NewsMax.com that in the two weeks since the Harken Oil story went critical, "the prestige press" (Limbacher's odd phrase, which presumably means he's excluding the *National Enquirer*) has given the affair fifty times more coverage than it gave the Whitewater deal after the *New York Times* broke that story on March 8, 1992.

Limbacher moans that Whitewater showed up only 14 times in the wake of the *Times'* story, while from June 28 to July 12 of this year there have been over 700 stories on the Harken sale.

C'mon, Carl. The reason Whitewater got off to a slow start was because for months no one could figure out what the *New York Times'* Jeff Gerth was writing about. Reading any Gerth's story is like bicycling through wet sand, but in the case of Whitewater he surpassed himself. As readers sank up to their armpits in the sludge of Gerth-prose, interest in Whitewater for that electoral year flickered and died. Gerth saved Clinton's ass. Ultimately Whitewater did make it into the headlines, but in truth it always lacked appeal. There just wasn't that much meat in the stew. Not like Hillary's commodity trades. Just like those trades, Harken is really easy to understand.

Same way with Cheney. No need to put in those daunting phrases like "complex transactions." The simple numbers have serious panache. Here's one précis of the situation that's going the rounds:

- Cheney's 2000 income from Halliburton: $36,086,635.

- Increase in government contracts while Cheney led Halliburton: 91 per cent.
- Minimum size of "accounting irregularity" that occurred while Cheney was CEO: $100,000,000.
- Number of the seven official U.S. "State Sponsors of Terror" that Halliburton contracted with: 2 out of 7.
- Pages of energy plan documents Cheney refused to give congressional investigators: 13,500.
- Amount energy companies gave the Bush/Cheney presidential campaign: $1,800,000.

But if anyone can save Bush and Cheney, it will be Gerth. He and another *Times* reporter called Richard Stevenson, managed the truly amazing feat of making the Harken story complicated and boring. Here was the first paragraph: "President Bush received two low-interest loans to buy stock from an oil company where he served as a board member in the late 1980s. He then benefited from the company's relaxation of the terms of one loan in 1989 as he was engaged in the most important business deal of his career."

Only 52 words and already the air is whistling out of the tire. On and on the story trundled, until it approached the famous SEC non-probe. You'll recall from the 700-plus stories lamented by Limbacher that Bush Jr.'s prolonged failure to report to the SEC the sale that netted him $840,000 was viewed with indulgence by that agency, whose boss had been appointed by President G.H.W. Bush, and whose counsel had worked for Bush Jr. negotiating the purchase of the Texas Rangers. It's hard to bore people with material like that, as Paul Krugman is discovering each week. Here's how Gerth and Stevenson approached this bit of the saga:

> The June 1990 Harken stock sale led to an investigation by the Securities and Exchange Commission—during his father's administration—of whether Mr. Bush had knowingly sold the stock in advance of worse-than-expected financial results that

temporarily drove down Harken's share price. The SEC took no
action against Mr. Bush.

Harken is not a new story. Charles Lewis of the Center for
Public Integrity dealt with it long ago in his book, *The Buying
of the President: 2000.* Even back then Lewis speculated that the
mysterious institutional buyer of Bush's stock might have been
Harvard Management, the overseer of the school's multi-billion
dollar endowment. Lewis wrote that "a month after Bush came
on board, Harvard Management agreed to invest at least $20
million in Harken. It would come to own some ten million shares
of Harken stock, making it one of the company's largest investors. The Bush name may have helped seal the deal.... Harvard's
Harken investments in oil and gas would eventually generate
nearly $200 million in losses for the endowment."

The broker involved, Ralph Smith of Sutro & Company, has
refused to name the buyer of Bush shares, though he has said it
was an institutional investor. Lewis reported that "at the bottom
of a spreadsheet Smith used to record his calls to Bush was the
name of Michael Eisenson, along with the telephone number of
Harvard Management."

In other words, Harvard Management lost staggering amounts
in a bum investment that saved the president's son.

None of this alluring stuff holds appeal for Gerth and his colleague, who simply wrote, "In the case of the sale of his Harken
stock, Mr. Bush benefited from the action of an investor who
remains unknown even today."

A few days later, Gerth and Don van Natta Jr. were at it again,
this time paralyzing *Times* readers with a narcotic narrative about
Halliburton. The lead was promising.

"The Halliburton Company, the Dallas oil services company
bedeviled lately by an array of accounting and business issues, is
benefiting very directly from the United States efforts to combat
terrorism.

"From building cells for detainees at Guantanamo Bay in
Cuba to feeding American troops in Uzbekistan, the Pentagon is

increasingly relying on a unit of Halliburton called KBR, sometimes referred to as Kellogg Brown & Root."

Reading the story was a bit like walking around some familiar
room in the dark, tripping over and then gradually recognizing
bits of furniture. Through the fog of Gerth-prose one could dimly
descry the familiar landscape of Pentagon corruption, with cost-
plus bids, non-competitive contract awards, manic over-billing,
and so forth. Senator Charles Grassley's staff will be only too glad
to send you thousands of pages of testimony on such endemic
corruption and fraud, a goodly part of which stemmed from Al
Gore's efforts to reinvent government by having recourse to the
discipline and efficiency of the private sector.

Another reason for the sense of familiarity was that the story
was broken, and furthermore told in an exciting and accessible way several months ago by Jordan Green of the Institute
for Southern Studies, published in *Facing South*, the Institute's
Internet newsletter, with a shorter version in the Institute's
Southern Exposure magazine. Contrast Gerth-tedium with Green's
pioneering and far richer treatment, under the title "To the
Victors Go the Markets: Halliburton's Claim On Central Asia":

> Last December, the U.S. Department of Defense made a no-
> cap, cost-plus-award contract to Halliburton KBR's Government
> Operations division. The Dallas-based company is contracted to
> build forward operating bases to support troop deployments for
> the next nine years wherever the president chooses to take the
> anti-terrorism war... The Pentagon posts all contract announce-
> ments exceeding $5 million on its Website, but in Halliburton's
> case declined to disclose the estimated value of the award. A
> spokesperson for Halliburton gave $2.5 billion as the amount
> the company earned from base support services in the 1990s,
> acknowledging that the contract value could exceed that number
> assuming that the scope of U.S. military actions widens in the
> next decade... The first increment of Halliburton's award is being
> subcontracted to Oshkosh Truck Corporation in Wisconsin and
> King Trailers in Market Harborough, England. Because of Prime
> Minister Tony Blair's invaluable service of persuading Britain's
> reluctant public to go along with the American campaign and in

providing British peacekeepers to secure Afghanistan, America's junior partner has been rewarded with a boost to its manufacturing base.

But the major rewards are reserved for the Texas oil oligarchy.

Halliburton Company has close connections with the Bush family. Aside from Cheney, there is Lawrence Eagleburger, a Halliburton director and former deputy secretary of defense under Bush Sr. during the Gulf War.

In its earlier incarnation as Brown & Root Services, the company sponsored Texan and future president Lyndon B. Johnson's stolen election to the U.S. Senate in 1948, building the state's spectacular political-industrial muscle.

That's how to write a story. (But surely, you'll be asking, Gerth and his associate reminded *Times'* readers of the colorful saga of Brown & Root? No they didn't.)

2002

Judith Miller:
Weapon of Mass Destruction
Alexander Cockburn

As for the Weapons of Mass Destruction, their non-appearance has become a huge embarrassment for both Bush and Blair. Last Sunday's British *Independent* carried the following huge front page banner headlines: "So where are they, Mr. Blair? Not one illegal warhead. Not one drum of chemicals. Not one incriminating document. Not one shred of evidence that Iraq has weapons of mass destruction in more than a month of war and occupation."

The days passed, and each excited bellow of discovery of WMD caches on the road north from Kuwait yielded to disappointment. Then came Judith Miller's story on the front page of the *New York Times*, April 21, 2003. The smoking gun at last! Not exactly, as we shall see. But first a word about the reporter. If ever someone has an institutional interest in finding WMD in Iraq it's surely Miller, who down the years has established a corner in creaking Tales of Terrorism, most of them bottle-fed to her by Israeli and U.S. intelligence.

It was Miller who served up Khidir Hamza, the self-proclaimed nuclear bomb maker for Saddam, later exposed as a fraud. It was Miller who last year whipped up an amazing confection in the *Times*, blind-sourced from top to toe, about a Russian bio-war scientist (sounding suspiciously like Lotte Lenya in *From Russia With Love*, and since deceased) ferrying Russian smallpox to Saddam. At least the *Times'* headline writer tried to keep things honest this time. "Illicit Arms Kept Till Eve of War, an Iraqi Scientist is Said to Assert."

What did who say and who did the asserting? It turns out that Miller, embedded with the entire 101 Airborne, had been told by "American weapons experts" in a group called MET Alpha that they have been talking to "a scientist who claims to have worked in Iraq's chemical weapons program," that the Iraqis destroyed chemical weapons days before the war and that "Iraq had secretly sent unconventional weapons and technology to Syria, starting in the mid-1990s, and that more recently Iraq was cooperating with Al Qaeda."

Now isn't that just what an Iraqi scientist looking for quick passage out of Iraq to the U.S.A. would say, in a series of unverifiable claims?

Miller does concede that the MET Alpha group would not tell her who the scientist was, would not allow her to question him (assuming it wasn't a "her," maybe Lotte Lenya in a later incarnation), or do anything more than look at him from a great distance as he stood next to what was billed to Miller as a dump for "precursors" for chemical weapons.

Furthermore, she wasn't allowed to write about the unnamed Iraqi scientist for three days, and even then U.S. military censors went over her copy line by line. What convenient disclosures this Iraqi allegedly offers, tailor-made to buttress Rumsfeld's fist-shaking at Syria and Bush and Powell's claims that Saddam and Osama bin Laden worked hand in glove, a claim that depended originally on an article by Jeffrey Goldberg in the *New Yorker* last year. At least Goldberg talked to the man claiming Osama/Saddam ties, although he made no effort to check the man's "evidence," subsequently discredited by less gullible journalists.

With Miller we sink to the level of straight press handout. Lay all Judith Miller's *New York Times* stories end to end, from late 2001 to June 2003, and you get a desolate picture of a reporter with an agenda, both manipulating and being manipulated by U.S. government officials, Iraqi exiles and defectors, an entire Noah's Ark of scam-artists.

And while Miller, either under her own single byline (or with *NYT* colleagues), was touting the bioterror threat, her book *Germs*, co-authored with *Times'* men Steven Engelberg and William Broad, was in the bookstores and climbing the bestseller lists. The same day that Miller opened an envelope of white powder (which turned out to be harmless) at her desk at the *New York Times*, her book was No. 6 on the *New York Times* bestseller list. The following week (October 21, 2001), it reached No. 2. By October 28—at the height of her scare-mongering campaign—it was up to No. 1. If we were cynical...

We don't have full 20/20 hindsight yet, but we do know for certain that all the sensational disclosures in Miller's major stories between late 2001 and early summer 2003, promoted disingenuous lies. There were no secret bio labs under Saddam's palaces; no nuclear factories across Iraq secretly working at full tilt. A huge percentage of what Miller wrote was garbage, garbage that powered the Bush administration's propaganda drive towards invasion.

What does that make Miller? She was a witting cheerleader for war. She knew what she was doing.

And what does Miller's performance make the *New York Times*? Didn't any senior editors at the *New York Times* or even the boss, A.O. Sulzberger, ask themselves whether it was appropriate to have a trio of *Times'* reporters touting their book *Germs* on TV and radio, while simultaneously running stories in the *New York Times* headlining the risks of bio-war and thus creating just the sort of public alarm beneficial to the sales of their book? Isn't that the sort of conflict of interest prosecutors have been hounding Wall Street punters for?

The knives are certainly out for Miller. Leaked internal email traffic disclosed Miller's self-confessed reliance on Ahmed Chalabi, a leading Iraqi exile with every motive to produce imaginative defectors eager to testify about Saddam's bio war, chemical and nuclear arsenal. In late June, Howard Kurtz of the *Washington Post* ran a long story about Miller's ability in recent months to make the U.S. Army jump, merely by threatening to go straight to Rumsfeld.

It was funny, but again, the conflicts of interest put the *New York Times* in a terrible light. Here was Miller, with a contract to write a new book on the post-invasion search for "weapons of mass destruction," lodged in the Army unit charged with that search, fiercely insisting that the unit prolong its futile hunt, while simultaneously working hand-in-glove with Chalabi. Journalists have to do some complex dance steps to get good stories, but a few red flags should have gone up on that one.

A brisk, selective timeline:

DECEMBER 20, 2001. HEADLINE: "Iraqi Tells of Renovations at Sites For Chemical and Nuclear Arms." Miller rolls out a new Iraqi defector, in the ripe tradition of her favorite, Khidir Hamza, the fraud who called himself Saddam's bomb maker.

STORY: "An Iraqi defector who described himself as a civil engineer said he personally worked on renovations of secret facilities for biological, chemical and nuclear weapons in underground wells, private villas, and under the Saddam Hussein Hospital in Baghdad as recently as a year ago.

"The defector, Adnan Ihsan Saeed al-Haideri, gave details of the projects he said he worked on for President Saddam Hussein's government in an extensive interview last week in Bangkok.... The interview with Mr. Saeed was arranged by the Iraqi National Congress, the main Iraqi opposition group, which seeks the overthrow of Mr. Hussein.

"If verified, Mr. Saeed's allegations would provide ammunition to officials within the Bush administration who have been arguing that Mr. Hussein should be driven from power partly because of his unwillingness to stop making weapons of mass destruction..."

Notice the sedate phrase "if verified." It never was verified. But the story served its purpose.

SEPTEMBER 7, 2002. HEADLINE: "U.S. Says Hussein Intensifies Quest for A-bomb Parts." This one was by Miller and Michael

Gordon, promoting the aluminum tube nonsense: "In the last 14 months, Iraq has sought to buy thousands of specially designed aluminum tubes, which American officials believe were intended as components of centrifuges to enrich uranium." All lies of course. Miller and Gordon emphasize: "Mr. Hussein's dogged insistence on pursuing his nuclear ambitions, along with what defectors described in interviews as Iraq's push to improve and expand Baghdad's chemical and biological arsenals."

Another of Miller's defectors takes a bow:

> Speaking on the condition that neither he nor the country in which he was interviewed be identified, Ahmed al-Shemri, his pseudonym, said Iraq had continued developing, producing and storing chemical agents at many mobile and fixed secret sites throughout the country, many of them underground.
>
> "All of Iraq is one large storage facility," said Mr. Shemri. Asked about his allegations, American officials said they believed these reports were accurate...

A final bit of brazen chicanery from Gordon and Miller:

> Iraq denied the existence of a germ warfare program entirely until 1995, when United Nations inspectors forced Baghdad to acknowledge it had such an effort. Then, after insisting that it had never weaponized bacteria or filled warheads, it again belatedly acknowledged having done so after Hussein Kamel, Mr. Hussein's brother-in-law, defected to Jordan with evidence about the scale of the germ warfare program.

What Gordon and Miller leave out (or lacked the enterprise or desire to find out) is that Hussein Kamel told U.N. inspectors, and the CIA and MI6 in separate sessions, that he had destroyed all Iraq's WMDs, on Saddam Hussein's orders.

SEPTEMBER 13, 2002. HEADLINE: "White House Lists Iraq Steps to Build Banned Weapons."

Miller and Gordon again, taking at face value the administration's claims that it was "the intelligence agencies' unanimous view that the type of [aluminum] tubes that Iraq has been seeking are used to make such centrifuges." If nothing else this shows what rotten reporters Miller and Gordon are, because it now turns out the intelligence analysts across Washington were deeply divided on precisely this issue.

SEPTEMBER 18, 2002. HEADLINE: "Verification is Difficult at Best, Say the Experts, and Maybe Impossible." This is Miller helping the War Party lay down a pre-emptive barrage against the U.N. inspectors: "Verifying Iraq's assertions that it has abandoned weapons of mass destruction, or finding evidence that it has not done so, may not be feasible, according to officials and former weapons inspectors..."

A cameo appearance by Khidhir Hamza, reporting his supposed knowledge that "Iraq was now at the 'pilot plant' stage of nuclear production and within two to three years of mass producing centrifuges to enrich uranium for a bomb."

DECEMBER 3, 2002. HEADLINE: "CIA Hunts Iraq Tie to Soviet Smallpox." A Classic Miller fragment: "The CIA is investigating an informant's accusation that Iraq obtained a particularly virulent strain of smallpox from a Russian scientist who worked in a smallpox lab in Moscow during Soviet times..."

JANUARY 24, 2003. HEADLINE: "Defectors Bolster U.S. Case Against Iraq, Officials Say." Another Miller onslaught on the U.N. inspectors: "Former Iraqi scientists, military officers and contractors have provided American intelligence agencies with a portrait of Saddam Hussein's secret programs to develop and conceal chemical, biological and nuclear weapons that is starkly at odds with the findings so far of the United Nations weapons inspectors."

Al-Haideri is still in play: "Intelligence officials said that some of the most valuable information has come from Adnan Ihsan Saeed al-Haideri, a contractor who fled Iraq in the summer of 2001. He later told American officials that chemical and biological weapons laboratories were hidden beneath hospitals and inside presidential palaces. Mr. Haideri was relocated anonymously to a small town in Virginia."

We'll leave al-Haideri in well-earned retirement and Miller heading towards her supreme triumph of April 20, 2003, relaying the allegations of chemical and bio-weapon dumps made by an unnamed Iraqi scientist she'd never met.

Revoke Judith Miller's Pulitzer Prize

Now that the *New York Times'* own ombudsman has weighed in with a scathing critique of Judith Miller's lies and deceptions about her WMD and Al Qaeda reporting, including a recommendation that the paper not allow her back in its newsroom, it's time to call for an independent investigation into her much trumpeted Pulitzer Prize, which she won jointly in 2002 with several other *Times'* reporters for her articles in 2001 about Al Qaeda.

Clearly, Miller was no independent journalist looking for truth in her incarnation as "Ms. Run Amok," pushing the Bush administrations line for war with Iraq in the post-9/11 run-up to the invasion of that country. Her breathless and terrifying stories claiming that Saddam Hussein was sitting on masses of WMDs—biological and chemical weapons and perhaps even nuclear bombs—and that his regime was tight with Osama bin Laden and his merry band of bombers and terrorists—were at best single-sourced propaganda and, at worst, deliberate fabrications.

Miller would go to Iraq conman and convicted embezzler Ahmed Chalabi, who would give her his latest wild fabrications about WMDs and Al Qaeda links. Chalabi would also go to the White House with the same information, which would be assimilated by the White House Iraq Group, a war-marketing enterprise set up and run by Andrew Card and Karl Rove, and then Miller, who knew all this, would go to WHIG for "confirmation" of the information she'd gotten from Chalabi, which she would then portray, to *Times'* editors and readers, as "confirmed" by White House sources.

It was all very neat.

And all extremely costly in terms of blood (the Iraqi death toll is over 450,000 and the U.S. military death toll is about to pass the 3,000 mark) and taxpayer money (in excess of a trillion and counting).

As Russ Baker put it in the *Nation*, "I am convinced there would not have been a war (against Iraq) without Judith Miller."

The case for challenging and calling for the revocation of Miller's Pulitzer—and also of her Emmy and Dupont awards for stories on WMDs and Al Qaeda in *Times* television specials—is that once one discovers a reporter is a fraud and a liar, it raises questions about their earlier work, which should be gone over with a fine-toothed comb for signs of the same pattern of behavior.

Her Pulitzer, after all, was for a series of articles she and several other *Times'* reporters wrote about Al Qaeda right after 9/11, and likely represent the earliest examples of her Chalabi deception campaign and her embed with the White House Iraq Group.

Challenging Miller's Pulitzer wouldn't be the first time a *Times* reporter's Pulitzer Prize has been called into question.

Right-wingers have long been calling for the revocation of a Pulitzer Prize awarded in 1932 to *Times'* Russia correspondent Walter Duranty, who has been accused posthumously of having been too credulous in his coverage of the Soviet Union under Joseph Stalin, and of soft-pedaling the 1930s famine that killed millions of Ukrainian and Russian peasants.

Duranty's work, as a result of the calls for his head, was subjected to an investigation by historian Mark Van Hagen, who concluded that the articles, which won the reporter his prize, were "dull and largely uncritical recitations of Soviet sources." So what would an independent historian looking at Miller's 2001–2004 oeuvre say? Not, perhaps, that her pieces were dull, for they were designed to terrify, but surely that they were "largely uncritical recitations of White House sources."

If Duranty, who at least mentioned the problems Soviet citizens were facing under Stalin's rule, can be considered credulous and one-sided in his Russian reports, what is one to say about Miller, who has been little more than a mouthpiece for the neocon cabal running Middle East policy for the Bush administration?

2005

"Maybe We Did Screw Up... a Little"

Alexander Cockburn and Jeffrey St. Clair

O N MAY 26, 2006, THE *New York Times* FINALLY HITCHED up its pants, took a deep breath, and issued an editorial declaration of moderate regret for its role in boosting the case for war on Iraq. There was a bit of dutiful trumpet-tootling at the start ("we found an enormous amount of journalism that we are proud of... accurate reflection of the state of our knowledge at the time") and then a manly confession that perhaps, maybe, conceivably, the *Times'* reporting was a shade less than perfect.

"We have found a number of instances of coverage that was not as rigorous as it should have been. In some cases, information that was controversial then, and seems questionable now, was insufficiently qualified or allowed to stand unchallenged." Given that the paper printed tens of thousands of words of willful balderdash from 2001 to early 2003, the admission leaves something to be desired, but that's scarcely surprising.

Remember this one? "Passages of some articles also posed a problem of tone. In place of a tone of journalistic detachment from our sources, we occasionally used language that adopted the sense of alarm that was contained in official reports." That was the *Times* issuing an exceptionally graceless admission in 2000 that it might have done better in the Wen Ho Lee affair.

The most the *Times* could manage then were a few strangled croaks, wishing it had portrayed his character in greater depth. It never had words of specific admonition for the instigators of Lee's persecution, reporters Jeff Gerth and James Risen and the columnist William Safire.

It's the same now. Nowhere in the editorial note of May 26 does the difficult name Judith Miller crop up. The editors cite, as examples of inadequate reporting, five stories from 2001 to 2003, without naming authors. Miller wrote or co-wrote three of them.

The climb-down is 1,100 words long. Here is no methodical review, such as the 7,200-word, unsparing scrutiny of Jayson Blair's insignificant fabrications. Given the fact that the *Times* helped launch a war, now shaping up to be a world-historical disaster, proportionality surely demands something the length of the *Times'* stories on the selling of another war, the Pentagon Papers.

The editors find no room to examine a story Miller wrote with Michael Gordon, another seasoned fabricator. Their September 8, 2002, article, "U.S. Says Hussein Intensifies Quest for A-Bomb Parts," was mostly nonsense about those notorious aluminum tubes, though there was a cameo role for another defector, a rogue offered to readers under the pseudonym Ahmed al-Shemri, who is quoted saying Iraq was "developing, producing and storing chemical agents. 'All of Iraq is one large storage facility,' said Shemri. Asked about his allegations, U.S. officials said they believed these reports were accurate."

Then Miller and Gordon wrote some of the most brazenly misleading lines in the history of war propaganda: "After insisting that it had never weaponized bacteria or filled warheads, [Iraq] again belatedly acknowledged having done so after Hussein Kamel, Hussein's brother-in-law [sic], defected to Jordan with evidence about the scale of the germ warfare program." What's missing from this brisk evocation of Hussein Kamel's debriefings by the UNSCOM inspectors, the CIA and MI6 in the summer of 1995 is that Kamel told them all, with corroboration from aides who had also defected, that on Saddam Hussein's orders his son-in-law had destroyed all of Iraq's WMDs years earlier, right after the Gulf War. If Miller and Gordon cite some of the debrief, why not all?

This brings us to the now popular scapegoat for the fictions about WMDs, touted by *Times'* editors, by other reporters, and by U.S. intelligence agencies. It was all the fault of the smooth-tongued Ahmed Chalabi, now fallen from grace and stigmatized as a cat's paw of Iranian intelligence. But was there ever a moment when Chalabi's motives and the defectors he efficiently mass-produced should not have been questioned by experienced reporters, editors, and intelligence analysts? Furthermore, it wasn't all Chalabi's doing. We have yet to see an apology from the *New Yorker* for publishing Jeffrey Goldberg's carefully wrought fantasies about the supposed links between Saddam and Al Qaeda. These were among the most effective pieces of propaganda, widely flourished by the Bush administration. Chalabi had nothing to do with that, nor with most of the "slam dunk" case on WMDs invoked by CIA Director George Tenet and dutifully parroted in the press.

2005

When Divas Collide:
Maureen Dowd vs. Judith Miller

Alexander Cockburn

WOULD YOU PAY $49.95 TO WATCH WOMEN WRESTLING IN mud? I did October 22, 2005, and it was well worth the expense. I get the *New York Times* online and until a couple of weeks ago all the features were free. Then, as some of you have no doubt discovered, the *NYT*'s columnists started to have only their opening sentences on free display. To get the full columns of Krugman, Rich, Dowd, and the others you have to pony up $49.95 a year's subscription to *Times Select*.

I held off until today when the *Times* nailed the sale with Dowd's column titled, "Woman of Mass Destruction," and her ominous opening sentence, "I've always liked Judith Miller."

Miller has been the sport of a million stories and there was nothing much by way of startling revelations in what Dowd wrote, but in operatic terms it was as though Maria Callas had suddenly rushed onto the stage and slugged Elizabeth Schwartzkopf.

After that enticing lead, designed to make online readers fish out their credit cards, Dowd spent five paragraphs sketching Miller's profile as a power-mad egomaniac (demanding Dowd's chair at a White House briefing), before drop-kicking her in the face with the blunt accusations that she's a liar and—a thought first expressed by this writer the day Miller went behind bars— that "her stint in the Alexandria jail was in part a career rehabilitation project."

Then, with Judith down on the canvas, Dowd came flying down from the corner post, with her knee on Judith's throat:

> Judith told the *Times* that she plans to write a book and intends
> to return to the newsroom, hoping to cover "the same thing I've
> always covered—threats to our country." If that were to happen,
> the institution most in danger would be the newspaper in your
> hands.

Moral: Don't ever take Maureen Dowd's chair at a White
House briefing.

Dowd mentions an internal memo to the staff from the *Times'*
editor, Bill Keller, in which—to use Dowd's words—"Judith
seemed to have 'misled' the Washington bureau chief, Phil
Taubman, about the extent of her involvement in the Valerie
Plame leak case."

What Keller actually wrote was the following:

> If I had known the details of Judith's entanglement with Libby,
> I'd have been more careful in how the paper articulated its
> defense and perhaps more willing than I had been to support
> efforts aimed at exploring compromises.

"Entanglement" is a curiously suggestive word, given the notoriously rich and varied texture of Judith Miller's personal resume
whose imagined contours have been the sport of newsrooms and
hotel bars around the world. Certainly Miller took it that way,
writing in response, "As for your reference to my 'entanglement'
with Mr. Libby, I had no personal, social, or other relationship
with him except as a source." Welcome to the *Times* as Pay-Per-
View Reality TV.

Keller's sniveling "internal" memo throwing Miller over the
side, which he obviously knew would be forwarded to Howard
Kurtz ten seconds after he hit the SEND key, was disgusting. The
Times nailed Miller's colors to its mast many years ago. There
are decades' worth of her atrocious mendacities in its archives,
and decades' worth of accurate refutations of her news stories
ignored by *Times'* editors.

Miller's game was the *Times'* game. They were witting co-con-
spirators. When Miller co-wrote (with Stephen Engelberg and
William Broad) *Germs: Biological Weapons and America's Secret War*,

the *Times* was happy to print her stories in the paper designed to push the book up into bestseller status, in a staggering conflict of interest that earned the paper plenty of money.

It's too late in the game for *Times'* editors to start whining that Judith misled them. They printed her rubbish because they were disposed to believe it, and for Keller to turn on her now in an "internal" memo designed for public consumption is cowardly and despicable. The gentlemanly thing for Keller to do would be to keep a stiff upper lip, let Dowd and the reporters toss Miller on their horns and, if circumstances warrant, fall upon his sword, accompanied in this act by the publisher, unless the *Times'* shareholders shoot him first for presiding over the 53 per cent drop in profits this year.

I never cared much for the whole Plame scandal, mostly on the aesthetic grounds that outing Plame as a CIA agent seemed such a moronic way for the White House to try to discredit Joe Wilson, also because outing CIA agents is an act for which—for radicals at least—applause should be the default setting. But in that odd way that scandals acquire critical mass by dint of larger social and political discontent, the Plame scandal is severely wounding the Bush regime and the *New York Times*, and we certainly applaud that.

And with the *Times* now publicly dismembering itself, the scandal has at last become fun. Not as much fun as the Lewinsky scandal of course, but what scandal will ever match those magic years?

2005

Gordon's Surge

Alexander Cockburn

NO TASK IS MORE IMPORTANT FOR ANY NEWSPAPER THAN TO impart the news convincingly to the people and their government that a war is lost or futile or wrong. The failure of America's major newspapers in 2005 and 2006 to disclose the U.S.'s defeat in Iraq has been as disastrous as the earlier failure to challenge the government on Iraq's weapons of mass destruction.

Because of Judith Miller's high profile in the WMD fabrications, other *Times* reporters like Michael Gordon, the *Times'* military correspondent, have garnered little of the criticism they richly deserve. Gordon has played a particularly pernicious role. Having co-written with Miller the infamous aluminum tubes-for-nukes story of September 8, 2002, that mightily assisted the administration in its push to war, Gordon has, as a careful reading of his reports suggests, strongly pushed his own agenda in his recent reports on Iraq, so much so as to provide a significantly misleading picture of the situation on the ground there. In the latter part of 2006 he became the prime journalistic agitator for a "surge" in troop strength.

In late July, Gordon laid down a preliminary salvo in a story about Gen. Abizaid's plans to move more troops into Baghdad. "It is not yet clear," Gordon wrote, "whether the increased violence will prompt American commanders to modify their longer-term plans for troop reductions."

On September 11 Gordon was more emphatic, in a story eliciting the headline, "Grim Outlook Seen in West Iraq Without More Troops and Aid." Gordon cited a senior officer in Iraq saying more

American troops were necessary to stabilize Anbar province. A story on October 22 emphasized that "the sectarian violence [in Baghdad] would be far worse if not for the American efforts…" There were, of course, plenty of Iraqis and some Americans Gordon could also have found, eager to say the exact opposite.

When John Murtha—advocate of immediate withdrawal—was running for the post of House majority leader in the new Democratic-controlled Congress, Gordon rushed out two stories, both front-paged by the *New York Times*. In "Get Out Now? Not So Fast, Some Experts Say" (11/14/06) Gordon sought out the now retired General Anthony Zinni and others, who "say the situation in Baghdad and other parts of Iraq is too precarious to start thinning out the number of American troops," while "some military experts said that while the American military is stretched thin, the number of American troops in Iraq could be increased temporarily…"

The next day, November 15, 2006, a second Gordon story was headlined "General Warns of Risks in Iraq if GIs Are Cut" Gordon cited Gen. Abizaid's warnings that phased withdrawal of troops would lead to an increase of sectarian violence, and that more troops might be necessary temporarily.

By December 4, with the Iraq Study Group about to issue its report, Gordon returned to General Zinni. In a story headlined "Blurring Political Lines in the Military Debate" Gordon embraced Gen. Zinni's plan for temporary increase of troops to offset Iranian influence, suggesting that any quick pull-out would destabilize Middle East and leave Iraq in chaos.

On December 7, Pearl Harbor Day, Gordon was at it again, flailing away at Baker and Hamilton's Report. Headline: "Will it Work on the Battlefield?" Lead: "The military recommendations issued yesterday by the Iraq Study Group are based more on hope than history and run counter to assessments made by some of its own military advisors." Precipitous withdrawal, Gordon charged, would leave Iraqi armed forces unprepared to take over security burden.

Reporters with a propaganda mission can always find the mouthpieces to say what they want. Gordon's "troop surge" campaign was particularly striking—and politically much more influential in Congress than the mad-dog ravings of the right-wing broadcasters.

At the *Washington Post*, which also editorialized against Murtha's bid, David Ignatius similarly fostered the impression of feasible options in Iraq. "With enough troops and aggressive tactics," Ignatius wrote earlier in 2006, "American forces can bring order to even the meanest streets." In Iraq, in March 2002, Ignatius, claimed to find "unmistakable signs here this week that Iraq's political leaders are taking the first tentative steps towards forming a broad government of national unity that could reverse the country's downward slide." His keen eye detected a "new spirit of accord."

So here we have the *Times*' and *Post*'s lead reporter/commentators on the war diligently promulgating the core fantasy: that the United States has options beyond accepting defeat. The vast majority of Iraqis want U.S. forces out. Militarily, the United States has been defeated. There is nothing sane left for the U.S.A. to do, beyond remove its troops at the earliest possible moment. No task is more important for any newspaper than to impart that news convincingly to the people and their government. The failure of the major newspapers in this regard has been as absolute and as disastrous as the failure to challenge the government on Iraq's weapons of mass destruction.

2006

Kid Glove Journalism:
the New York Times
and the NSA's Illegal Spying

Alexander Cockburn and Jeffrey St. Clair

The first duty of the press is to obtain the earliest and most correct intelligence of the events of the time, and instantly, by disclosing them, to make them the common property of the nation. The statesman collects his information secretly and by secret means; he keeps back even the current intelligence of the day with ludicrous precautions... The press lives by disclosures... For us, with whom publicity and truth are the air and light of existence, there can be no greater disgrace than to recoil from the frank and accurate disclosure of facts as they are. We are bound to tell the truth as we find it, without fear of consequences— to lend no convenient shelter to acts of injustice or oppression, but to consign them at once to the judgment of the world.
—*Robert Lowe, editorial,* London Times, *1851*

LOWE'S MAGNIFICENT EDITORIAL WAS WRITTEN IN RESPONSE to the claim of a government minister that if the press hoped to share the influence of statesmen it "must also share in the responsibilities of statesmen." It's a long, sad decline from what Lowe wrote in 1851 to the disclosure by the *New York Times* on Friday, Dember 16, 2005 that it sat for over a year on a story revealing that the Bush administration had sanctioned a program of secret, illegal spying on U.S. citizens here in the homeland, by the National Security Agency.

And when it comes to zeal in protecting the Bill of Rights, between December 22, 1974, and December 16, 2005, it's been a steady run down hill for the *New York Times*. Thirty-one years ago, almost to the day, here's how Seymour Hersh's lead, on the front page of the *Times*, began:

> The Central Intelligence Agency, directly violating its charter, conducted a massive, illegal domestic intelligence operation during the Nixon Administration against the antiwar movement and other dissident groups in the United States, according to well-placed Government sources.

And here's the lead paragraph of the *NYT*'s page one story December 16, 2006, by James Risen and Eric Lichtblau:

> Months after the September 11 attacks, President Bush secretly authorized the National Security Agency to eavesdrop on Americans and others inside the United States to search for evidence of terrorist activity without the court-approved warrants ordinarily required for domestic spying, according to government officials.

Government illegality is the sinew of Hersh's first sentence. He says that what the CIA did was illegal and that it violated the CIA's charter. What the NSA has been doing is also illegal. Its warrantless domestic eavesdropping is in direct violation of the 1978 law which came about as a direct result of Hersh's exposé and the congressional hearings that followed. The eavesdropping also violates the NSA's charter, which gives the Agency no mandate to conduct domestic surveillance.

Yet in the *Times'* story it wasn't until the end of the third paragraph that Risen and Lichtblau wrote timidly, "Some officials familiar with the continuing operation have questioned whether the surveillance has stretched, if not crossed, constitutional limits on legal searches."

In the eighth paragraph of Risen and Lichtblau's story comes the shameful disclosure alluded to above:

> The White House asked the *New York Times* not to publish this article, arguing that it could jeopardize continuing investigations and alert would-be terrorists that they might be undergoing scrutiny. After meeting with senior administration officials, the newspaper delayed publication for a year to conduct addi-

tional reporting. Some information that administration officials
argued could be useful to terrorists has been omitted.

Hersh put the word "massive" in his first sentence, and drew
undeserved fire for exaggerating the extent of surveillance, which
a presidential panel finally admitted was "considerable... large-
scale... substantial." Risen and Lichtblau shirk any direct estimate
of how big the NSA's domestic spying has been, though one can
deduce from the ninth paragraph of the story that probably many
thousands of people had their phone conversations and emails
and faxes illegally spied upon by the NSA.

The *Times* suggests that it held up the story for a year partly
to do "additional reporting." This "additional reporting" seems
to have yielded sparse results. Risen and Lichtblau's story was
extremely long, but pretty thin, once the basic fact of NSA eavesdropping had been presented. The year's work doesn't seem to
have taken the reporters beyond what was urgently leaked to
them in 2004 by twelve different government officials concerned
about the illegality of what the NSA was doing and the lack of
congressional oversight.

Indeed, the *Washington Post* featured a much more compact
story by Dan Eggan that not only stressed the illegality in its
first paragraph but had material that Risen and Lichtblau missed,
namely that the NSA had begun its illegal program right after
9/11, even before Bush signed the executive order okaying the
surveillance, some time in 2002. It was Eggan who reported that
faxes had also been spied upon by the NSA.

And again, it was Eggan in the *Post* who put the NSA story in a
larger context, namely the fact that in the past week the Pentagon
has been forced to admit that military intelligence agencies such
as the Defense Intelligence Agency have also been illegally sur-
veilling U.S. citizens within the U.S.A.

In the TALON Program (Threat and Local Observation Notice),
a Pentagon unit called Counter Intelligence Field Activity (CIFA)
has been amassing thousands of files on potential threats to U.S.
military installations. Many of the subjects of these files have

turned out to be antiwar groups and anti-recruiting activists. For example, when CIA director George Tenet visited a campus and encountered protests, the CIFA unit would immediately open files on the protesters. The unit was supposed to purge its files of all names and organizations caught in its drift nets that failed to meet the test of being any form of threat. But of course no such purge took place.

Eggan also reported that "teams of Defense Intelligence Agency personnel stationed in major U.S. cities [have been] conducting the type of surveillance typically performed by the FBI: monitoring the movements and activities—through high-tech equipment of individuals and vehicles."

The impression one gets from the *Washington Post*'s story is that the Bush administration had given the green light to a truly massive program of warrantless domestic surveillance by the NSA and military agencies. The *New York Times'* reporters suggested no such context, setting the spying activities in a more forgiving light, as part of the war on terror.

Who designed this policy? Deep in the *Times'* story hardy readers trudging through Risen and Lichtblau's leaden prose would have tripped over Vice President Cheney's name in the twenty-fifth paragraph, where he is described as bringing congressional leaders to his office to brief them on the program. Only at the very end of the story, in the forty-eighth paragraph, do such readers as have survived the trek learn that the legal brief justifying this onslaught on the U.S. Constitution was written by Professor John Yoo, at that time at the Department of Justice. Such readers would not have learned—as they did from the *Washington Post*—that Yoo had written the notorious memos justifying torture. The *Times* didn't make it clear that Cheney and Yoo were key players in the administration's insistence that the Executive Branch has the inherent powers to sanction domestic spying without oversight from either of the other two branches of the government.

In fact members of Congress, aside from Senator Jay Rockefeller, raised no demur. It was the judiciary, in the form of the judge, Colleen Kollar-Kotelly, presiding over the secret intelligence court established by FISA, who reprimanded Justice Department lawyers for trying to get legal warrants from her, using as "probable cause" data from the illegal surveillance, although not admitting this.

In fact it's something of a puzzle why the *Times* finally did publish the story, after sitting on the information leaked to it by the NSA officials worried that they might get prosecuted for illegal surveillance. It is true that Friday's publication came in the closing hours of the battle in the U.S. Senate over reauthorization of the Patriot Act. And it's probably true that the publication of the story pushed enough wavering senators into the ranks of those who on Friday successfully fought to get the bill shelved, in a major defeat for the White House.

It's also true that all year Risen has been hard at work on a book about the conduct of U.S. intelligence agencies in the "war on terror" after 9/11, slated for release next spring. The book's launch will no doubt be accompanied by some new disclosure by Risen, designed to give the book lift up the charts. Perhaps that too will be a story he's been keeping in the larder for months.

This lamentable synergy featured in Bob Woodward's journalistic calculations and also in the promotional circumstances of the book written by Judith Miller, Stephen Engelberg, and William Broad, *Germs: Biological Weapons and America's Secret War.* Risen, we should remind our readers, is one of the reporters who smeared the late Gary Webb with the charge that Webb had over-hyped his 1996 *San Jose Mercury News* series on the CIA/Contra/cocaine connections. Webb didn't pace his disclosures to suit a book-writing schedule. He only wrote his book *Dark Alliance* after he'd been forced out of his job.

Risen was also one of the *New York Times'* reporters, along with Jeff Gerth, who raced into print with baseless smears that cost Wen Ho Lee almost a year of his life in solitary confinement, being threatened with the death penalty by FBI interrogators. On that occasion, Risen and Gerth didn't wait a year to do additional reporting and fact checking. They rushed to do the government's bidding (relaying the smears of an Energy Department official who had it in for Wen Ho Lee) just as Risen and the *New York Times* clicked their heels in the NSA case, sitting on an explosive story through the 2004 election and for months thereafter, and even then agreeing to withhold certain facts.

Such submissiveness on the part of the *Times* harks back to self-censorship by the paper in the early 1950s, covering up CIA plans for coups in Guatemala and Iran; also to the paper's behavior in 1966 when it had information about CIA shenanigans in Singapore and through southeast Asia. The editors submitted the story for review by CIA director John McCone, who made editorial deletions.

In its NSA story, the *New York Times* meekly agreed not to identify the "senior White House official" who successfully petitioned them to spike the story for a year. The fact that no one was specifically named allowed Bush to discount the entire story when he went the *Lehrer News Hour* on Friday evening.

2005

Join the 14 Per Cent Club! We Won!

Alexander Cockburn

IGN HERE TO BECOME A MEMBER OF THE 14 PER CENT CLUB. Twenty bucks plus shipping and handling gets you the T-shirt. Credentials for membership derive from a recent study from the Pew Research Center disclosing, in the words of Katharine Seelye of the *New York Times* on May 9, 2005, that a recent study from the Pew Research Center found that 45 per cent of Americans believe little or nothing of what they read in their daily newspapers.

When specific newspapers were mentioned, the *Times* fared about average, with 21 per cent of readers believing all or most of what they read in the *Times* and 14 per cent believing almost nothing. Chalk up another victory for the left. We're been at it for thirty years at least, saying that most things in the *Times* are distortions of reality or outright lies and here is a robust slice of the American people agreeing with us. Of course the faint hearts who believe that the left can never win anything will say that the credit should go to moles at the *New York Times*, boring from within, hollowing out the mighty edifice with year upon year of willful falsehoods until at last the whole ponderous structure is crumbling into dust crushing all within.

True to a point.

Heroic moles, entombed in the rubble of your own making, Judith Miller and all the others, back through to the suzerain of sappers, A.M. Rosenthal, we salute you all! As with any empire on the brink of collapse, frantic commands are issuing from the command bunker. Seelye divulges the program of proposed "reform" devised by the editors. "Encourage reporters to confirm the accuracy of articles with sources before publication and to solicit feedback from sources after publication. Set up an error-tracking system to detect patterns and trends. Encourage the development of software to detect plagiarism when accusations arise. Increase coverage of middle America, rural areas and religion. Establish a system for evaluating public attacks on the *Times'* work and determining whether and how to respond."

Can there be any better evidence of the panic that has settled in? If this trend continues, they'll be forcing Tom Friedman to install preventive software based on the works of Noam Chomsky that freezes his hard drive every time he types an untrue sentence.

The *Times'* "reform" package veers between apologetic sniveling about improved coverage of the heartland (fatter slabs of patronizing nonsense about god-fearing kulaks in Iowa) and quavering barks of defiance at "the relentless public criticism of the paper... Mr. Keller [the *NYT*'s editor] asked the committee to consider whether it was 'any longer possible to stand silent and stoic under fire.'"

"'We need to be more assertive about explaining ourselves— our decisions, our methods, our values, how we operate,' the committee said, acknowledging that 'there are those who love to hate the *Times* and suggesting a focus instead on people who do not have 'fixed' opinions about the paper."

This is like reading a strategy memo from the dying embers of the Dukakis Campaign in 1988. I'm glad to say I have no constructive recommendations to offer to the editors of the *New York Times*, except maybe one suggested by my *Nation* intern, Mark Hatch-Miller whom I canvassed for his opinions: "Stop bringing up Jayson Blair every time you screw up. Every time the *Times* talks about why people don't trust them, they have to mention Blair, but we all would have forgotten him by now if they'd shut up about him for a second. His story is only used to distract us from the real problems at the *Times*." Aye to that. So far as I know, the *Times* has never named its reporter, Judith Miller, as a prime agent in fomenting what has become the most thoroughly discredited propaganda campaign in the entire history of war scares.

Daniel Okrent, the *Times'* ombudsman through its crisis months, departs this week loosing a Parthian shot or two at his erstwhile employer. Okrent tells Salon.com that the *Times* could have done a lot more in the way of self-criticism for its role in selling Saddam's supposed WMDs, though he says he doesn't know whether or not the *Times* actually "disciplined" Miller. Of course history has performed that function more than adequately. Her name is up there alongside Piggott, author of the famous Parnell forgeries.

On the matter of constructive versus destructive criticism, I'll always opt for the latter. Keep things clean and simple, like "U.S. out of Iraq now." My only quibble with Chomsky down the years has been the implication in all his trenchant criticisms of the *Times* that somehow the *Times* should be getting things right, and that it would be better if it did so.

This has always seemed to me to be a contradiction in terms. The role devised for itself by the *New York Times* was to be the credible organ of capitalism ("newspaper of record"), with its reports and editorials premised on the belief that American capitalism can produce a just society in which all can enjoy the fruits of their labor in peaceful harmony with their environment and the rest of the planet.

The evidence is in. The case is proved a million different ways. American capitalism can't do that. It's produced an unjust society run by a tiny slice of obscenely rich people (including the real estate developers owning the *New York Times*) with a vested and irreversible interest in permanent war and planetary destruction.

Given those premises, how can the *Times* ever get it right? Why would we want the *Times* to get it right? It's like a parody I wrote here a decade ago, when the *Times* said that henceforth it would issue corrections "for the sake of balance:"

"A *New York Times* Business Day report published two days ago quoted sources confident of America's continued economic expansion, but the report failed to provide adequate balance to these optimistic views. The report markedly failed to represent the views of the Marxist school. According to the Marxist school, the capitalist economy of the United States will suffer increasing crises of accumulation and a falling rate of profit. These phenomena will aggravate social and economic contradictions to a degree that will be ultimately fatal to capitalism. Failure to note the theories of the German economic and social critic Karl Marx violated the *Times'* standards of fairness."

Get the idea?

We won! On the left we've always said that the corporate press tells lies and now, for a variety of reasons, most people believe us. The corporate media are discredited, the same way the corporate political parties are. They have zero credibility. Newspapers are dying. The main TV networks have lost a third of their audience over the past twenty years. There's no need for whining that the problem consists of narrowing ownership. The corporate press was just as bad when there were five hundred different newspaper owners instead of five. And, for now at least, we have the web. We're infinitely better off than we were thirty years ago.

The only trouble is, the left hasn't got too many ideas. We should stop whining about the corporate press and get on with a new program. If it's credible, then the people who don't trust the *New York Times* may start trusting us.

For "14 per cent" t-shirts, contact *CounterPunch@CounterPunch.org* or call 1-800-840-3683.

2005

Part 3

White on Black
In Black and White

What You Can't Say

Alexander Cockburn

EW SPECTACLES IN JOURNALISM IN THE MID-1990S WERE more disgusting than the onslaughts on Gary Webb in the *New York Times, Washington Post*, and *Los Angeles Times*. Squadrons of hacks, some of them with career-long ties to the CIA, sprayed thousands of words of vitriol over Webb and his paper, the *San Jose Mercury News*, for besmirching the Agency's fine name by charging it with complicity in the importing of cocaine into the U.S.A.

There are certain things you aren't meant to say in public in America. The systematic state sponsorship of torture by agencies of the U.S. government used to be a major no-no, but that went by the board this year (even though Seymour Hersh treated the CIA with undue kindness in *Chain of Command*). A prime no-no is saying that the U.S. government has used assassination down the years as an instrument of national policy; also that the CIA's complicity with drug-dealing criminal gangs stretches from the Afghanistan of today back to the year the Agency was founded in 1947. That last one is the line Webb stepped over. He paid for his presumption by undergoing one of the unfairest batterings in the history of the U.S. press.

Friday, December 10, 2005, Webb died in his Sacramento apartment by his own hand, or so it certainly seems. The notices of his passing in many newspapers were as nasty as ever. The *Los Angeles Times* took care to note that even after the "Dark Alliance" uproar, Webb's career had been "troubled," offering as evidence the fact that "while working for another legislative committee in Sacramento, Webb wrote a report accusing the California

Highway Patrol of unofficially condoning and even encouraging racial profiling in its drug interdiction program." The effrontery of the man! "Legislative officials released the report in 1999," the story piously continued, "but cautioned that it was based mainly on assumptions and anecdotes," no doubt meaning that Webb didn't have dozens of CHP officers stating under oath, on the record, that they were picking on blacks and Hispanics.

There were similar fountains of outrage in 1996 that the CIA hadn't been given enough space in Webb's series to solemnly swear that never a gram of cocaine had passed under its nose but that it had been seized and turned over to the Drug Enforcement Agency or U.S. Customs.

In 1998, Jeffrey St. Clair and I published our book, *Whiteout*, about the relationships between the CIA, drugs, and the press since the Agency's founding. We also examined the Webb affair in detail. On a lesser scale, at lower volume it elicited the same sort of abuse Webb drew. It was a long book stuffed with well-documented facts, over which the critics lightly vaulted to charge us, as they did Webb, with "conspiracy-mongering," though, sometimes in the same sentence, of recycling "old news." Jeffrey and I came to the conclusion that what really affronted the critics, some of them nominally left-wing, was that our book portrayed Uncle Sam's true face. Not a "rogue" Agency but one always following the dictates of government, murdering, torturing, poisoning, drugging its own subjects, approving acts of monstrous cruelty, following methods devised and tested by Hitler's men, themselves whisked to America after the Second World War.

One of the CIA's favored modes of self-protection is the "uncover-up." The Agency first denies with passion, then later concedes in muffled tones, the charges leveled against it. Such charges have included the Agency's recruitment of Nazi scientists and SS officers; experiments on unwitting American citizens; efforts to assassinate Fidel Castro; alliances with opium lords in Burma, Thailand, and Laos; an assassination program in Vietnam; complicity in the toppling of Salvador Allende in

Chile; the arming of opium traffickers and religious fanatics in Afghanistan; the training of murderous police in Guatemala and El Salvador; and involvement in arms-for-drugs shuttles between Latin America and the U.S.A.

True to form, after Webb's series raised a storm, particularly on black radio, the CIA issued categorical denials. Then came the solemn pledges of an intense and far-reaching investigation by the CIA's inspector general, Fred Hitz. On December 18, 1997, stories in the *Washington Post* by Walter Pincus and in the *New York Times* by Tim Weiner appeared simultaneously, both saying the same thing: Inspector General Hitz had finished his investigation. He had found "no direct or indirect" links between the CIA and the cocaine traffickers. As both Pincus and Weiner admitted in their stories, neither of the two journalists had actually seen the report.

The actual report itself, so loudly heralded, received almost no examination. But those who took the time—as we did—to examine the 149-page document, the first of two volumes, found Inspector General Hitz making one damning admission after another including an account of a meeting between a pilot who was making drug/arms runs between San Francisco and Costa Rica with two Contra leaders who were also partners with the San Francisco-based Contra drug smuggler Norwin Meneses. Present at this encounter in Costa Rica was a curly-haired man who said his name was Ivan Gomez, identified by one of the Contras as CIA's "man in Costa Rica." The pilot told Hitz that Gomez said he was there to "ensure that the profits from the cocaine went to the Contras and not into someone's pocket."

The second volume of CIA Inspector General Fred Hitz's investigation released in the fall of 1998 buttressed Webb's case even more tightly, as James Risen conceded in a story in the *New York Times* on October 12 of that year.

So why did the top-tier press savage Webb and parrot the CIA's denials? It comes back to this matter of Uncle Sam's true face. Another *New York Times'* reporter, Keith Schneider, was asked by

In These Times back in 1987 why he had devoted a three-part series in the *New York Times* to attacks on the Contra hearings chaired by Senator John Kerry. Schneider said such a story could "shatter the Republic. I think it is so damaging, the implications are so extraordinary, that for us to run the story, it had better be based on the most solid evidence we could amass." Kerry did uncover mountains of evidence. So did Webb. But neither of them got the only thing that would have satisfied Schneider, Pincus, and all the other critics: a signed confession of CIA complicity by the Director of Central Intelligence himself. Short of that, I'm afraid we're left with "innuendo," "conspiracy mongering," and "old stories." We're also left with the memory of some great work by a very fine journalist who deserved a lot better than he got from the profession he loved.

2005

How the Press and the CIA Killed Gary Webb's Career

Alexander Cockburn and Jeffrey St. Clair

THE ATTACK ON GARY WEBB AND HIS "DARK ALLIANCE" SERIES in the *San Jose Mercury News* remains one of the most venomous and factually inane assaults on a professional journalist's competence in living memory. In the mainstream press he found virtually no defenders, and those who dared stand up for him, themselves became the object of virulent abuse and misrepresentation. L.J. O'Neale, the prosecutor for the Justice Department who was Contra drug runner Danilo Blandón's patron and black crack dealer Ricky Ross' prosecutor, initially formulated the polemical program against Webb. When one looks back on the assault in the calm of hindsight, what is astounding is the way Webb's foes in the press mechanically reiterated those attacks.

There was a disturbing racist thread underlying the attacks on Webb's series and on those who took his findings seriously. It's clear, looking through the onslaughts on Webb in the *Los Angeles Times*, the *Washington Post*, and the *New York Times*, that the reaction in black communities to the series was extremely disturbing to elite opinion. This was an eruption of outrage, an insurgency not just of very poor people in South Central L.A. and kindred areas, but of almost all blacks and many whites as well. In the counterattacks, one gets the sense that a kind of pacification program was in progress. Karen De Young, an assistant editor at the *Washington Post*, evoked just such an impulse when Alicia Shepard of the *American Journalism Review* interviewed her. "I looked at [the *Mercury News* series] when it initially came out and decided it was something we needed to follow up on. When it became an issue in the black community and on talk shows, that seemed to be a different phenomenon." Remember too that the O.J. Simpson jury decision had also been deeply disturbing to white opinion. In that case, blacks had rallied around a man most whites believed to be a vicious killer, and there was a "white opinion riot" in response. Now blacks were mustering in support of a story charging that their profoundest suspicions of white malfeasance were true. So, in the counterattack there were constant, patronizing references to "black paranoia," decorously salted with the occasional concession that there was evidence from the past to support the notion that such paranoia might have some sound foundation.

Another factor lent a particular edge to the onslaughts. This was the first occasion on which the established press had to face the changing circumstances of the news business, in terms of registering mass opinion and allowing popular access. Webb's series coincided with the coming of age of the Internet. The *Miami Herald*, another *Knight Ridder* paper in the same corporate family as the *Mercury News*, had been forced to change editorial course in the mid-1980s by the vociferous, highly conservative Cuban-American presence in Miami. The *Herald* chose not to reprint Webb's series. However, this didn't prevent anyone in south Florida from finding the entire series on the Internet, along with all the supporting documents.

The word "pacification" is not inappropriate to describe the responses to Webb's story. Back in the 1980s, allegations about Contra drug running, also backed by documentary evidence, could be ignored with impunity. Given the Internet and black radio reaction, in the mid-1990s this was no longer possible, and the established organs of public opinion had to launch the fiercest of attacks on Webb and on his employer. This was a campaign of extermination: the aim was to destroy Webb and to force the *Mercury News* into backing away from the story's central premise.

At the same time, these media manipulators attempted to minimize the impact of Webb' s story on the black community.

Another important point in the politics of this campaign is that Webb's fiercest assailants were not on the right. They were mainstream liberals, such as Walter Pincus and Richard Cohen of the *Washington Post* and David Corn of the *Nation*. There has always been a certain conservative suspicion of the CIA, even if conservatives—outside the libertarian wing—heartily applaud the Agency's imperial role. The CIA's most effective friends have always been the liberal center, on the editorial pages of the *Washington Post* and the *New York Times* and in the endorsement of a person like the *Washington Post*'s president, Katharine Graham. In 1988 Graham had told CIA recruits: "We live in a dirty and dangerous world. There are some things the general public does not need to know, and shouldn't. I believe democracy flourishes when the government can take legitimate steps to keep its secrets and when the press can decide whether to print what it knows."

By mid-September of 1996 the energy waves created by Webb's series were approaching critical mass and beginning to become an unavoidable part of the national news agenda. For example, NBC's *Dateline*, a prime-time news show, had shot interviews with Webb and Ricky Ross and had sent a team down to Nicaragua, where they filmed an interview with Norwin Meneses and other figures in the saga. Webb tells of a conversation with one of the *Dateline*'s producers, who asked him, "Why hasn't this shit been on TV before?"—"You tell me," Webb answered. "You're the TV man."

A couple of weeks after this exchange, the program was telling Webb that it didn't look as though they would be going forward with the story after all. In the intervening weeks, the counterattack had been launched, and throughout the networks the mood had abruptly shifted. On November 15, NBC's Andrea Mitchell (partner of the Federal Reserve's chairman, Alan Greenspan, about as snugly ensconced a member of the Washington elite as you could hope to find) was saying on NBC that Webb's story "was a conspiracy theory" that had been "spread by talk radio."

The storm clouds began to gather with the CNN-brokered exchange between Webb and Ron Kessler. Kessler had had his own dealings with the Agency. In 1992, he had published *Inside the FBI*, a highly anecdotal and relatively sympathetic book about the Agency, entirely devoid of the sharp critical edge that had characterized Kessler's *The FBI*. A couple of CIA memos written in 1991 and 1992 record the Agency's view of the experience of working with Kessler and other reporters.

The 1991 CIA note discusses Kessler's request for information and brags that a close relationship had been formed with Kessler, "which helped turn some 'intelligence failure' stories into 'intelligence success' stories." Of course this could have been merely self-serving fluff by an Agency's officer, but it is certainly true that Kessler was far from hard on the Agency. That same CIA memo goes on to explain that the Agency maintains "relationships with reporters from every major wire service, newspaper, news weekly and TV network." The memo continues, "In many instances we have persuaded reporters to postpone, change, hold or even scrap stories that could have adversely affected national security interests or jeopardized sources or methods."

The next attack on Webb came from another long-time friend of the Agency, Arnaud de Borchgrave, who had worked for *Newsweek* as a columnist for many years and made no secret of the fact that he regarded many of his colleagues as KGB dupes. He himself boasted of intimate relations with French, British, and U.S. intelligence agencies and was violently right-wing in his views. In recent years he has written for the *Washington Times*, a conservative paper owned by the Rev. Sun Myung Moon.

The thrust of de Borchgrave's attack, which appeared in the *Washington Times* on September 24, 1996, was that Webb's basic thesis was wrong, because the Contras had been rolling in CIA money. Like almost all other critics, de Borchgrave made no effort to deal with the plentiful documents, such as federal grand jury transcripts, that Webb had secured and that were available on the *Mercury News'* website. Indeed, some of the most experienced reporters in Washington displayed, amid their criticisms, a marked aversion to studying such source documents. De Borchgrave did remark that when all the investigations were done, the most that would emerge would be that a couple of CIA officers might have been lining their own pockets.

That same September 24, 1996, a more insidious assault came in the form of an interview of Webb by Chris Matthews on the CNBC cable station. There are some ironies here. Matthews had once worked for Speaker of the House Tip O'Neill. O'Neill had been sympathetic to the amendment against Contra funding offered by his Massachusetts colleague, Edward Boland. On the other hand, O'Neill had swiftly reacted to a firestorm of outrage about cocaine after the death of the Celtics' draftee Len Bias, a star basketball player at the University of Maryland. At that time, he rushed through the House some appalling "War on Drugs" legislation whose dire effects are still with us today.

Matthews left O'Neill's office with a carefully calculated career plan to market himself as a syndicated columnist and telepundit. Positioning himself as a right-of-center liberal, Matthews habitually eschews fact for opinion, and is regarded by many op-ed editors as a self-serving blowhard with an exceptionally keen eye for the main chance. Clearly sensing where the wind was blowing, Matthews used his show to launch a fierce attack on Webb. First, he badgered the reporter for supposedly producing no evidence of "the direct involvement of American CIA officers." "Who said anything about American CIA agents?" Webb responded. "That's the most ethnocentric viewpoint I've ever seen in my life. The CIA used foreign nationals all the time. In this operation they were using Nicaraguan exiles."

Matthews had clearly prepped himself with de Borchgrave's article that morning. His next challenge to Webb was on whether the Contras needed drug money. Matthews' research assistants had prepared a timeline purporting to show that the Contras were flush with cash during the period when Webb's stories said they were desperate for money from any source.

But Webb, who had lived the chronology for eighteen months, stood his ground. He patiently expounded to Matthews' audience how Meneses and Blandón's arms-for-drugs operation was at its peak during the period when Congress had first restricted, then later totally cut off U.S. funding to the Contra army based in Honduras. Webb told Matthews, "When the CIA funding was restored, all these guys got busted." After the interview, Webb says Matthews stormed off the set, berating his staff, "This is outrageous. I've been sabotaged."

The tempo now began to pick up. On October 1, Webb got a call in San Diego from Howard Kurtz, the *Washington Post*'s media reporter. "Kurtz called me," Webb remembers, "and after a few innocuous questions I thought that was that." It wasn't. Kurtz's critique came out on October 2 and became a paradigm for many of the assaults that followed. The method was simplicity itself: a series of straw men swiftly raised up, and as swiftly demolished. Kurtz opened by describing how blacks, liberal politicians, and "some" journalists have been trumpeting a *Mercury News* story that they say links the CIA to drug trafficking in the United States. Kurtz told how Webb's story had become "a hot topic," through intrinsically unreliable media such the Internet and black talk radio. "There's just one problem," Kurtz went on. "The series doesn't actually say the CIA knew about the drug trafficking." To buttress this claim, Kurtz then wrote that Webb had "admitted" as much in their brief chat with the statement, "We'd never pretended otherwise. This doesn't prove the CIA targeted black people. It doesn't say this was ordered by the CIA. Essentially, our trail stopped at the door of the CIA. They wouldn't return my phone calls."

What Webb had done in the series was show in great detail how a Contra funding crisis had engendered enormous sales of crack in South Central Los Angeles, how the wholesalers of that cocaine were protected from prosecution until the funding crisis ended, and how these same wholesalers were never locked away in prison, but were hired as informants by federal prosecutors. It could be argued that Webb's case is often circumstantial, but prosecutions on this same amount of circumstantial evidence have seen people put away on life sentences. Webb was telling the truth on another point as well: the CIA did not return his phone calls. And unlike Kurtz's colleagues at the *Washington Post* or *New York Times'* reporter Tim Golden, who offered twenty-four off-the-record interviews in his attack, Webb refused to run quotes from officials without attribution. In fact, Webb did have a CIA source. "He told me," Webb remembers, "he knew who these guys were and he knew they were cocaine dealers. But he wouldn't go on the record so I didn't use his stuff in the story. I mean, one of the criticisms is we didn't include CIA comments in [the] story. And the reason we didn't is because they wouldn't return my phone calls and they denied my Freedom of Information Act requests."

But suppose the CIA had returned Webb's calls? What would a spokesperson have said, other than that Webb's allegations were outrageous and untrue? The CIA is a government entity pledged to secrecy about its activities. On scores of occasions it has remained deceptive when under subpoena before a government committee. Why should the Agency be expected to answer frankly a bothersome question from a reporter? Yet it became a fetish for Webb's assailants to repeat, time after time, that the CIA denied his charges and that he had never given this denial as the Agency's point of view.

The CIA is not a kindergarten. The Agency has been responsible for many horrible deeds, including killings. Yet journalists kept treating it as though it was some above-board body, like the U.S. Supreme Court. Many of the attackers assumed that Webb had been somehow derelict in not unearthing a signed order from William Casey mandating Agency's officers to instruct Enriqué Bermúdez to arrange with Norwin Meneses and Danilo Blandón to sell "x kilos of cocaine." This is an old tactic, known as "the hunt for the smoking gun." But, of course, such a direct order would never be found by a journalist. Even when there is a clearly smoking gun, like the references to cocaine paste in Oliver North's notebooks, the gun rarely shows up in the news stories. North's notebooks were released to the public in the early 1990s. There for all to see was an entry on July 9, 1984, describing a conversation with CIA man Dewey Clarridge: "Wanted aircraft to go to Bolivia to pick up paste." Another entry on the same day stated: "Want aircraft to pick up 1,500 kilos."

"In Bolivia they have only one kind of paste," says former DEA agent Michael Levine, who spent more than a decade tracking down drug smugglers in Mexico, Southeast Asia, and Bolivia. "That's cocaine paste. We have a guy working for the NSC talking to a CIA agent about a phone call to Adolfo Calero. In this phone call they discuss picking up cocaine paste from Bolivia and wanting an aircraft to pick up 1,500 kilos." None of Webb's attackers mentioned these diary entries.

A sort of manic literalism permeated the attacks modeled on Kurtz's chop job. For instance, critics repeatedly returned to Webb's implied accusation that the CIA had targeted blacks. As we have noted, Webb didn't actually say this, but merely described the sequence that had led to blacks being targeted by the wholesaler. However, we shall see that there have been many instances where the CIA, along with other government bodies, has targeted blacks quite explicitly—in testing the toxicity of disease organisms, or the effects of radiation and mind-altering drugs. Yet Webb's critics never went anywhere near the well-established details of such targeting. Instead, they relied on talk about "black paranoia," which liberals kindly suggested could be traced to the black historical experience, and which conservatives more brusquely identified as "black irrationality."

Kurtz lost no time in going after Webb's journalistic ethics and denouncing the *Mercury News* for exploitative marketing of the series. As an arbiter of journalistic morals, Kurtz castigated Webb for referring to the Contras as "the CIA's army," suggesting that Webb used this phrase merely to implicate the Agency. This charge recurs endlessly in the onslaughts on Webb, and it is by far the silliest. One fact is agreed upon by everyone except a few berserk Maoists-turned-Reaganites, like Robert Leiken of Harvard. That fact is that the Contras were indeed the CIA's army, and that they had been recruited, trained and funded under the Agency's supervision. It's true that in the biggest raids of all—the mining of the Nicaraguan harbors and the raids on the Nicaraguan oil refineries—the Agency used its own men, not trusting its proxies. But for a decade the main Contra force was indeed the CIA's army, and followed its orders obediently.

In attacks on reporters who have overstepped the bounds of political good taste, the assailants will often make an effort to drive a wedge between the reporter and the institution for which the reporter works. For example, when Ray Bonner, working in Central America for the *New York Times*, sent a dispatch saying the unsayable—that U.S. personnel had been present at a torture session—the *Wall Street Journal* and politicians in Washington attacked the *Times* as irresponsible for running such a report. The *Times* did not stand behind Bonner and allowed his professional credentials to be successfully challenged.

The fissure between Webb and his paper opened when Kurtz elicited a statement from Jerry Ceppos, executive editor of the *Mercury News*, that he was "disturbed that so many people have leaped to the conclusion that the CIA was involved." This apologetic note from Ceppos was not lost on Webb's attackers, who successfully worked to widen the gap between reporter and editor.

Another time-hallowed technique in such demolition jobs is to charge that this is all "old news"—as opposed to that other derided commodity, "ill-founded speculation." Kurtz used the "old news" ploy when he wrote, "The fact that Nicaraguan rebels were involved in drug trafficking has been known for a decade." Kurtz should have felt some sense of shame in writing these lines, since his own paper had sedulously avoided acquainting its readers with this fact. Kurtz claimed, ludicrously, that "the Reagan Administration acknowledged as much in the 1980s, but subsequent investigations failed to prove that the CIA condoned or even knew about it." This odd sentence raised some intriguing questions. When had the Reagan administration "acknowledged as much?" And if the Reagan administration knew, how could the CIA have remained in ignorance? Recall that in the 1980s, the Reagan administration was referring to the Contras as the "moral equivalent of the Founding Fathers," and accusing the Sandinistas of being drug runners.

Kurtz also slashed at Webb personally, stating that he "appeared conscious of making the news." As illustration, Kurtz quoted a letter that Webb had written to Ricky Ross in July 1996 about the timing of the series. Webb told Ross that it would probably be run around the time of his sentencing, in order to "generate as much public interest as possible." As Webb candidly told Ross, this was the way the news business worked. So indeed it does, at the *Washington Post* far more than at the *Mercury News*, as anyone following the *Post*'s promotion of Bob Woodward's books will acknowledge. But Webb is somehow painted as guilty of self-inflation for telling Ross a journalistic fact of life.

On Friday, October 4, the *Washington Post* went to town on Webb and on the *Mercury News*. The onslaught carried no less than 5,000 words in five articles. The front page featured a lead article by Roberto Suro and Walter Pincus, headlined "CIA and Crack: Evidence is Lacking of Contra-Tied Plot." Also on the front page was a piece by Michael Fletcher on "black paranoia." The A section carried another piece on an inside page, a profile of Norwin Meneses by Douglas Farah. A brief sidebar by Walter Pincus was titled, "A Long History of Drug Allegations," compressing the entire history of the CIA's involvement with drug production in Southeast Asia—a saga that Al McCoy took 634 pages to chart in his book *The Politics of Heroine*—into 300 words. Finally, the front page of the *Post*'s Style section that Friday morning contained an article by Donna Britt headlined, "Finding the Truest Truth." Britt's topic was how blacks tell stories to each other and screw things up in the process.

Connections between Walter Pincus and the intelligence sector are long-standing and well known. From 1955 to 1957, he worked for U.S. Army Counter-Intelligence in Washington, D.C. Pincus himself is a useful source about his first connections with the CIA. In 1968, when the stories about the CIA's penetration of the National Student Association had been broken by the radical magazine *Ramparts*, Pincus wrote a rather solemn exposé of himself in the *Washington Post*. In a confessional style, he reported how the Agency had sponsored three trips for him, starting in 1960. He had gone to conferences in Vienna, Accra, and New Delhi, acting as a CIA observer. It was clearly an apprenticeship in which—as he well knew—Pincus was being assessed as officer material. He evidently made a good impression, because the CIA asked him to do additional work. Pincus says he declined, though it would be hard to discern from his reporting that he was not, at the least, an Agency asset. The *Washington Times* describes Pincus as a person "who some in the Agency refer to as 'the CIA's house reporter.'"

Since Webb's narrative revolved around the central figures of Blandón and Meneses, Pincus and Suro understandably focused on the Nicaraguans, claiming that they were never important players in Contra circles. To buttress this view, the *Post*'s writers hauled out the somewhat dubious assertions of Adolfo Calero. As with other CIA denials, one enters a certain zone of unreality here. Journalists were using as a supposedly reliable source someone with a strong motivation to deny that his organization had anything to do with the cocaine trafficking of which it was accused. Pincus and Suro solemnly cited Calero as saying that when he met with Meneses and Blandón, "We had no crystal ball to know who they were or what they were doing." Calero's view was emphasized as reliable, whereas Blandón and Meneses were held to be exaggerating their status in the Contra army.

Thus, we have Webb, based on Blandón's sworn testimony as a government witness before a federal grand jury, reporting that FDN leader Colonel Enriqué Bermúdez had bestowed on Meneses the title of head of intelligence and security for the Contra army in California. On the other hand, we have the self-interested denials to Pincus and Suro of a man who has been denounced to the FBI as "a pathological liar" by a former professor at California State University-Hayward, Dennis Ainsworth.

Just as Kurtz had done, Pincus and Suro homed in on the charge that Webb had behaved unethically. This time the charge was suggesting certain questions that Ross' lawyer, Alan Fenster, could ask Blandón. Webb's retort has always been that it would be hard to imagine a better venue for reliable responses than a courtroom with the witness under oath.

But how did all the *Washington Post*'s writers come to focus in so knowledgeably on this particular courtroom scene?

Kurtz never mentions his name, and Pincus and Suro refer to him only in passing, but Assistant U.S. District Attorney L.J. O'Neale was himself being questioned by Los Angeles Sheriff's Department investigators on November 19, 1996. The department's transcript of the interview shows O'Neale reveling in his top-secret security clearance with the CIA, and saying that "his personal feelings were that Mr. Webb had become an active part of Ricky Ross' defense team. He said that it was his personal opinion that Webb's involvement was on the verge of complicity." While he was speaking, O'Neale was searching for a document. As the investigators put it in their report, "In our presence he called Howard Kurtz, the author of the first *Washington Post*'s article, but nobody answered." Thereupon, also in their presence, he talked to Walter Pincus.

This hint of pre-existing relations between the *Washington Post* and the federal prosecutor suggests that O'Neale had rather more input into the *Post*'s attacks on Webb than the passing mention of his name might suggest. And indeed, a comparison between O'Neale's court filings and the piece by Pincus and Suro shows that the *Washington Post* duo faithfully followed the line of O'Neale's attack. Once again, motive is important. O'Neale had every reason to try to subvert a reporter who had described in great detail how the U.S. District Attorney had become the patron and handler of Danilo Blandón. Webb had described how O'Neale had saved Blandón from a life term in prison, found him a job as a government agent, and used him as his chief witness in a series of trials. O'Neale had an enormous stake in discrediting Webb.

O'Neale's claim, reiterated by Pincus and Suro, is that Blandón mainly engaged in sending cocaine profits to the Contras in late 1981 and 1982, before hooking up with Ricky Ross. Furthermore, the amount of cocaine sold by Blandón was a mere fraction of the national market for the drug, and thus could not have played a decisive role in sparking a crack plague in Los Angeles. In other words, according to the O'Neale line in the *Post*, Blandón had sold only a relatively insignificant amount of cocaine in 1981 and 1982 (later the magical figure $50,000 worth became holy writ among Webb's critics). His association with Ross had begun after Blandón had given up his charitable dispensations to the Contras, and thus was a purely criminal enterprise with no political ramifications. Therefore, even by implication, there could be no connection between the CIA and the rise of crack.

O'Neale had reversed the position he had taken in the days when he was prosecuting Blandón and calling him "the largest Nicaraguan cocaine dealer in the United States." Now he was claiming that Blandón's total sales of cocaine amounted to only five tons, and thus he could not be held accountable for the rise of crack. This specific argument was seized gratefully by Pincus and Suro. "Law enforcement estimates," Pincus and Suro wrote, "say Blandón handled a total of only about five tons of cocaine during a decade-long career."

Imagine if the *Washington Post* had been dealing with a claim by Mayor Marion Barry that during his mayoral terms "only" about 10,000 pounds of crack had been handled by traffickers in the blocks surrounding his office!

Webb was attacked for claiming, in the opening lines of his series, that "millions" had been funneled back to the Contras. In his statements to the Los Angeles Sheriff's Department investigators, O'Neale said: "Blandón dealt with a total of 40 kilos of cocaine from January to December 1982. The profits of the sales were used to purchase weapons and equipment for the Contras." O'Neale was trying to narrow the window of "political" cocaine sales. However, during that time Blandón was selling cocaine worth over $2 million—in only a fraction of the period that Webb identified as the time the cocaine profits were being remitted to Honduras.

The degree of enmity directed toward Webb can be gauged not only by O'Neale's diligent briefings of Webb's antagonists, but also by the raid on the office of Gary Webb's literary agent, Jody Hotchkiss of the Sterling Lord Agency, by agents of the Department of Justice and the DEA. The government men came brandishing subpoenas for copies of all correspondence between the Sterling Lord Agency, Ricky Ross, Ross' lawyer Alan Fenster, and Webb. The DEA justified the search on the grounds that it wanted to see if Ross had any assets it could seize to pay his hefty fines. But Webb reckons "they were really looking for some sort of business deal between me and Ross. They wanted to discredit me as a reporter by saying he's making deals with drug dealers." The raid produced no evidence of any such deal, because there was none.

Cheek by jowl with Pincus and Suro on the *Washington Post's* front page that October 4 was Fletcher's essay on the sociology of black paranoia. Blacks, Fletcher claimed, cling to beliefs regardless of "the shortage of factual substantiation" and of "denials by government officials." Fletcher duly stated some pieties about the "bitter" history of American blacks. Then he bundled together some supposed conspiracies (that the government deliberately infected blacks with the AIDS virus, that Church's fried chicken and Snapple drinks had been laced with chemicals designed to sterilize black men), and implied that allegations about the CIA and cocaine trafficking were of the same order. It is true, Fletcher conceded, that blacks had reasons to be paranoid. "Many southern police departments," he wrote delicately, "were suspected of having ties to the Ku Klux Klan." He mentioned in passing the FBI snooping on Martin Luther King Jr. and the sting operation on Washington, D.C.'s Mayor Marion Barry. He also touched on the syphilis experiments conducted by the government on blacks in Tuskegee, Alabama. "The history of victimization of black people allows myths—and, at times, outright paranoia—to flourish." In other words, the black folk get it coming and going. Terrible things happen to them, and then they're patronized in the *Washington Post* for imagining that such terrible things might happen again. "Even if a major investigation is done," Fletcher concluded, "it is unlikely to quell the certainty among many African Americans that the government played a role in bringing the crack epidemic to black communities."

A few days later, a *Post* editorial followed through on this notion of black irrationality and the lack of substance in Webb's thesis. The writer observed that "the *Mercury* [had] borrowed heavily from a certain view of CIA rogue conduct that was widespread ten years ago." The "biggest shock," the editorial went on, "wasn't the story but the credibility the story seems to have generated when it reached some parts of the black community." This amazing sentence was an accurate rendition of what really bothered the *Washington Post*, which was not charges that the CIA had been complicit in drug running, but that black people might be suspicious of the government's intentions toward them. The *Post*'s editorial said solemnly that "[i]f the CIA did associate with drug pushers its aim was not to infect Americans but to advance the CIA' s foreign project and purposes."

In the weeks that followed, *Post*'s columnists piled on the heat. Mary McGrory, the doyenne of liberal punditry, said that the *Post* had successfully "discredited" the *Mercury News*. Richard

Cohen, always edgy on the topic of black America, denounced Rep. Maxine Waters for demanding an investigation after the *Washington Post* had concluded that Webb's charges were "baseless." "When it comes to sheer gullibility—or is it mere political opportunism?—Waters is in a class of her own."

One story in that October 4 onslaught in the *Post* differed markedly from its companion pieces. That was the profile of Meneses by Douglas Farah, which actually advanced Webb's story. Farah, the *Post*'s man in Central America, filed a dispatch from Managua giving a detailed account of Meneses' career as a drug trafficker, going back to 1974. Farah described how Meneses had "worked for the Contras for five years, fundraising, training and sending people down to Honduras." He confirmed Meneses' encounter with Enriqué Bermúdez and added a detail—the gift of a crossbow by Meneses to the colonel. Then Farah produced a stunner, lurking in the twelfth paragraph of his story. Citing "knowledgeable sources," he reported that the DEA had hired Meneses in 1988 to try to set up Sandinista political and military leaders in drug stings. Farah named the DEA agent involved as Federico Villareal. The DEA did not dispute this version of events. In other words, Farah had Meneses performing a political mission for the U.S. government, side by side with the story by his colleagues Pincus and Suro claiming Meneses had no such connections.

Shortly after the *Post*'s offensives on October 2 and October 4, the *Mercury News'* editor, Jerry Ceppos, sent a detailed letter to the *Post* aggressively defending Webb and rebutting the criticisms. "The *Post* has every right to reach different conclusions from those of the *Mercury News*," Ceppos wrote. "But I'm disappointed in the 'what's the big deal' tone running through the *Post*'s critique. If the CIA knew about illegal activities being conducted by its associates, federal law and basic morality required that it notify domestic authorities. It seems to me that this is exactly the kind of story that a newspaper should shine a light on."

The *Post* refused to print Ceppos' letter. Ceppos called Stephen Rosenfeld, the deputy editor of the editorial page, who suggested that Ceppos revise his letter and resubmit it. Ceppos promptly did this, and again the *Post* refused to print his response. Rosenfeld said Ceppos' letter was "misinformation." Ceppos later wrote in the *Mercury News*:

> I was stunned when the *Washington Post* rejected my request to reply to its long critique of "Dark Alliance." The *Post* at first encouraged me, asking me to rewrite the article and then to agree to other changes. I did. Then, a few days ago, I received a one-paragraph fax saying that the *Post* is "not able to publish" my response. Among other reasons, the *Post* said [that] other papers "essentially" confirmed the *Post*'s criticism of our series. I've insisted for years that newspapers don't practice "groupthink." I'm still sure that most don't. But the *Post*'s argument certainly gives ammunition to the most virulent critics of American journalism. The *Post* also said I had backed down "elsewhere" from positions I took in the piece I wrote for the *Post*. But I didn't. I shouted to anyone who would listen (and wrote that, in another letter to the *Post*). It was too late. On the day that the *Post* faxed me, the *Los Angeles Times* incorrectly had written that reporter Gary Webb, who wrote the "Dark Alliance" series, and I had backed down on several key points. Fiction became fact. As if I had no tongue, and no typewriter, I suddenly had lost access to the newspaper that first bitterly criticized our series.

The *Post*'s sordid procedures in savaging Webb were examined by its ombudsman, Geneva Overholzer, on November 10. Ultimately she found her own paper guilty of "misdirected zeal," but first she took the opportunity to stick a few more knives into poor Webb. "The San Jose series was seriously flawed. It was reported by a seemingly hot-headed fellow willing to have people leap to conclusions his reporting couldn't back up—principally that the CIA was knowingly involved in the introduction of drugs into the United States." That said, Overholzer then turned her sights on the *Post*'s editors, saying that the *Post* showed more energy for protecting the CIA than for protecting the people from government excesses. "*Post* editors and reporters knew there was strong evidence that the CIA at least chose to overlook Contra involvement in the drug trade. Yet when those revelations came out in the 1980s they had caused 'little stir,' as the *Post* delicately noted. Would that we had welcomed the surge of public interest as an occasion to return to a subject the *Post* and the public had given short shrift. Alas, dismissing someone else's story as old news comes more naturally."

1998

The History of "Black Paranoia"

Alexander Cockburn and Jeffrey St. Clair

HE FURY AMONG AMERICAN BLACKS SPARKED BY WEBB'S "Dark Alliance" series was powerful enough to cause serious concern to the U.S. government, urban mayors, and major newspapers, and even prompted CIA Director John Deutch to make an extraordinary appearance at a town meeting in South Central Los Angeles, where Rep. Maxine Waters was accused of fanning the flames of "black paranoia." We will now briefly outline why this "paranoia" is amply justified and why Webb's series very reasonably struck a chord in the black community.

In all discussions of "black paranoia" during the Webb affair, white commentators invariably conceded—as indeed they had to—that the one instance where such fears were entirely justified was the infamous Tuskegee experiments. Yet in the press coverage no more than a sentence or two was devoted to any account of what actually happened at Tuskegee.

The facts are terrible. In 1932, 600 poor black men from rural Macon County, Alabama, were recruited for a study by the United States Public Health Service and the Tuskegee Institute. The researchers found 400 out of the 600 infected with syphilis, and the 200 uninfected men were monitored as the control group. The other 400 men were told they were being treated for "bad blood" and were given a treatment the doctors called "pink medicine," which was actually nothing more than aspirin and an iron supplement. No effective medical treatment was ever given to the Tuskegee victims because the researchers wanted to study the natural progress of venereal disease. When other physicians diagnosed syphilis in some of the men, the Public Health Service researchers intervened to prevent any treatment. When penicillin was developed as a cure for syphilis in 1943, it was not provided to the patients. Indeed, the development of a cure only seemed to spur on the Tuskegee researchers, who, in the words of historian James Jones, author of *Bad Blood*, saw Tuskegee as a "never-again-to-be-repeated opportunity."

As an inducement to continue in the program over several decades the men were given hot meals, a certificate signed by the surgeon general, the promise of free medical care, and a $50 burial stipend. This stipend was far from altruistic because it allowed the Health Service researchers to perform their own autopsies on the men after they died. The experiments continued until 1972, and were canceled only after information about them had leaked to the press. Over the course of the experiments more than 100 of the men died of causes related to syphilis, but even after exposure, the lead researchers remained unapologetic. "For the most part, doctors and civil servants simply did their job," said Dr. John Heller, who had headed the U.S. Public Health Services Division of Venereal Diseases. "Some merely followed orders, others worked for the glory of science."

In 1996, President Clinton issued a public apology to the Tuskegee victims. Nor was this an entirely disinterested act of governmental contrition. Earlier in the year, Clinton had been approached by Secretary of Health and Human Services Donna Shalala regarding the scarcity of blacks willing to volunteer as research subjects. Shalala attributed this reluctance to "unnatural fears" arising from the Tuskegee experiments. George Annas, who runs the Law, Ethics and Medicine program at Boston University, notes that the apology was skewed and that Clinton and Shalala should have been finding ways of recruiting more blacks as medical students rather than research subjects. "If you were to look at the historical record, you will see that blacks' distrust predated Tuskegee," according to Dr. Vanessa Gamble, an associate professor of the history of medicine at the University of

Wisconsin at Madison. "There were experiments dating back to more than a hundred years that were more often done by whites on slaves and free blacks than on poor whites."

Another oft-cited explanation for the readiness of blacks to believe the worst about the white man's intentions is briskly referred to as "the FBI's snooping on Martin Luther King Jr.," as Tim Golden put it amid his reflections on black paranoia in the *New York Times*. The government's interest in Dr. King went considerably beyond "snooping," however, to constitute one of the most prolonged surveillances of any family in American history. In the early years of the 20th century, Ralph Van Deman created an Army Intelligence network targeting four prime foes: the Industrial Workers of the World, opponents of the draft, Socialists, and "Negro unrest." Fear that the Germans would take advantage of black grievances was great, and Van Deman was much preoccupied with the role of black churches as possible centers of sedition.

By the end of 1917, the War Department's Military Intelligence Division had opened a file on Martin Luther King Jr.'s maternal grandfather, the Rev. A.D. Williams, pastor of Ebenezer Baptist Church and first president of the Atlanta NAACP. King's father, Martin Sr., Williams' successor at Ebenezer Baptist, also entered the army files. Martin Jr. first shows up in these files (kept by the 111th Military Intelligence Group at Fort McPherson in Atlanta) in 1947, when he attended Dorothy Lilley's Intercollegiate School; the army suspected Lilley of having ties to the Communist Party.

Army Intelligence officers became convinced of Martin Luther King Jr.'s own Communist ties when he spoke in 1950 at the twenty-fifth anniversary of the integrated Highlander Folk School in Monteagle, Tennessee. Ten years earlier, an Army Intelligence officer had reported to his superiors that the Highlander school was teaching a course of instruction to develop Negro organizers in the southern cotton states.

By 1963, as Tennessee journalist Stephen Tompkins reported in the Memphis *Commercial Appeal*, U-2 planes were photographing disturbances in Birmingham, Alabama, capping a multilayered spy system that by 1968 included 304 intelligence offices across the country, "subversive national security dossiers" on 80,731 Americans, plus 19 million personnel dossiers lodged at the Defense Department's Central Index of Investigations.

A more sinister thread derives from the anger and fear with which the Army's high command greeted King's denunciation of the Vietnam War at Riverside Church in 1967. Army spies recorded Stokely Carmichael telling King, "The Man don't care you call ghettos concentration camps, but when you tell him his war machine is nothing but hired killers you got trouble."

After the 1967 Detroit riots, 496 black men under arrest were interviewed by agents of the Army's Psychological Operations group, dressed as civilians. It turned out King was by far the most popular black leader. That same year Maj. Gen. William Yarborough, assistant chief of staff for intelligence, observing the great antiwar march on Washington from the roof of the Pentagon, concluded that the Empire was coming apart at the seams. There were, Yarborough reckoned, too few reliable troops to fight in Vietnam and hold the line at home.

In response, the army increased its surveillance of King. Green Berets and other Special Forces veterans from Vietnam began making street maps and identifying landing zones and potential sniper sites in major U.S. cities. The Ku Klux Klan was recruited by the 20th Special Forces Group, headquartered in Alabama as a subsidiary intelligence network. The Army began offering 30-06 sniper rifles to police departments, including that of Memphis.

In his fine investigation, Tompkins detailed the increasing hysteria of Army Intelligence chiefs over the threat they considered King to pose to national stability. The FBI's J. Edgar Hoover was similarly obsessed with this threat, and King was dogged by spy units through early 1967. A Green Beret special unit was operating in Memphis on the day he was shot. He died from a bullet from a 30-06 rifle purchased in a Memphis store, a murder for which James Earl Ray was given a 99-year sentence in a Tennessee prison. A court-ordered test of James Earl Ray's rifle raised questions as to whether it in fact had fired the bullet that killed King.

Notable black Americans, from the boxing champion Jack Johnson to Paul Robeson to W. E. B. Du Bois, were all the object of relentless harassment by the FBI. Johnson, the first black superstar, was framed by the FBI's predecessor under the Mann Act. Johnson ultimately served a year for crossing state lines with his white girlfriend (who later became his wife). Du Bois, founder of the NAACP, was himself under surveillance for nearly seventy years and was arrested and shackled for urging peace talks with North Korea.

Still fresh in the minds of many blacks is the FBI's COINTEL-PRO program, started in 1956 and conceived as a domestic counterinsurgency program. Though its ambit extended to the New Left, Puerto Rican revolutionaries, and Native Americans, the most vigorous persecutions under COINTELPRO were those of black leaders. A memo from FBI Director J. Edgar Hoover described the program as it stood in August 1967: the purpose of COINTELPRO was to "expose, disrupt, misdirect, discredit or otherwise neutralize" black organizations the FBI didn't care for. And if any black leader emerged, Hoover's order was that the Bureau should "pinpoint potential troublemakers and neutralize them before they exercised their potential for violence."

"Neutralize" has long been a euphemism for assassination. At least six or seven Black Panther leaders were killed at the instigation of the FBI, the most infamous episode being the assassination of Fred Hampton and Mark Clark in Chicago. These two Panther leaders were shot in their beds, while asleep, by Chicago police who had been given a detailed floor plan of the house by an FBI informant who had also drugged Hampton and Clark.

During the mid-1970s hearings chaired by Idaho Senator Frank Church, the FBI was found to have undertaken more than

200 so-called "black bag" jobs, in which FBI agents broke into offices, homes, and apartments to destroy equipment, steal and copy files, take money, and plant drugs. The FBI was also linked to the arson fire that destroyed the Watts Writers' Workshop in Los Angeles.

In all the stories about "black paranoia" trolled forth by Webb's assailants, one topic was conspicuously ignored: the long history of the racist application of U.S. drug laws. The first racist application of drug laws in the United States was against Chinese laborers. After the U.S. Civil War, opium addiction was a major problem: wounded soldiers used it to dull pain and then became habituated. One study estimates that by 1880, one in every 400 adults in the United States had such an addiction to opium. Chinese laborers had been brought into the United States in the wake of the Civil War to build the transcontinental railroad and, in California, to haul rock in the gold mines in the Sierras. Thousands of Chinese were also brought into the South to replace slave labor on the cotton and rice plantations. The Chinese brought opium smoking with them, their addiction having actively fostered in the Opium Wars by the British, who had successfully beaten down efforts by the Chinese government to curb the habit.

Then came the recession of the 1870s. The Chinese were now viewed as competitors for the dwindling number of jobs available. In 1875, San Francisco became the first city to outlaw opium smoking with legislation clearly aimed at the Chinese, who smoked the narcotic, as opposed to the main group of users, white men and women, who took opium in liquid form. This was the era when the use of opium-based patent medicines was pervasive. Women used them in "tonics" to alleviate pain in childbirth, and also to "soothe" their nerves. Unlike the "yellow dope fiends," however, the white users were politely termed "habitués." In 1887, the U.S. Congress weighed in with the Chinese Exclusion Act, which among other things) allowed Chinese opium addicts to be arrested and deported.

Similarly, racist attitudes accompanied the rise of cocaine use. Cocaine had been mass marketed in the United States in the late 1880s by the Parke-Davis Company (which many decades later had contracts to provide the CIA with drugs in the MK-ULTRA program). The company also sold a precursor to crack, marketing cocaine-laden cigarettes in the 1890s. In that same decade the Sears & Roebuck catalogue, which was distributed to millions of homes, offered a syringe and a small amount of cocaine for $1.50. But by the turn of the century the attitude of the medical and legal establishment to cocaine was beginning to change. In 1900 the *Journal of the American Medical Association* printed an editorial alerting its readers to a new peril: "Negroes in the South are reported as being addicted to a new form of vice—that of 'cocaine sniffing' or the 'coke habit.'"

President Theodore Roosevelt responded to the new scare by creating the nation's first drug czar, Dr. Hamilton Wright. Wright was a fanatic racist, announcing that "[i]t is been authoritatively stated that cocaine is often the direct incentive to the crime of rape by the Negroes of the South and other regions." One of Wright's favored authorities was Dr. Christopher Koch of the State Pharmacy Board of Pennsylvania. Koch testified before Congress in 1914 in support of the Harrison Bill, shortly to pass into law as the first criminalization of drug use. Said Koch: "Most of the attacks upon the white women of the South are the direct result of a cocaine-crazed Negro brain."

At the same hearing, Wright alleged that drugs made blacks uncontrollable, gave them superhuman powers, and prompted them to rebel against white authority. These hysterical charges were trumpeted by the press, in particular the *New York Times*, which on February 8, 1914, ran an article by Edward Hunting Williams reporting how Southern sheriffs had upped the caliber of their weapons from .32 to .38 in order to bring down black men under the influence of cocaine. The *Times'* headline for the article read: "Negro Cocaine 'Fiends' are New Southern Menace:

Murder and Insanity Increasing Among Lower-Class Blacks." Amid these salvoes, the Harrison Act passed into law.

In 1930, a new department of the federal government, the Bureau of Narcotics and Dangerous Drugs, was formed under the leadership of Harry Anslinger to carry on the war against drug users. Anslinger, another racist, was an adroit publicist and became the prime shaper of American attitudes to drug addiction, hammering home his view that this was not a treatable dependency but one that could only be suppressed by harsh criminal sanctions. Anslinger's first major campaign was to criminalize the drug commonly known at the time as hemp. But Anslinger renamed it "marijuana" to associate it with Mexican laborers who, like the Chinese before them, were unwelcome competitors for scarce jobs in the Depression. Anslinger claimed that marijuana "can arouse in blacks and Hispanics a state of menacing fury or homicidal attack. During this period, addicts have perpetrated some of the most bizarre and fantastic offenses and sex crimes known to police annals."

Anslinger linked marijuana with jazz and persecuted many black musicians, including Thelonius Monk, Dizzy Gillespie, and Duke Ellington. Louis Armstrong was also arrested on drug charges, and Anslinger made sure his name was smeared in the press. In Congress he testified that "[c]oloreds with big lips lure white women with jazz and marijuana."

By the 1950s, amid the full blast of the Cold War, Anslinger was working with the CIA to charge that the newborn People's Republic of China was attempting to undermine America by selling opium to U.S. crime syndicates. (This took a good deal of chutzpa on the part of the CIA, whose planes were then flying opium from Chiang Kai-shek's bases in Burma to Thailand and the Philippines for processing and export to the U.S.A.) Anslinger convinced the U.S. Senate to approve a resolution stating that "subversion through drug addiction is an established aim of Communist China."

In 1951, Anslinger worked with Democrat Hale Boggs to marshal through Congress the first minimum mandatory sentences for drug possession: two years for the first conviction of possession of a Schedule 1 drug (marijuana, cocaine), five to ten years for a second offense, and ten to twenty years for a third conviction. In 1956, Anslinger once again enlisted the help of Boggs to pass a law allowing the death penalty to be imposed on anyone selling heroin to a minor, the first linking of drugs with Death Row.

This was Anslinger's last hurrah. Across John Kennedy's New Frontier charged sociologists attacking Anslinger's punitive philosophy. The tempo of the times changed, and federal money began to target treatment and prevention as much as enforcement and prison. But the interim did not last long. With the waning of the war in Southeast Asia, millions of addicted GIs came home to meet the fury of Nixon's War on Drugs program. Nixon picked up Anslinger's techniques of threat inflation, declaring in Los Angeles: "As I look over the problems of this country I see that one stands out particularly: the problem of narcotics."

Nixon pledged to launch a war on drugs, to return to the punitive approach, and not let any quaint notions of civil liberties and constitutional rights stand in the way. After a Nixon briefing in 1969, his top aide, H.R. Haldeman, noted in his diary: "Nixon emphasized that you have to face the fact that the whole problem is really the blacks. The key is to devise a system that recognizes this while not appearing to."

But for all his bluster, Nixon was a mere prelude to the full fury of the Reagan-Bush-Clinton years, when the War on Drugs became explicitly a war on blacks. The first move of the Reagan administration was to expand the forfeiture laws passed during the Carter administration. In 1981, Reagan's drug policy advisers outlined a plan they thought would be little more than good PR, a public display of the required toughness. They proposed allowing the Justice Department to seize real property and so-called "substitute property" (that is, legally acquired assets equal in value to illegal monetary gains). They also proposed that the federal government seize attorneys' fees that they suspected might have been funded by drug proceeds. They even proposed to allow attorneys to be summoned by federal prosecutors before grand juries to testify about the source of their clients' money. The Reagan plan was to permit forfeitures on the basis of a "probable cause showing" before a federal judge. This meant that seizures could be made against people neither charged nor convicted, but only suspected, of drug crimes.

Contrary to the administration's expectations, this plan sailed through Congress, eagerly supported by two Democratic Party liberals, Senators Hubert H. Humphrey and Joe Biden, the latter being the artificer, in the Carter era, of a revision to the RICO act, a huge extension of the federal conspiracy laws. Over the next few years, the press would occasionally report on some exceptionally bizarre applications of the new forfeiture laws, such as the confiscation of a $2.5 million yacht in a drug bust that netted only a handful of marijuana stems and seeds. But typically the press ignored the essential pattern of humdrum seizures, which more often focused on such ordinary assets as houses and cars. In Orange County, California, fifty-seven cars were seized in drug-related cases in 1989: "Even if only a small amount of drugs is found inside," an Orange County narcotics detective explained, "the law permits seized vehicles to be sold by law enforcement agencies to finance anti-drug law enforcement programs."

In fact, the forfeiture program became a tremendous revenue stream for the police. From 1982 to 1991, the U.S. Department of Justice seized more than $2.5 billion in assets. The Justice Department confiscated $500 million in property in 1991 alone, and 80 per cent of these seizures were from people who were never charged with a crime.

On June 17, 1986, University of Maryland basketball star Len Bias died, reportedly from an overdose of cocaine. As Dan Baum put it in his excellent *Smoke and Mirrors: The War on Drugs and the Politics of Failure*, "In life, Len Bias was a terrific basketball player.

In death, he became the Archduke Ferdinand of the Total War on Drugs." It was falsely reported that Bias had smoked crack cocaine the night before his death. (He had in fact used powder cocaine and, according to the coroner, there was no clear link between this use and the failure of his heart.)

Bias had just signed with the Boston Celtics and amid Boston's rage and grief, Speaker of the House Tip O'Neill, a representative from Massachusetts, rushed into action. In early July he convened a meeting of the Democratic Party leadership. "Write me some goddam legislation," he ordered. "All anybody in Boston is talking about is Len Bias. They want blood. If we move fast enough we can get out in front of the White House." The White House was itself moving fast. Among other things, the DEA had been instructed to allow ABC News to accompany it on raids against crack houses. "Crack is the hottest combat-reporting story to come along since the end of the Vietnam War," the head of the New York office of the DEA exulted.

All this fed into congressional frenzy to write tougher laws. House Majority Leader Jim Wright called drug abuse "a menace draining away our economy of some $230 billion this year, slowly rotting away the fabric of our society and seducing and killing our young." Not to be outdone, South Carolina Republican Thomas Arnett proclaimed that "drugs are a threat worse than nuclear warfare or any chemical warfare waged on any battlefield." The 1986 Anti-Drug Abuse Act was duly passed. It contained twenty-nine new minimum mandatory sentences. Up until that time in the history of the Republic there had been only 56 mandatory minimum sentences in the whole penal code.

The new law had a death penalty provision for drug "kingpins" and prohibited parole for even minor possession offenses. But the chief target of the bill was crack cocaine. Congress established a 100-to-1 sentencing ratio between possession of crack and powder cocaine. Under this provision, possession of 5 grams of crack carries a minimum five-year federal prison sentence. The same mandatory minimum is not reached for any amount of powder cocaine less than 500 grams. This sentencing disproportion was based on faulty testimony that crack was fifty times as addictive as powder cocaine. Congress then doubled this ratio as a so-called "violence penalty." There is no inherent difference in the drugs, as Clinton drug czar Barry McCaffery conceded. The federal Sentencing Commission, established by Congress to review sentencing guidelines, found that so-called "crack violence" is attributable to the drug trade and has more to do with the setting in which crack is sold: crack is sold on the street, while powder cocaine is vended by house calls. As Nixon and Haldeman would have approvingly noted about the new drug law, it was transparently aimed at blacks, reminiscent of the early targeting of Chinese smoking opium rather than white ladies sipping their laudanum-laced tonics.

In 1995, the U.S. Sentencing Commission reviewed eight years of application of this provision and found it to be undeniably racist in practice: 84 per cent of those arrested for crack possession were black, while only 10 per cent were white and 5 per cent Hispanic. The disparity for crack-trafficking prosecutions was even wider: 88 per cent blacks, 7 per cent Hispanics, 4 per cent whites. By comparison, defendants arrested for powder cocaine possession were 58 per cent white, 26 per cent black, and 15 per cent Hispanic.

In Los Angeles, all twenty-four federal defendants in crack cases in 1991 were black. The Sentencing Commission recommended to Congress and the Clinton administration that the ratio should be one-to-one between sentences for offenses involving crack and powder cocaine, arguing that federal law allows for other factors to be considered by judges in lengthening sentences (such as whether violence was associated with the offense). But for the first time in its history the Congress rejected the Sentencing Commission's recommendation and retained the 100-to-1 ratio. Clinton likewise declined the advice of his drug czar and his attorney general, and signed the bill.

One need only look at the racial makeup of federal prisons to appreciate the consequences of the 1986 drug law. In 1983, the total number of prisoners in federal, state and local prisons and jails was 660,800. Of those, 57,975—8.8 per cent—were incarcerated for drug-related offenses. In 1993, the total prison population was 1,408,000, of whom 353,564—25.1 per cent—were inside for drug offenses. The Sentencing Project, a Washington, D.C.-based watchdog group, found that the increase was far from racially balanced. Between 1986 and 1991, the incarceration rate for white males convicted on drug crimes increased by 106 per cent. But the number of black males in prison for kindred offenses soared by a factor of 429 per cent, and the rate for black women went up by an incredible 828 per cent.

The queen of the drug war, Nancy Reagan, said amid one of her innumerable sermons on the issue: "If you're a casual drug user, you're an accomplice to murder." In tune with this line of thinking, Congress moved in 1988 to expand the crimes for which the federal death penalty could be imposed. These included drug-related murders, and murders committed by drug gangs, which would allow any gang member to face the death penalty if one member of the gang was linked to a drug killing. The new penalties were inscribed in an update of the Continuing Criminal Enterprises Act. The figures arising from implementation of the act suggest that "black paranoia" has in fact a sound basis in reality.

Convictions under the act between 1989 and 1996 were 70 per cent white and 24 per cent black—but 90 per cent of the times the federal prosecutors sought the death penalty it was against non-whites: of these, 78 per cent were black and the rest Hispanic. From 1930 to 1972 (when the U.S. Supreme Court found the federal death penalty unconstitutional), 85 per cent of those given death sentences were white. When it was reapplied in 1984, with the Anti-Drug Abuse Act, the numbers for black death penalty convictions soared. Whether the offense is drug-related or not, a black is far more likely to end up on Death Row. Of those on

Death Row, both federal and state, 50 per cent are black. Blacks constitute 16 per cent of the population. Since 1976, 40 per cent of the nation's homicide victims have been black, but 90 per cent of death sentences handed down for homicide involved white victims.

In the drug war, Los Angeles was Ground Zero. On the streets of Los Angeles, gang-related killings were a constant presence to the residents of the mostly poor areas in which they occurred, as gangs fought out turf battles for distribution rights to the crack supplied by Ricky Ross and his associates in an operation connived at by the CIA. As long as it was confined to black areas of Los Angeles, little official attention was paid to this slaughter—an average of one murder per day from 1988 through 1990. However, in December 1987 a gang mistakenly killed 27-year-old Karen Toshima outside a cinema complex in Westwood, near the UCLA campus, prompting outrage from the city's government: "The continued protection of gang activity under the guise of upholding our Constitution is causing a deadly blight on our city," cried Los Angeles City Attorney Kenneth Hahn.

LAPD Chief Darryl Gates promptly rolled out his campaign to pacify inner-city Los Angeles, Operation Hammer. Even before this campaign, the LAPD was not known for its sensitivity to black people. In the 1970s, there had been more than 300 killings of non-whites by the LAPD, and Gate's own racism was notorious. Responding to complaints about a string of choke-hold deaths, Gates blamed them on the physiology of blacks: "We may be finding that in some blacks, when [the choke-hold] is applied, the veins or arteries do not open as fast as they do on normal people."

Operation Hammer was a counterinsurgency program that sometimes resembled the Phoenix program in Vietnam. There were hundreds of commando-style raids on "gang houses." More than 50,000 suspected gang members were swept up for interrogation based on factors such as style of dress and whether the suspect was a young black male on the street past curfew. Of those caught up in such Hammer sweeps, 90 per cent were later released without charge, but their names were held in a computer database of gang members that was later shown to have included twice as many names as there were black youths in Los Angeles. Gates sealed off large areas of South Central as "narcotics enforcement zones." There was a strict curfew, constant police presence, and on-the-spot strip searches for those caught outside after curfew.

In this war there were many innocent casualties. In 1989, the LAPD shotgunned to death an 81-year-old man they wrongly believed to be a crack dealer. Witnesses claimed that the old man had his hands up when he was blown away. In 1989, 75 per cent of all cases in the Los Angeles criminal courts were drug-related.

It would be difficult to find any documentary evidence that this War on Drugs had anything other than a deleterious effect. By 1990, black youth unemployment in the greater Los Angeles area was 45 per cent. Nearly half of all black males under the age of twenty-five had been in the criminal justice system. Life expectancy for blacks was falling for the first time in this century, and infant mortality in the city was rising. Some 40 per cent of black children were born into poverty.

Among those white people concerned by the awful conditions of life in the inner cities was government psychiatrist Fred Goodwin. In 1992, he was director of the umbrella agency ADAMHA, the Alcohol, Drug Abuse, and Mental Health Administration. Goodwin was an eager crusader for a national biomedical program to control violence, the core notion being the search for a "violence" gene. In the quest for this supposed biological basis for social crisis in the poverty-stricken and crime-ridden ghettoes, Goodwin was replicating all the Malthusian obsessions of late-nineteenth and early-twentieth century white American intellectuals and politicians. Many of supposedly enlightened people like Woodrow Wilson believed that sterilization was the best way to maintain the cleanliness in the national gene pool. It was too late to stop the arrival of Africans, but these Malthusians inspired the race exclusion laws of 1923, designed to keep out genetically dubious Slavs, Jews, Italians, and other rabble—legislation admired by the Nazis.

On February 11, 1992, Goodwin gave a speech to the National Mental Health Advisory Council on the future of federal mental health policy, calling for an approach that would focus on presumed genetic and biomedical factors. Among Goodwin's observations in his address:

> There are discussions of "biological correlates" and "biological markers." The individuals have defective brains with detectable prefrontal changes that may well be predictive of later violence. The individuals have impaired intelligence, in this case "cognitive deficit."... Now, one could say that if some of the loss of social structure in this society, and particularly within the high impact inner city areas, has removed some of the civilizing evolutionary things that we have built up and that maybe it isn't just the careless use of the word when people call certain areas of certain cities jungles, that we may have gone back to what might be more natural, without all of the social controls that we have imposed upon ourselves as a civilization over thousands of years in our evolution.
>
> If you look, for example, at male monkeys, especially in the wild, roughly half of them survive to adulthood. The other half die by violence. That is the natural way of it for males, to knock each other off and, in fact, there are some interesting evolutionary implications of that because the same hyperaggressive monkeys who kill each other are also hypersexual, so they copulate more and therefore they reproduce more to offset the fact that half of them are dying.

Goodwin called for early identification of these dangerous monkey-men. "There will be emphasis on the earliest detection of behavioral patterns which have predictor value, and two, what do we know and what can we learn about preventive interventions."

Goodwin did not address treatment issues further, but a news story in the *Washington Post* by Boyce Rensberger noted that

NIMH psychiatrists who supported Goodwin and his violence initiative were testing new medications to correct the biochemical imbalances supposedly found in both violent monkeys and men.

Goodwin's remarks were reported in the press and created a commotion. There was a brief spasm of official admonition, and he was "demoted" to the post of director of the National Institute of Mental Health, a position for which he had been already slated.

Would black men or women, already "paranoid" about the idea of the problem of poverty being addressed by government chemists carrying "rebalancing" agents in their syringes, have been hyperbolically paranoid in seeing traces of a longer obsession on the part of the government agencies such as the CIA?

Goodwin was himself only following in the footsteps of Dr. Lewis "Jolly" West. West is a psychiatrist in UCLA who is well known for his suzerainty over the university's Neuropsychiatric Institute. Back in 1969, he leaped to prominence with disclosure of his plan to put electrodes in the brains of suspected violent offenders at a spin-off of the institute called the Center for the Study and Reduction of Violence. Public uproar forced West to abandon this scheme. In 1973, West once again sought to set up a center for human experimentation, this time at a former Nike missile base in the Santa Monica Mountains. In this pastoral setting, the work of scientific experimentation would proceed undisturbed. "The site is securely fenced," West wrote excitedly to the California state legislature. "Comparative studies could be carried out there, in an isolated but convenient location, of experimental model programs, for alteration of undesirable behavior."

West had long worked with CIA chemists and kindred boffins on the use of LSD in altering human behavior—and not just that of humans, either. In 1962 West killed Tusko, a renowned elephant at the Oklahoma City zoo. He shot the mighty pachyderm full of LSD, and Tusko swiftly succumbed. West claimed that the zookeeper had brought him the elephant for treatment.

In the late 1960s and early 1970s, neurologists and psychiatrists were much taken with the problems of urban violence. One of West's mentors was Dr. Ernst Rodin, a Dr. Strangelove-type, heading up the Neurology Department at the Lafayette Clinic, who recommended psychosurgery and castration as appropriate medical technologies to apply to the dangerous classes.

Rodin equated "dumb young males who riot" to oxen and declared that "the castrated ox will pull his plow" and that "human eunuchs, although at times quite scheming entrepreneurs are not given to physical violence. Our scientific age tends to disregard this wisdom of the past."

West made similar statements after the Watts rebellion, but for the castrator's sickle he recommended the substitution of cyproterone acetate, a sterilizing chemical developed by the East Germans. By 1972, West was suggesting the use of prisoners as "subjects" in such treatment. There was a big stink about this, and in 1974 statewide protests led to cuts of state funding to West's project. In his book, *Operation Mind Control*, Walter Bowart wrote that West is "perhaps the chief advocate of mind control in America today."

West put his finger unerringly on the usefulness of drug laws as a way of imposing selective social control. "The role of drugs in the exercise of political control is also coming under increasing discussion," he wrote in *Hallucinations: Behavior, Experience and Theory*, a book he edited in 1975. "Control can be imposed either through prohibition or supply. The total or even partial prohibition of drugs gives government considerable leverage for other types of control. An example would be the selective application of drug laws... against selected components of the population such as members of certain minority groups or political organizations." As we have seen, sentencing patterns vindicate West's analysis.

It is not in the least paranoid for any black person to conclude that since the late-nineteenth century prominent white intellectuals and politicians have devoted much effort to reducing the number of black people by the expedient of sterilization, or selective medical assault, often chastely described as the "science" of eugenics.

Back in 1910, blunt as always, Home Secretary Winston Churchill used his position to secretly propose the sterilization of 100,000 "mental degenerates" in the U.K., using as intellectual buttress research by Dr. H. C. Sharp of the Indiana Reformatory in the U.S.A. In the first couple of decades of the twentieth century, American elites also were much concerned about the national gene pool (the founders of Cal Tech, for example, were rabid eugenicists). Between 1907 and 1913, starting with Indiana, twelve states put sterilization statutes on their books. Indiana's Governor J. Frank Hanley signed a law authorizing the compulsory sterilization of any confirmed criminal, idiot, rapist, or imbecile in a state institution whose condition was determined to be "unimprovable" by a panel of physicians.

Allan Chase in *The Legacy of Malthus* reports that 63,678 people were compulsorily sterilized between 1907 and 1964 in thirty states and one colony with such laws. But he also points out that these victims represent "the smallest part of the actual number of Americans who have this century been subjected to forced eugenic sterilization operations by state and federal agencies." Chase quotes Federal Judge Gerhard Gessell as saying in 1974 in a suit brought on behalf of poor victims of involuntary sterilization: "Over the last few years an estimated 100,000 to 150,000 low-income persons have been sterilized annually in federally funded programs." This rate, as Chase points out, equals that achieved in Nazi Germany. Across the twelve years of the Third Reich, after the German Sterilization Act of 1933 (inspired by U.S. laws) went into effect, 2 million Germans were sterilized as social inadequates.

Gesell said that though Congress had been insistent that all family planning programs function on a purely voluntary basis, "an indefinite number of poor people have been improperly coerced into accepting a sterilization operation under the threat that various federally supported welfare benefits would be withdrawn unless they submitted to irreversible sterilization. Patients receiving Medicaid assistance at childbirth are evidently the most frequent targets of this pressure." Among the plaintiffs in this action was Katie Relf of Alabama, who fought off the advancing sterilizers by locking herself in her room. Writing toward the end of the 1970s, Chase reckoned that probably at least 200,000 Americans per year were the victims of involuntary and irreversible sterilization.

In the great program of sterilization, the note of commonsensical do-goodism was relentlessly sounded. Take the California sterilizer and racist Paul Popenoe, a man close to the Chandler family, who owned the *Los Angeles Times*. In a 1930 pamphlet, "Sterilization for Human Betterment," Popenoe and his co-author E.S. Gosney cautioned thus:

> One of the greatest dangers in the use of sterilization is that overzealous persons who have not thought through the subject will look on it as a cure-all, and apply it to all sorts of ends for which it is not adapted. It is only one of many measures that the state can and must use to protect itself from racial deterioration. Ordinarily it is merely adjunct to supervision of the defective or diseased.
>
> The objection is sometimes made that sterilization will at least deprive the world of many useful, law-abiding, self-supporting citizens. They may not be brilliant, it is admitted; but isn't there a need for a large portion of dull people in modern civilization, to do the rough and routine work that the intellectuals are unwilling to do? If the breeding of all the morons is stopped, who will dig the sewers and collect the garbage?
>
> Fortunately or unfortunately, there is no possibility of stopping production of morons altogether. Many of them are born in families of normal intelligence, simply through unfavorable combination of genes which carry the heredity. There will

always be enough of them produced to dig sewers and collect
the garbage, without encouraging the reproduction of people
who are likely to produce only morons.

Though race-specific terms were usually avoided by eugenicists, who preferred words like "weak-minded," or "imbeciles" (a favorite of that enthusiast for sterilizing, Oliver Wendell Holmes, a jurist much admired by liberals), the target was, by and large, blacks. What direct sterilization could not prevent, incarceration or medically justified confinement has also sought to achieve.

So far as medical confinement is concerned, the magazine *Southern Exposure* has documented the excessively large number of blacks locked up in state-run mental hospitals in the southern U.S.A. In 1987, nearly 37 per cent of those involuntarily committed were black. The blacks were consistently diagnosed with more serious illnesses, more frequently subjected to sedative medicine, and held in greater numbers for indefinite confinement without judicial review. The pattern, so the article suggested, may extend beyond the South.

The history of bio-chemical warfare is also suggestive. The U.S. use of bio-weapons goes back to the distribution of smallpox-infected blankets to American Indian tribes in the 1860s. In 1900, U.S. Army doctors in the Philippines infected five prisoners with a variety of plague and 29 prisoners with beriberi. At least four of the subjects died. In 1915, a doctor working with government grants exposed 12 prisoners in Mississippi to pellagra, an incapacitating condition that attacks the nervous system.

In 1942, U.S. Army and Navy doctors infected 400 prisoners in Chicago with malaria in experiments designed to get "a profile of the disease and develop a treatment for it." Most of the inmates were black and none was informed of the risks of the experiment. Nazi doctors on trial at Nuremberg cited the Chicago malaria experiments as part of their defense.

In 1951, the U.S. Army secretly contaminated the Norfolk Naval Supply Center in Virginia with infectious bacteria. One type of bacterium was chosen because blacks were believed to be more susceptible to it than whites. Savannah, Georgia, and Avon Park, Florida, were the targets of repeated army bio weapons experiments in 1956 and 1957. Army CBW researchers released millions of mosquitoes on the two towns in order to test the ability of insects to carry and deliver yellow fever and dengue fever. Hundreds of residents fell ill, suffering from fevers, respiratory distress, stillbirths, and encephalitis. Several deaths were reported.

The harmonious collaboration between the CIA and racist regimes of an overall Nazi outlook began with the importing of Nazi scientists. Among the CIA's friends in later years was South Africa's apartheid regime. It was, for example, a CIA tip that led the arrest of Nelson Mandela and his imprisonment for more than twenty years. Close CIA cooperation with South Africa's intelligence agencies continued unabated and indeed mounted during the Reagan years, with close collaboration in attacks on Mozambique and other neighbors of South Africa deemed to be threats to South African and U.S. interests.

In a 1970 article in *Military Review*, a journal published by the U.S. Army Command and General Staff College, a Swedish geneticist at the University of Lund named Carl Larson discussed genetically selective weapons. Larson stated that though the study of drug-metabolizing enzymes was in its infancy, "observed variations in drug responses have pointed to the possibility of great innate differences in vulnerability to chemical agents between different populations." Larson went on to speculate that in a process similar to mapping the world's blood groups, "we may soon have a grid where new observations of this kind can be pinpointed." In the same vein, a January 1975 U.S. Army report noted in its conclusion that "[i]t is theoretically possible to develop so-called 'ethnic weapons' which would be designed to exploit naturally occurring differences in vulnerability among specific population groups."

1998

How the Media Use Blacks
to Chastise Blacks
Ishmael Reed

REPLAY DON IMUS AS MUCH AS I CAN BECAUSE HIS PUTRID RACIST offerings are said to represent the secret thinking of the cognoscenti. Maybe that's why journalists like Jeff Greenfield and others admire him so much. He says what they think in private.

On any day, you might find Bernard McGirk, the man, who, according to 60 *Minutes*, Imus hired to do "nigger jokes," doing a lame imitation of New Orleans Mayor Ray Nagin, using a plantation-type dialect. The blacks who are satirized by McGirk and others are usually displayed as committing malapropisms, but, though white writers appear daily on the show, I've rarely seen a black author.

In the last twenty years, black authors have received every prize available to authors. His idea of a black author must be the same as the producers of the movie, *The Tenants*, Snoop Dogg.

Recently, McGirk referred to Rev. Joseph Lowery as a "shameless skunk," and a joke was made about the manner in which Betty Shabazz, Malcolm X's widow, was murdered. Black athletes are referred to as "knuckle draggers," which, the Irish and Scots-Irish members of Imus' crew—they discussed their ethnic heritage on C-SPAN—might be surprised to learn, was the way that the British referred to their groups. When an exhibition of great apes was presented in London, the British commentators said that the exhibition showed the Irish to be the link between ape and man. But their being Irish and Scots-Irish makes sense because it was members of these groups who used to entertain the Anglos by blackening up. Maybe that's why Imus has listeners in Kennebunkport. Bush Senior is a fan.

Another fan is Congressman Harold Ford (D-TN), whom Imus endorses so as to deflect attention from the show's lowbrow racism. I'm sure that Ford understands what Imus is all about, but he needs the country and western vote in rural Tennessee in order to gain a senate seat. Imus has a big following among this constituency. So did James Earl Ray. But why pick on Imus? His approach to the treatment of black issues and personalities has become mainstream, the only difference being that instead of using the Irish and Scots-Irish, the traditional white-trash mercenaries, who stand between the Other and the Anglos, when, given their social and economic position, they should strike common cause with blacks, the network and newspaper executives use people who resemble blacks to chastise blacks. This colored auxiliary functions as their mind doubles and iPod people.

I'll bet the executives got the idea from the cynical packagers of President Bush's political strategies. The administration's advocates of torture are Vietnamese, Chinese, and Mexican Americans. The former domestic policy advisor who was recently arrested for scamming a department store is black, and the secretary of state is black. When they come before congressional committees, the idea is that congressmen would be reluctant to submit them to harsh questioning for fear of being called racist. That way, they can promote the administration's megalomaniac foreign policy with very little criticism. I'm sure that's Karl Rove's thinking. Unlike Ms. Rice, whom I, in a heated public exchange with her, dubbed "the Manchurian Candidate" about a year before she joined the Bush campaign, journalist Barbara Reynolds is a progressive. She said that she was fired from *USA Today* because she didn't appeal to the demographic group from which the paper gets its sales: Angry White Males. Those black syndicated columnists who have remained must fit the bill. They have become the gofers for backlash journalism, all of them competing with each other to blame the country's social problems on black behavior.

Clarence Page and others are regularly blaming the victim. Harvard's Orlando Patterson is also brought in by the neocon op-ed editors at the *Times* to characterize the problems of African Americans as self-inflicted, using the kind of argument that would be ripped to shreds in a freshman classroom.

Even Bob Herbert, a liberal and the token black on the *New York Times'* neocon editorial page, has to take the brothers and sisters to the woodshed from time to time in order to maintain credibility with his employers. He too says that Gangsta Rap is the cause of society's woes. (David Brooks, who promotes some of the same ideas as David Duke, but has a more opaque writing style, even blamed the riots in France on Gangsta Rap).

For these writers, black peoples' style is the irritant. If we could only get Rep. Cynthia McKinney to a new hair stylist. Michel Martin, who was assigned to beat up on Ms. McKinney by the producers of *Nightline*, spent half the interview on Ms. McKinney's hair even though Ms. McKinney has been outspoken on a number of serious issues. Can you imagine Ms. Martin conducting an interview with Trent Lott, the last person on the planet to use Wild Root Cream Oil, or Joe Biden, and spending half the time on his hair?

If *Nightline*'s Martin had subjected a white male congressman to this kind of hostile sarcastic interview, sarcastic not only in words but in body language, to which she subjected Cynthia McKinney, Martin would have gotten the same treatment from her bosses that Connie Chung received when she interviewed Newt Gingrich's mom, who denounced Hillary Clinton as "a bitch." (Ms. Martin knows whom to aggress upon. When she appeared on a program with "white militant" Joe Klein, and Klein, who lied about his authorship of *Primary Colors*, talked about "the poverty of values within the inner city," she just sat there and took it.)

Before Chung's interview with Newt's mom, the network executives, according to a media publication issued by the Freedom Forum, wanted someone like Connie Chung for their shows. She still hasn't recovered and has been assigned to a Saturday morning show on MSNBC. Oblivion.

Cynthia Tucker of the *Atlanta Journal-Constitution* was also solicited by *Nightline* to join in on the ambush of Ms. McKinney. Ms. Tucker, who blames the Hudlin brothers, producers at Black Entertainment Network, for the problems confronting some black kids, is the syndicated columnist who relied on the usual inflammatory and racist reporting to describe those who sought refuge in the New Orleans Superdome as "bestial." The *New York Times*, the *New Orleans Time-Picayune*, and the *Los Angeles Times* all discounted these rumors, and the *LA Times* even apologized, saying that such reporting would never have occurred had there been white middle class inhabitants of the Superdome.

Ms. Tucker never retracted her false accusation, nor did Jeff Koinange, the reporter whom CNN has assigned to cover all of Africa. He replaced the black reporter who was covering the Superdome because this reporter presumably wasn't sensational enough.

While one can see African leaders, intellectuals, and scientists, sessions of parliaments, cultural events on the BBC, CNN's view of Africa is on par with that found in the Tarzan movies. When CNN bade Koinange farewell on the occasion of his new assignment, they presented the highlights of his Africa coverage. One picture showed him staring at a crocodile. Another showed him grinning at a monkey. No wonder the American public's knowledge of the world is on par with that of their president's.

You'll also notice that the moderator of the *Nightline* show where Rep Cynthia McKinney was grilled was of South Asian origin. According to a memo I have from a Cuban reporter, who was fired from CNN, the executives there, led by Jonathan Klein (the new head of CNN who is trying to boost his ratings by running mug shots of black males all day, while dropping the story about the middle class white kids, who were caught on video beating up homeless people, killing one of them; they were sent to psychiatric counseling), prefer South Asians as anchors, especially the women, and particularly on CNN International.

CNN Atlanta features a South Asian anchorwoman who giggles while the male correspondents exchange remarks with her that are loaded with sexual innuendo, certainly an issue that feminists should take up. Even C-SPAN, the only network where you can obtain a variety of viewpoints from African Americans, though they give disproportionate time to think-tank blacks like Shelby Steele, has gone Imus. Recently, Jadish Bhaghati, a South Asian professor at Columbia who supports Bush's plan to bring Mexican slave labor into the United States to serve his big agribusinesses contributors, shared laughs with host Pedro Echevarria and a caller, a white employer, who was voicing the kind of jokes about black work habits that one reads at the Klan's "Nigger Watch" website. Both Bhaghati and host Echevarria are black, but that didn't prevent them from enjoying the kind of barbs against African Americans one hears on the Imus show.

Of course, one should avoid generalizing about South Asians, but obviously the British, who referred to them as "niggers," trained some of them very well and they're not the only "people of color" who serve as stooges for the corporate media. Michel Malkin, instead of a hard-hitting anti-establishment writer like Emil Gulliermo of *Asia Week*, represents Filipino-Americans. For Muslim Americans they give us Irshad Manji, who refuses to debate the young playwright Wajahat Ali. For Mexican-Americans we are awarded the syndicated columnist Ruben Navarrette Jr., who believes that black people are too dumb to compete with the cheap Mexican labor that has been brought into New Orleans. People who work off the books, for less than the minimum wage, and who are subject to blackmail by their employers. People who threaten to wipe out all of the gains that American workers have fought for over the last one hundred years. Apparently, there is no room for the views of Patricia Gonzales and Roberto Rodriquez, who are to the left of Navarrette Jr.

African Americans have a number of individuals who are willing to serve as mind doubles. Some are supported by right-wing think tanks like the Manhattan Institute's John McWhorter, black front man for the eugenics movement. The Manhattan Institute boasts that they can provide enormous publicity for their fellows—the kind of clout that enables them to impose their viewpoints upon discussions about black issues—by using proxies who are unknown to black Americans. When McWhorter attacks me in *Commentary*, a magazine that praised Charles Murray's *The Bell Curve*, or in his books, where do I go to get equal time? He once challenged me to a debate, threatening "to wipe up the floor with me," but when I accepted, he backed out.

Another proxy person-of-color intellectual for right-wing interests is Shelby Steele of the Hoover Institute. He just got three hours on C-SPAN to explain his one-note theory that blacks complain too much about their "victimization." He accused blacks of expressing "victimization" when they complained about being robbed of their votes in Florida during the presidential election of 2000, even though there is abundant evidence that they *were* victimized.

But even Shelby Steele isn't as popular with the right as Ward Connerly who is so firmly associated with Proposition 209, the measure that ended Affirmative Action in California, that lazy journalists claim he started the drive that led to its passage. He didn't. He was brought on when the real sponsors suffered a lapse in their notion of a color-blind society long enough to realize that a black face on their proposition would aid in its adoption. Before Connerly came on, the proposition was failing. (One of the two white founders of the proposition said that he did so because a woman got the job that he was qualified for. Lydia Chavez, the author of *The Color Bind: The Campaign to End Affirmative Action*, April 1998, an excellent book about the sinister maneuvering that led to Proposition 209, says the woman has never been found.)

Connerly, viewed by the media as a martyr who braved the scorn of his black accusers to follow his conscience, only agreed to support the proposition if its supporters raised $500,000. Newt Gingrich helped to raise the money. He was also supported financially by President Clinton's nemesis, Richard Mellon Scaife. Rupert Murdoch contributed $200,000 and the Pioneer Fund contributed $35,000 to the campaign to end Affirmative Action in California, so that now Duke University and "Old Miss" have a higher black enrollment than the University of California and California State University.

In his book, *The Nazi Connection*, Stefan Kuhl says that "today, the Pioneer Fund is the most important financial supporter of research concerning the connection between race and heredity in the United States." Its largest contributor, until the 1960s, was textile magnate Wickliffe Draper, who worked with the United States House Un-American Activities Committee to demonstrate that blacks were genetically inferior and ought to be "repatriated" to Africa. The Pioneer Fund also supported Charles Murray's *The Bell Curve*, the book beloved by publications that hate Minister Louis Farrakhan so much. In this book, Charles Murray floats some of the same stereotypes about blacks that were once aimed at his Scots-Irish ancestors.

Another supporter was Andrew Sullivan, who came to the attention of the mainstream electronic media after he did such a good job bashing blacks at the *New York Times Magazine*, which describes blacks as cannibals and crack addicts.

Obviously Ward Connerly, who has made millions from being associated with Proposition 209, is supported so lavishly by such ultra-right individuals and groups that he has been reluctant to list his contributors.

Such is the power of their right-wing backers that Steele, Connerly, and McWhorter get more media attention than black elected officials. When Congressman Jesse Jackson Jr. and

Connerly appeared on C-SPAN, on the same day, it was Connerly who was featured.

I remember the press conference held by David Duke when he announced that he was abandoning his quest for the presidency.

Only a few news people attended. Duke complained that he had to quit because the mainstream candidates had co-opted his program all about a growing black underclass threatening civilization. (His Nazi colleague, Tom Metzger, disagreed with him. He said on Larry King's show that the average woman on welfare is a white woman whose husband has abandoned her.)

The same might happen to Don Imus, whose "nigger jokes" are sponsored by American Express and other famous brand names. Who needs a white man when there are plenty of people of color willing to take up the slack?

Ishmael Reed is a poet, novelist, and essayist who lives in Oakland. He is also the editor of the online zine Konch.

2005

What You Didn't Read About the Black Vote in Florida

Jeffrey St. Clair

O N THE ONE HAND, THE CALLS FOR "CLOSURE," "FINALITY," and "national unity." On the other, Justice John Paul Stevens' bitter summation: "in the interests of finality however the majority [of the U.S. Supreme Court] effectively orders the disenfranchisement of an unknown number of voters whose ballots reveal their intent, and are therefore legal votes under [Florida] state law, but were for some reason rejected by the ballot-counting machines. Although we may never know with complete certainty the identity of the winner of this year's presidential election the identity of the loser is perfectly clear. It is the nation's confidence in the judge as an impartial guardian of the law."

Back in the 1980s, radicals used to write about "demonstration elections," conducted in Central American countries such as El Salvador at the instigation of the U.S. government and micromanaged by the CIA. After the money was appropriately spread around, the opposition's more tenacious and principled leaders either butchered by death squads or driven underground, and the unruly poor thoroughly intimidated, the election ritual would take place amid complacent orations about the democratic way from North American commentators.

We've just had a peaceful and non-lethal version of these "demonstration elections" in the state of Florida and no calls for closure will erase that national disgrace, least of all in the minds of those who were denied their democratic rights. Don't forget, beyond those who made it to the polls in Florida, there were those denied even the dubious benefits of that access.

Beyond the obsession about defiant punch card machines, obstacle course ballots, and pregnant or hanging chads,there are more serious issues that, in the miles of print published about the election in Florida, have received barely a mention: the systematic intimidation of poor people, blacks, Hispanics, immigrants, and the disabled.

Consider this story from Ron Davis of Miami-Dade County. "Our family always votes together. This year it was my turn to drive. After work, my wife Lisa and I borrowed a van from a friend and picked up my brother, my parents, and my uncle and aunt. About a block away from the polling place, we were pulled over by a county sheriff. He looked in the van and asked me if I had a chauffeur's license. I said, this is my family and we're going to vote. He said, 'You can't take all those people to the polling place without a license. Go home and I won't write you a ticket.' I was tired of arguing. We went home and all tried to vote later. But it was too late."

Or how about this account told to us by Dave Crawford of Broward County: "I showed up at the polling place with my 5-year-old daughter. I was stopped at the door by an election official. He asked me my name. I told him. He said, 'Son, we've got a problem. You're not allowed to vote.' I asked him what the hell he was talking about. He said, 'Son, says here you're a convict. Convicts can't vote.' He had this list in his hand. And I told him that I'd never even been arrested in my life. I handed him my voter ID card. He just shook his head, smiled and pointed at a list. He never showed me my name. My daughter began to cry and I left in disgust."

On November 7, blacks and Hispanics turned out to vote in record numbers. But tens of thousands were shunted away before they reached the polling booth. The scenes, many of them narrated during an extraordinary 5-hour hearing sponsored by the NAACP and the Lawyers Committee for Civil Rights Under

Law, harked back to the pre-Voting Rights Act South, when black voters were denied the franchise through a variety of schemes, from the poll tax and character vouchers to loyalty oaths and literacy tests.

Across Florida, black voters were turned away from the polls by hostile election workers who demanded voter ID cards, even though those weren't required from white voters. Police set up roadblocks in black precincts around Tallahassee. Other police intimidated voters by asking if they were felons. Polls in black precincts closed early, often with dozens of voters waiting in line. Other polls were moved from their original locations without notice. Dozens of black college students who had registered in the summer weren't permitted to vote. Other voters were told that their names weren't on the voter rolls only to find out later that they were. Haitian voters were often asked for two forms of identification.

Stacey Powers, a former cop who is now a news director at a Tampa radio station, spent the day visiting different polling places in Tampa's black neighborhoods. She said dozens of black voters were turned away after being told that their names didn't appear on the voting registers. Powers said that when she reminded some voters that they could sign an affidavit and then vote, she was booted out of the polling place.

"There were illegal poll watchers, threatening people, telling them: 'I know where you work. You're going to get fired,'" reported Charles Weaver, publisher of the Fort Myers-based *Community Voice*.

A catalog of these accounts was assembled and shipped off to Janet Reno, who, as attorney general, is charged with enforcing the Voting Rights Act. The Clinton Justice Department didn't take one step to investigate the charges. "This is a strange stance from the Justice Department," said Kwesi Mfumi, head of the NAACP. "They just seem to get colder to civil rights as the administration draws to a close."

Then there were more than 12,000 largely black voters who were evicted from the Florida voter rolls in May, supposedly because they were ex-felons. In the Sunshine State, the system functioned in a particularly devious way. Nearly all of those purged from the rolls turned out not to have had criminal records. But nearly all of them were black. Some 8,000 went through the legal red tape to assert their voting rights. The remaining 4,000 didn't bother. Nearly all of those votes would have gone to Gore. The list was prepared by a company known as Database Technologies, a firm picked by Secretary of State Katherine Harris. As the London *Guardian* reported, Database Techologies is a subsidiary of ChoicePoint, which is has been under investigation for misusing personal information gathered state computers. ChoicePoint's beleaguered CEO, Rick Bozar, made a timely $100,000 contribution to the Republican National Committee in early 2000.

Even those who made it inside the polling booth found out later that their votes didn't tally. While the press and the Gore PR machine raged about the injustices done to Jewish voters by the infamous Butterfly ballot, the real story, even in Palm Beach County, was the effort to suppress the black vote. Democratic pollster Patrick Caddell, who speaks venomously of the Gore machine, was one of the first to point this out. "I looked at those precincts," said Caddell. "And it struck me that most of them were in predominately black areas. Of course, they would be just as unlikely to vote for Buchanan as the Jewish retirees. But the Gore people made a deliberate effort to spin it as a case of 4,000 elderly Jewish Democrats being duped into voting for a Nazi." A similar point was made by Adora Ori, the president of the NAACP's Florida chapter. "A closer examination has to be made. The precincts that have the most irregularities at this point seem to be black and minority."

The Democratic Party has displayed a marked disinclination to make any political capital out of the denial of black and Haitian voting rights in Florida. After a couple of days hammering the issue, Jesse Jackson was evidently told to cool it.

In Duval County, a Republican stronghold, about 25,000 votes were tossed out by the canvassing board. More than 17,000 of those came from black precincts. "That so-called voter error rate raises real questions about what was going on up there," says Kendrick Meek, a Florida state senator from Miami. Duval County has one of the highest illiteracy rates in the United States. More than 47 per cent of the voting age population is considered functionally illiterate, making it nearly impossible for them to navigate Florida's obscure ballot. To top it off, according to numerous accounts, election workers regularly demeaned as being "dumb and retarded" those voters who asked for help.

Throughout Florida, more than 187,000 votes were dismissed, more than half of them from black precincts. Nationally more than 2.8 million ballots were eliminated, often because of some trifling error by the voter. A disproportionate percentage of these discarded votes originated in black and Hispanic precincts.

Although more than 95 per cent of blacks supported Gore, election offices controlled by Democrats seemed just as determined to suppress the black vote as Republicans. Listen to this account from Palm Beach County resident Mary Didier. "My husband and I moved to Palm Beach from New York City eight months ago. We had just retired as public school teachers. We registered to vote at the motor vehicle department when I got my license. Months went by, and we never received our voter cards. About six weeks before the election I began to get nervous and called the DMV. They said it wasn't their problem and that I should contact the election office. I drove down there. They had no record of us. I said, 'I want to re-register now.' The woman told me to wait a few weeks and see if the card came. We waited. It never came. The week before the election, I went in again. They said, 'Do you have any proof of how long you've lived in Florida.' I gave showed them my driver's license. They said that wasn't good enough. I got mad and left. Then I called the state election's office. They said they didn't have time to deal with a minor issue like this. It was the first time I haven't voted in 30 years."

Didier was not alone. In West Palm Beach, the votes of more than 2,000 recent Haitian immigrants were rejected because of the maze-like ballot and the lack of Creole interpreters. "There were lots of Spanish translators to make sure all of the Cubans voted, but none who spoke Creole," Ken Murtaugh, a poll watcher in West Palm Beach, told *CounterPunch*. "Most of them were utterly confused. Others just walked away. It was pathetic. They were treated as being subhuman."

In other counties, Haitians were harassed for their voter iden-tification cards or told that their names couldn't be found on the voter rolls. Others were threatened with deportation. In one precinct with Creole translators, election officials ordered the interpreters not to speak to Haitian voters or risk being tossed from the polling place.

There should be no closure on these outrages, even though it is hard to imagine George W. Bush's Justice Department exert-ing itself in this regard. Nor should there be closure on what Justice Stevens stigmatized as the refusal, endorsed by the 5-4 Supreme Court majority, to recognize the clear voting intentions of those who did manage to gain access to Florida's dubious voting machines.

The saga of shenanigans in Florida has been a bracing civic education, not least because we have learned to appreciate yet again that judges' politics weigh far more strongly upon their opinion-forming faculties than a thousand precedents in American constitutional law. A strict constructionist on states' rights, like Justice Scalia, can become a federalist overnight, when the chips are down.

This has been a year when some members of the U.S. Supreme Court have discredited themselves thoroughly. Justices Rehnquist, Kennedy, and Antonin Scalia all have sons who were involved in the Microsoft case, from which the justices nonetheless declined to recuse themselves.

So far as the Florida decisions are concerned, Scalia should certainly have recused himself since he had more than one conflict of interest. For example, on November 7, 2000 his son John joined the Miami law firm Greenberg, Traurig. The following day Barry Richard, a partner in that firm, said he was called to represent Bush in Florida.

Clarence Thomas' wife has been working for the Heritage Foundation, which is putting forward resumés for appointments in the Bush administration. Section 455 of Title 28 of the United States Code requires recusal if a spouse has "an interest that could substantially be affected by the outcome of the proceedings." Other family relations, such as Scalia's, can be cause for recusal. Scalia has leaked stories to the effect that if Gore were to be elected, he would leave the Court.

Here's a pewter lining for Al Gore. Paradoxically, the U.S. Supreme Court may have helped his political career. Despite a dismal campaign, he emerges as a man who can claim with some merit that he was the popular choice, winning nationally by nearly 300,000 votes; that he probably won the state of Florida, given the more than 30,000 votes in Duval and Palm Beach counties cast for him but disallowed because of double punching; that he may have well won the legal vote had it not been for the Republican strict obstructionists.

It is true that little in the way of substantive issues separated Bush from Gore. That is surely why the Florida imbroglio has been so mostly untroubling. Never has there been greater fuss over smaller stakes until we come to Justice Stevens' bottom line. If this has been a constitutional crisis, the fates gave us the right time to have one.

Al Gore made his call for unity after the ruling, for the "coming together," demanded on a nightly basis by Larry King and the others. It proves Ralph Nader's point and once again vindicates his candidacy, one that in Florida and New Hampshire denied Al Gore conclusive victory on November 7.

The weeks since November 7 have entirely proved the accuracy of Nader's assault on the corruption of the two-party system. We've seen Republicans toss aside their supposed dedication to states' rights, same as did Scalia as he bent his supposed principles to elect a president he hopes will make him Chief Justice. We've seen Democrats equally eager to assert states' rights, while exhibiting absolutely no disquiet about the actual application of states' rights in Florida, meaning the racist efforts described above to stop blacks and other minorities from voting at all. Not a word from Gore on this. Honesty is divisive. It was a "demonstration election" in every sense of the word. It demonstrated how rotten the whole system is.

2000

Juan Williams: Liar, Liar!

Bruce Dixon

FOX NEWS AND NPR TALKING HEAD JUAN WILLIAMS HAS A new book out. It's called *Enough*, with a long subtitle that will not be reproduced here, and is being heavily promoted in the establishment media. On the evidence of extensive promotional interviews on C-SPAN and NPR, in which the author lays out the book's thesis, this is one writer with no plans to buy or read the thing. Therefore, this is not a book review.

To hear Williams tell it, the book arose out of his disgust for what he calls "a generation of black leadership" which he says refuses to condemn crime and drug trafficking in African American communities, which champions unmarried motherhood, thug life, and the destruction of black family life as good things, and which advises young people to avoid education or gainful employment. These are black leaders, according to Williams, who embrace conspiracy theories, who needlessly insult the sensibilities of white America and who have contributed to what he and others call a culture of victimhood in black America.

So just who, in the estimation of Juan Williams, are these pro-drug and pro-thug black leaders? In a 17-minute NPR interview, the best Williams can do is to name Rev. Al Sharpton and former Newark Mayor Sharpe James. In an hour-long C-SPAN session, Williams managed to also point the finger at the Rev. Jesse Jackson. So what gives here? There is plenty of room for disagreement with all three of these guys, but none of them even remotely qualifies as an apologist for crime and deadbeat dadness. None of them are implacable foes of self-help and educational excellence or anything of the sort. Juan Williams is no fool, and certainly knows this. So if, as he says, he has a message for black America, Williams is shouting it from a place where reason and logic do not apply, and facts just plain don't matter.

Where is this place? Why is Mr. Williams there, and is there any reason we should think about joining him?

Juan Williams is in a place where marketing-style messaging has completely replaced any effort to educate the public, or to promote informed discussion. Marketing messages are necessarily completely independent of facts and logic. Can anyone seriously imagine consumers choosing brands of soap or models of car based on factual comparisons of their characteristics and features? Of course not. So it's commonplace for corporations to sell us SUVs by depicting vehicles that drive straight up the sides of cliffs and buildings, and that navigate the bottoms of lakes and rivers. The fruity components of the logo on one brand of underwear sing to us on TV, while Michael Jordan pitches a rival brand on another channel.

Growing corporate media consolidation, the disappearance of most local news coverage, and the consequent shrinkage of the ranks of full-time professional journalists has reduced political discussion in the mainstream media to battles of sound bytes, a terrain inherently more friendly to rightist political messaging, which, like its commercial cousins, endeavors to reach audiences not through their reasoning and critical faculties, but tries to grab them by their subconscious fears, their unfulfilled desires for status and belonging, their prejudices and loathings. Political messaging in this era is all about crafting potent propaganda, phrases and slogans completely independent of any facts, but calculated to appeal to things many people know deep down inside, but which are simply not true at all. Think "support the troops." Think the "war on terror." Think the "culture of victimhood."

Left and progressive politics, by comparison, demand a consistent degree of intellectual engagement from even the most humble among us, whether it's grappling with the fact of oppression, or visualizing oneself as a part of some larger community of interest, or empathizing with the struggles and sufferings of people like and unlike us. Left and progressive politics challenge us to imagine a better world and contribute somehow to making it happen.

It's not difficult to see what place the unhelpful rhetoric of Juan Williams has in the scheme of things. The man is, after all, a *Fox News* personality, and Fox is notorious for ideologically qualifying writers, producers, and on-air talent. Although the mainstream media promote Williams, and Williams promotes himself as a brave and sometimes lonely voice (along with Bill Cosby) administering much needed if little heeded advice to black America, the fact is that Juan Williams has long ago forgotten how to talk respectfully enough to black folks to merit listening to.

Arguably, as befits a *Fox News* celebrity, a very large fraction of Mr. Williams' audience is fundamentally opposed to the interests of African Americans and to anybody who might point out that white supremacy is still an active and adaptive force in American life today.

The Amazon.com page for every book has a revealing section titled, "People who bought this book also bought..." Among the top six selections of those who purchased Williams' latest book are choices by the notoriously self-hating black conservative Shelby Steele, another by the execrable John McWhorter of the right-wing Manhattan Institute, a third by some wingnut advocating U.S. withdrawal from the U.N. in order to more effectively wage war against all those ungrateful brown people, and the latest hateful screed by Ann Coulter, titled *Godless: the Church of Liberalism*.

A long cherished project of the right in America is to impose and popularize the blanket invalidation of any and all claims of racism, racial profiling, white skin privilege, and institutional white supremacy made by people on the receiving end of those practices. That's what the previous decade's phrase, "playing the race card," was about. It's what today's charges of victimhood, victimology, and the alleged "culture of victimhood" are about. Both are cases of PR terminology designed to facilitate a disregard of the facts of life as it is lived, and which appeal to beliefs many white Americans hold but would rather not admit to. Both de-legitimize and pathologize anybody who would dare call attention to their own mistreatment or the mistreatment of others. When Juan Williams denounces black leadership and fol-lowership for fostering an alleged culture of victimization, that's the team he is playing for.

There is no shortage of problems in black America, prob-lems that we alone can address by directing our own energies to projects of self-help and uplift. But a vision that calls those who point to the existence of active white privilege and white supremacy as continuing and often dominating factors in a sup-posedly color-blind America merely "apostles of victimhood," is not visionary at all. It's not factual at all. It's enemy propa-ganda.

Bruce Dixon is managing editor of Black Agenda Report, "the weekly African American political website for thought and action." (http://www.blackagendareport.com/) Here can be found Glen Ford and the core crew which in August 2006 left Black Commentator, which Ford conceived, co-founded, and edited for four years.

2006

Part 4

Dogs of War

How to Sell a War

Jeffrey St. Clair

HE WAR ON IRAQ WON'T BE REMEMBERED FOR HOW IT WAS waged so much as for how it was sold. It was a propaganda war, a war of perception management, where loaded phrases, such as "weapons of mass destruction" and "rogue state" were hurled like precision weapons at the target audience: us.

To understand the Iraq war you don't need to consult generals, but the spin doctors and PR flacks who stage-managed the countdown to war from the murky corridors of Washington where politics, corporate spin, and PSYOPS spooks cohabit.

Consider the picaresque journey of Tony Blair's plagiarized dossier on Iraq, from a grad student's website to a cut-and-paste job in the prime minister's bombastic speech to the House of Commons. Blair, stubborn and verbose, paid a price for his grandiose puffery. Bush, who looted whole passages from Blair's speech for his own clumsy presentations, has skated freely through the tempest. Why?

Unlike Blair, the Bush team never wanted to present a legal case for war. They had no interest in making any of their allegations about Iraq hold up to a standard of proof. The real effort was aimed at amping up the mood for war by using the psychology of fear.

Facts were never important to the Bush team. They were disposable nuggets that could be discarded at will and replaced by whatever new rationale that played favorably with their polls and focus groups. The war was about weapons of mass destruction one week, al-Qaeda the next. When neither allegation could be substantiated on the ground, the fall-back position became the mass graves (many from the Iran/Iraq war where the U.S.A. backed Iraq) proving that Saddam was an evil thug who deserved to be toppled. The motto of the Bush PR machine was: Move on. Don't explain. Say anything to conceal the perfidy behind the real motives for war. Never look back. Accuse the questioners of harboring unpatriotic sensibilities. Eventually, even the cagey Paul Wolfowitz admitted that the official case for war was made mainly to make the invasion palatable, not to justify it.

The Bush claque of neocon hawks viewed the Iraq war as a product and, just like a new pair of Nikes, it required a roll-out campaign to soften up the consumers. The same techniques (and often the same PR gurus) that have been used to hawk cigarettes, SUVs, and nuclear waste dumps were deployed to retail the Iraq war. To peddle the invasion, Donald Rumsfeld and Colin Powell and company recruited public relations gurus into top-level jobs at the Pentagon and the State Department. These spinmeisters soon had more say over how the rationale for war on Iraq should be presented than intelligence agencies and career diplomats. If the intelligence didn't fit the script, it was shaded, retooled, or junked.

Take Charlotte Beers whom Powell picked as undersecretary of state in the post-9/11 world. Beers wasn't a diplomat. She wasn't even a politician. She was a grand diva of spin, known on the business and gossip pages as "the queen of Madison Avenue." On the strength of two advertising campaigns, one for Uncle Ben's Rice and another for Head and Shoulders dandruff shampoo, Beers rocketed to the top of the heap in the PR world, heading two giant PR houses: Ogilvy and Mathers as well as J. Walter Thompson.

At the State Department Beers, who had met Powell in 1995 when they both served on the board of Gulf Airstream, worked on, in Powell's words, "the branding of U.S. foreign policy." She extracted more than $500 million from Congress for her Brand America campaign, which largely focused on beaming U.S. propaganda into the Muslim world, much of it directed at teens.

"Public diplomacy is a vital new arm in what will combat terrorism over time," said Beers. "All of a sudden we are in this position of redefining who America is, not only for ourselves, but for the outside world." Note the rapt attention Beers pays to the manipulation of perception, as opposed, say, to alterations of U.S. policy.

Old-fashioned diplomacy involves direct communication between representatives of nations, a conversational give and take, often fraught with deception (see April Glaspie), but an exchange nonetheless. Public diplomacy, as defined by Beers, is something else entirely. It's a one-way street, a unilateral broadcast of American propaganda directly to the public (domestic and international), a kind of informational carpet-bombing.

The themes of her campaigns were as simplistic and flimsy as a Bush press conference. The American incursions into Afghanistan and Iraq were all about bringing the balm of "freedom" to oppressed peoples. Hence, the title of the U.S. war: Operation Iraqi Freedom, where cruise missiles were depicted as instruments of liberation. Bush himself distilled the Beers equation to its bizarre essence: "This war is about peace."

Beers quietly resigned her post a few weeks before the first volley of tomahawk missiles battered Baghdad. From her point of view, the war itself was already won, the fireworks of shock and awe were all afterplay.

Over at the Pentagon, Donald Rumsfeld drafted Victoria "Torie" Clarke as his director of public affairs. Clarke knew the ropes inside the Beltway. Before becoming Rumsfeld's mouthpiece, she had commanded one of the world's great parlors for powerbrokers: Hill and Knowlton's D.C. office.

Almost immediately upon taking up her new gig, Clarke convened regular meetings with a select group of Washington's top private PR specialists and lobbyists to develop a marketing plan for the Pentagon's forthcoming terror wars. The group was filled with heavy-hitters and was strikingly bipartisan in composition. She called it the Rumsfeld Group and it included PR executive

Sheila Tate, columnist Rich Lowry, and Republican political consultant Rich Galen.

The brain trust also boasted top Democratic fixer Tommy Boggs, brother of NPR's Cokie Roberts and son of the late Congressman Hale Boggs of Arkansas. At the very time Boggs was conferring with top Pentagon brass on how to frame the war on terror, he was also working feverishly for the royal family of Saudi Arabia. In 2002 alone, the Saudis paid his Qorvis PR firm $20.2 million to protect its interests in Washington. In the wake of hostile press coverage following the exposure of Saudi links to the 9/11 hijackers, the royal family needed all the well-placed help it could buy. They seem to have gotten their money's worth. Boggs' felicitous influence-peddling may help to explain why the references to Saudi funding of al-Qaeda were dropped from the recent congressional report on the investigation into intelligence failures and 9/11.

According to the trade publication *PR Week*, the Rumsfeld Group sent "messaging advice" to the Pentagon. The group told Clarke and Rumsfeld that in order to get the American public to buy into the war on terrorism, they needed to suggest a link to nation states, not just nebulous groups such as al-Qaeda. In other words, there needed to be a fixed target for the military campaigns, some distant place to drop cruise missiles and cluster bombs. They suggested the scenario (already embedded in Rumsfeld's mind) of playing up the notion of so-called rogue states as the real masters of terrorism. Thus was born the Axis of Evil, which, of course, wasn't an "axis" at all, since two of the states, Iran and Iraq, hated each other, and neither had anything at all to do with the third, North Korea.

Tens of millions in federal money were poured into private public relations and media firms working to craft and broadcast the Bush dictat that Saddam had to be taken out before the Iraqi dictator blew up the world by dropping chemical and nuclear bombs from long-range drones. Many of these PR executives and image consultants were old friends of the high priests in the

Bush inner sanctum. Indeed, they were veterans, like Cheney and Powell, of the previous war against Iraq, another engagement that was more spin than combat.

At the top of the list was John Rendon, head of the D.C. firm, the Rendon Group. Rendon is one of Washington's heaviest hitters, a Beltway fixer who never let political affiliation stand in the way of an assignment. Rendon served as a media consultant for Michael Dukakis and Jimmy Carter, as well as Reagan and George H.W. Bush. Whenever the Pentagon wanted to go to war, he offered his services at a price. During Desert Storm, Rendon pulled in $100,000 a month from the Kuwaiti royal family. He followed this up with a $23-million contract from the CIA to produce anti-Saddam propaganda in the region.

As part of this CIA project, Rendon created and named the Iraqi National Congress and tapped his friend Ahmed Chalabi, the shady financier, to head the organization.

Shortly after 9/11, the Pentagon handed the Rendon Group another big assignment: public relations for the U.S. bombing of Afghanistan. Rendon was also deeply involved in the planning and public relations for the pre-emptive war on Iraq, though both Rendon and the Pentagon refuse to disclose the details of the group's work there.

But it's not hard to detect the manipulative hand of Rendon behind many of the Iraq war's signature events, including the toppling of the Saddam statue (by U.S. troops and Chalabi associates) and videotape of jubilant Iraqis waving American flags as the Third Infantry rolled by them. Rendon had pulled off the same stunt in the first Gulf War, handing out American flags to Kuwaitis and herding the media to the orchestrated demonstration. "Where do you think they got those American flags?" clucked Rendon in 1991. "That was my assignment."

The Rendon Group may also have had played a role in pushing the phony intelligence that has now come back to haunt the Bush administration. In December of 2002, Robert Dreyfuss reported that the inner circle of the Bush White House preferred the intelligence coming from Chalabi and his associates to that being proffered by analysts at the CIA.

So Rendon and his circle represented a new kind of off-the-shelf PSYOPS, the privatization of official propaganda. "I am not a national security strategist or a military tactician," said Rendon. "I am a politician, and a person who uses communication to meet public policy or corporate policy objectives. In fact, I am an information warrior and a perception manager."

What exactly is perception management? The Pentagon defines it this way: "actions to convey and/or deny selected information and indicators to foreign audiences to influence their emotions, motives and objective reasoning." In other words, lying about the intentions of the U.S. government. In a rare display of public frankness, the Pentagon actually let slip its plan (developed by Rendon) to establish a high-level den inside the Department Defense for perception management. They called it the Office of Strategic Influence and among its many missions was to plant false stories in the press.

Nothing stirs the corporate media into outbursts of pious outrage like an official government memo bragging about how the media are manipulated for political objectives. So the *New York Times* and *Washington Post* threw indignant fits about the Office of Strategic Influence; the Pentagon shut down the operation, and the press gloated with satisfaction on its victory. Yet, Rumsfeld told the Pentagon press corps that while he was shuttering the office, the same devious work would continue. "You can have the corpse," said Rumsfeld. "You can have the name. But I'm going to keep doing every single thing that needs to be done. And I have."

At a diplomatic level, despite the hired guns and the planted stories, this image war was lost. It failed to convince even America's most fervent allies and dependent client states that Iraq posed much of a threat. It failed to win the blessing of the U.N. and even NATO, a wholly owned subsidiary of Washington. At the end of the day, the vaunted coalition of the willing consisted of Britain, Spain, Italy, Australia, and a cohort of former Soviet bloc nations. Even so, the citizens of the nations that cast their lot with the U.S.A. overwhelmingly opposed the war.

Domestically, it was a different story. A population traumatized by terror threats and shattered economy became easy prey for the saturation bombing of the Bush message that Iraq was a terrorist state linked to al-Qaeda that was only minutes away from launching attacks on America with weapons of mass destruction.

Americans were the victims of an elaborate con job, pelted with a daily barrage of threat inflation, distortions, deceptions and lies, not about tactics or strategy or war plans, but about justifications for war. The lies were aimed not at confusing Saddam's regime, but the American people. By the start of the war, 66 per cent of Americans thought Saddam Hussein was behind 9/11 and 79 per cent thought he was close to having a nuclear weapon.

Of course, the closest Saddam came to possessing a nuke was a rusting gas centrifuge buried for 13 years in the garden of Mahdi Obeidi, a retired Iraqi scientist. Iraq didn't have any functional chemical or biological weapons. In fact, it didn't even possess any SCUD missiles, despite erroneous reports fed by Pentagon PR flacks alleging that it had fired SCUDs into Kuwait.

This charade wouldn't have worked without a gullible or a complicit press corps. Victoria Clarke, who developed the Pentagon plan for embedded reports, put it succinctly a few weeks before the war began: "Media coverage of any future operation will to a large extent shape public perception."

During the Vietnam War, TV images of maimed GIs and napalmed villages suburbanized opposition to the war and helped hasten the U.S. withdrawal. The Bush gang meant to turn the Vietnam phenomenon on its head by using TV as a force to propel the U.S.A. into a war that no one really wanted.

What the Pentagon sought was a new kind of living-room war, where instead of photos of mangled soldiers and dead Iraqi kids, they could control the images Americans viewed and to a large extent the content of the stories. By embedding reporters inside selected divisions, Clarke believed the Pentagon could count on the reporters to build relationships with the troops and to feel dependent on them for their own safety. It worked, naturally. One reporter for a national network trembled on camera that the U.S. Army functioned as "our protectors." The late David Bloom of NBC confessed on the air that he was willing to do "anything and everything they can ask of us." Call it a kind of journalistic Stockholm Syndrome.

When the Pentagon needed a heroic story, the press obliged. Jessica Lynch became the war's first instant celebrity. Here was a neo-gothic tale of a steely young woman wounded in a fierce battle, captured and tortured by ruthless enemies, and dramatically saved from certain death by a team of selfless rescuers, knights in camo and night-vision goggles. Of course, nearly every detail of her heroic adventure proved to be as fictive and maudlin as any made-for-TV-movie. But the ordeal of Private Lynch, which dominated the news for more than a week, served its purpose: to distract attention from a stalled campaign that was beginning to look a lot riskier than the American public had been hoodwinked into believing.

The Lynch story was fed to the eager press by a Pentagon operation called Combat Camera, the Army network of photographers, videographers, and editors that sends 800 photos and 25 video clips a day to the media. The editors at Combat Camera carefully culled the footage to present the Pentagon's montage of the war, eliding such unsettling images as collateral damage, cluster bombs, dead children and U.S. soldiers, napalm strikes and disgruntled troops.

"A lot of our imagery will have a big impact on world opinion," predicted Lt. Jane Larogue, director of Combat Camera in Iraq. She was right. But as the hot war turned into an even hotter occupation, the Pentagon, despite airy rhetoric from occupation supremo Paul Bremer about installing democratic institutions such as a free press, moved to tighten its monopoly on the flow images out of Iraq. First, it tried to shut down Al Jazeera, the Arab news channel. Then the Pentagon intimated that it would like to see all foreign TV news crews banished from Baghdad.

Few newspapers fanned the hysteria about the threat posed by Saddam's weapons of mass destruction as sedulously as did the *Washington Post*. In the months leading up to the war, the *Post*'s pro-war op-eds outnumbered the antiwar columns by a 3-to-1 margin.

Back in 1988, the *Post* felt much differently about Saddam and his weapons of mass destruction. When reports trickled out about the gassing of Iranian troops, the *Washington Post*'s editorial page shrugged off the massacres, calling the mass poisonings "a quirk of war."

The Bush team displayed a similar amnesia. When Iraq used chemical weapons in grisly attacks on Iran, the U.S. government not only didn't object, it encouraged Saddam. Anything to punish Iran was the message coming from the White House. Donald Rumsfeld himself was sent as President Ronald Reagan's personal envoy to Baghdad. Rumsfeld conveyed the bold message than an Iraq defeat would be viewed as a "strategic setback for the United States." This sleazy alliance was sealed with a handshake caught on videotape. When CNN reporter Jamie McIntyre replayed the footage for Rumsfeld in the spring of 2003, the secretary of defense snapped, "Where'd you get that? Iraqi television?"

The current crop of Iraq hawks also saw Saddam much differently then. Take the writer Laurie Mylroie, sometime colleague of the *New York Times'* Judith Miller, who persists in peddling the ludicrous conspiracy that Iraq was behind the 1993 car bombing of the World Trade Center.

How times have changed! In 1987, Mylroie felt downright cuddly toward Saddam. She wrote an article for the *New Republic* titled "Back Iraq: Time for a U.S. Tilt in the Mideast," arguing that the U.S. should publicly embrace Saddam's secular regime as a bulwark against the Islamic fundamentalists in Iran. The co-author of this mesmerizing weave of wonkery was none other than Daniel Pipes, perhaps the nation's most bellicose Islamophobe. "The American weapons that Iraq could make good use of include remotely scatterable and anti-personnel mines and counterartillery radar," wrote Mylroie and Pipes. "The United States might also consider upgrading intelligence it is supplying Baghdad."

In the rollout for the 2003 war, Mylroie seemed to be everywhere hawking the invasion of Iraq. She would often appear on two or three different networks in the same day. How did the reporter manage this quarklike feat? She had help in the form of Eleana Benador, the media placement guru who runs Benador Associates. Born in Peru, Benador parlayed her skills as a linguist into a lucrative career as media relations whiz for the Washington foreign policy elite. She also oversees the Middle East Forum, a fanatically pro-Zionist white paper mill. Her clients include some of the nation's most fervid hawks, including Michael Ledeen, Charles Krauthammer, Al Haig, Max Boot, Daniel Pipes, Richard Perle, and Judith Miller. During the Iraq war, Benador's assignment was to embed this squadron of pro-war zealots into the national media, on talk shows, and op-ed pages.

Benador not only got them the gigs, she also crafted the theme and made sure they all stayed on message. "There are some things, you just have to state them in a different way, in a slightly different way," said Benador. "If not, people get scared." Scared of intentions of their own government.

It could have been different. All of the holes in the Bush administration's gossamer case for war were right there for the mainstream press to expose. Instead, the U.S. press, just like the oil companies, sought to commercialize the Iraq war and profit from the invasions. They didn't want to deal with uncomfortable facts or present voices of dissent.

Nothing sums up this unctuous approach more brazenly than MSNBC's firing of liberal talk show host Phil Donahue on the eve of the war. The network replaced the *Donahue Show* with a running segment called *Countdown: Iraq*, featuring the usual nightly coterie of retired generals, security flacks, and other cheerleaders for invasion. The network's executives blamed the cancellation on sagging ratings. In fact, during its run Donahue's show attracted more viewers than any other program on the network. The real reason for the pre-emptive strike on Donahue was spelled out in an internal memo from anxious executives at NBC. Donahue, the memo said, offered "a difficult face for NBC in a time of war. He seems to delight in presenting guests who are anti-war, anti-Bush and skeptical of the administration's motives."

The memo warned that Donahue's show risked tarring MSNBC as an unpatriotic network, "a home for liberal anti-war agenda at the same time that our competitors are waving the flag at every opportunity." So, with scarcely a second thought, the honchos at MSNBC gave Donahue the boot and hoisted the battle flag.

It's war that sells.

There's a helluva caveat, of course. Once you buy it, the merchants of war accept no returns.

2005

All the News That's Fit to Buy

Alexander Cockburn and Jeffrey St. Clair

THE BUSH ERA HAS BROUGHT A ROBUST SIMPLICITY TO THE business of news management: where possible, buy journalists to turn out favorable stories and, as far as hostiles are concerned, if you think you can get away with it, shoot them or blow them up.

As with much else in the Bush era, the novelty lies in the openness with which these strategies have been conducted. Regarding the strategies themselves, there's nothing fundamentally new, both in terms of paid coverage and murder, as the killing in 1948 of CBS reporter George Polk suggests. Polk, found floating in the Bay of Salonika after being shot in the head, had become a serious inconvenience to a prime concern of U.S. covert operations at the time, namely the onslaught on communists in Greece.

Today we have the comical saga of the Pentagon turning to a Washington, D.C.-based subcontractor, the Lincoln Group, to write and translate for distribution to Iraqi news outlets booster stories about the U.S. military's successes in Iraq. I bet the Iraqi newspaper reading public was stunned to learn the truth at last.

More or less simultaneously comes news of Bush's plan, mooted to Tony Blair in April of 2004, to bomb the headquarters of Al Jazeera in Qatar. Blair argued against the plan, not, it seems, on moral grounds but because the assault might prompt retaliation.

Earlier assaults on Al Jazeera came in the form of a 2001 strike on the channel's office in Kabul. In November 2002, the U.S. Air Force had another crack at the target and this time managed to blow it up. The U.S. military claimed that they didn't know the target was an Al Jazeera office, merely "a terrorist site."

In April 2003, a U.S. fighter plane targeted and killed Tariq Ayub, an Al Jazeera reporter on the roof of Al Jazeera's Baghdad office. The Arab network had earlier attempted to head off any "accidental" attack by giving the Pentagon the precise location of its Baghdad premises. That same day in Iraq, U.S. forces killed two other journalists, from Reuters and a Spanish TV station, and bombed an office of Abu Dhabi TV.

On the business of paid placement of stories in the Iraqi press there's been some pompous huffing and puffing in the U.S.A. among the opinion-forming classes about the dangers of "poisoning the well" and the paramount importance of instilling in the Iraqi mind respect for the glorious traditions of unbiased, unbought journalism as practiced in the U.S. homeland. Christopher Hitchens, tranquil in the face of torture, indiscriminate bombing and kindred atrocities, yelped that the U.S. instigators of this "all-the-news-that's fit-to-buy" strategy should be fired.

Actually, it's an encouraging sign of the resourcefulness of those Iraqi editors that they managed to get paid to print the Pentagon's handouts. Here, in the homeland, editors pride themselves in performing the same service, without remuneration.

Did the White House slip Judith Miller money under the table to hype Saddam's weapons of mass destruction? I'm quite sure it didn't and the only money Miller took was her regular *Times'* paycheck and those book advances.

But this doesn't mean that we, the taxpayers, weren't ultimately footing the bill for Miller's propaganda. We were, since Miller's stories mostly came from the defectors proffered her by Ahmed Chalabi's group, the Iraqi National Congress,which even as late as the spring of 2004 was getting $350,000 a month from the CIA, said payments made in part for the INC to produce "intelligence" from inside Iraq.

It also doesn't mean that when she was pouring her nonsense into the *NYT*'s news columns, Judith Miller (or her editors) didn't know that the INC's defectors were linked to the CIA by a money trail. This same trail was laid out in considerable detail in *Out of the Ashes*, written by my brothers, Andrew and Patrick Cockburn, and published in 1999.

In this fine book, closely studied (and frequently plagiarized without acknowledgement) by journalists covering Iraq, the authors described how Chalabi's group was funded by the CIA, with huge amounts of money—$23 million in the first year alone—invested in an anti-Saddam propaganda campaign, subcontracted by the Agency to John Rendon, a Washington PR operator with good CIA connections.

Almost from its founding in 1947, the CIA had journalists on its payroll, a fact acknowledged in ringing tones by the Agency in its announcement in 1976, when G.H.W. Bush took over from William Colby, that "effective immediately, the CIA will not enter into any paid or contract relationship with any full-time or part-time news correspondent accredited by any U.S. news service, newspaper, periodical, radio or television network or station."

Though the announcement also stressed that the CIA would continue to "welcome" the voluntary, unpaid cooperation of journalists, there's no reason to believe that the Agency actually stopped covert payoffs to the Fourth Estate.

Its practices in this regard before 1976 have been documented to a certain degree. In 1977, Carl Bernstein attacked the subject in *Rolling Stone*, concluding that more than 400 journalists had maintained some sort of alliance with the Agency between 1956 and 1972.

In 1997, the son of a well-known CIA senior man in the Agency's earlier years said emphatically, though off the record, to a CounterPuncher that "of course" the powerful and malevolent columnist Joseph Alsop "was on the payroll."

Press manipulation was always a paramount concern of the CIA, as with the Pentagon. In his *Secret History of the CIA*, published in 2001, Joe Trento described how in 1948 CIA man Frank Wisner was appointed director of the Office of Special Projects, soon renamed the Office of Policy Coordination (OPC). This became the espionage and counterintelligence branch of the Central Intelligence Agency; the very first in its list of designated functions was "propaganda."

Later that year Wisner set an operation code-named "Mockingbird," to influence the domestic American press. He recruited Philip Graham of the *Washington Post* to run the project within the industry.

Trento writes that "one of the most important journalists under the control of Operation Mockingbird was Joseph Alsop, whose articles appeared in over 300 different newspapers." Other journalists willing to promote the views of the CIA included Stewart Alsop (*New York Herald Tribune*), Ben Bradlee (*Newsweek*), James Reston (*New York Times*), Charles Douglas Jackson (*Time*), Walter Pincus (*Washington Post*), William C. Baggs (*Miami News*), Herb Gold (*Miami News*), and Charles Bartlett (*Chattanooga Times*).

By 1953, Operation Mockingbird had a major influence over 25 newspapers and wire agencies, including the *New York Times*, *Time*, and CBS News. Wisner's operations were funded by siphoning of funds intended for the Marshall Plan. Some of this money was used to bribe journalists and publishers.

In his book, *Mockingbird: The Subversion Of The Free Press By The CIA*, Alex Constantine writes that in the 1950s "some 3,000 salaried and contract CIA employees were eventually engaged in propaganda efforts."

Senate Armed Services Chairman John Warner said recently, apropos the stories put into the Iraqi press by the Lincoln Group, that it wasn't clear whether traditionally accepted journalistic practices were violated. Warner can relax. The Pentagon, and the Lincoln Group, were working in a rich tradition, and their only mistake was to get caught.

2005

Have Journalists Been Deliberately Murdered By The U.S. Military?

Christopher Reed

THE WORD "MURDER" CROPS UP SOONER OR LATER IN SERIOUS discussions—scanty though they are—about American forces in Iraq and the many foreign journalists they have killed there. So, in order not to be later, let us ask the question now: Is the U.S. military deliberately murdering non-American media in the Iraqi war?

Many answer affirmatively, especially the families, eyewitnesses, colleagues, and employers of those who died violently in circumstances not explained satisfactorily, despite three years of requesting information. Others, including several international journalists' organizations, voice the charge of "war crimes" to describe these killings.

A third interpretation comes in various, shockingly descriptive phrases such as "criminal negligence, malicious manslaughter, reckless neglect, wanton savagery, intentional homicide, random murders, cowboy-killers, crazy killers," and so on.

It all amounts to a searing condemnation, but comes mainly from abroad. In America a tired, uninformed cynicism predominates with clichés such as: "Shit happens, what d'you expect, it's war for chrissake, they all do it."

Except they do not. Americans do. The Iraq war is the worst such conflict for wrongful deaths of journalists in modern memory. Proportionately, more have been killed than in any other conflict. In August 2003, when American troops shot dead a Reuters news agency cameraman in Iraq, Mazen Dana, he was the 17th journalist to die since the invasion started in March that year. During that time U.S. military casualties totaled less than 300—an astonishing comparative statistic. At the close of 2006 the total number of journalists and assistants killed in Iraq exceeded 130. Of these, another shocking figure is the number of journalists apparently killed deliberately.

These dead, including interpreters and technicians, total at least 20 as counted by the International Federation of Journalists (IFJ) in Brussels, the world's largest such organization representing more than 100 nations. At the very least it involves an outrageous scandal that is deliberately ignored by the U.S. government. For more than three years the Pentagon has dismissed, obstructed, delayed, or neglected attempts to seek justice in these killings. It has consistently concealed the truth and, in at least one instance, tampered with evidence.

The lack of cooperation means no satisfactory verdict in any single instance, but one case has come near and could finally— with the help of a more sympathetic new Congress?—lead to at least a semblance of justice. Yet even here, the preliminary finding emerged not because of the U.S. military, but despite it. British military allies also obstructed inquiries and failed to cooperate.

The case centers upon British reporter Terry Lloyd, the senior war correspondent of Independent Television News (ITN), BBC TV's main rival in the U.K. He was aged 50 with two children from his 19-year marriage, when he was killed by U.S. forces on the third day of the Iraq invasion in March of 2003 near Basra in the south. It happened along what they call the Highway of Hell when Lloyd, already wounded in the shoulder by Iraqi gunfire, lay in a minibus makeshift ambulance about to rush him to hospital.

But before that could happen, a bullet from an M63 machine gun fired by a U.S. marine tank crew shattered Lloyd's skull. His Lebanese interpreter Hussein Osman, married in his 30s, had been killed already, probably in earlier crossfire that caused Lloyd's wound. Their French cameraman, Frederic Nerac, 42 and married, was officially "presumed dead" by the French government in October 2005. His remains have yet to be found after more than three years.

The case of the dead Briton is important, even although most of the 20 suspected murdered journalists are Arab, because it happens to be the only one examined by a court of law with high standards of evidence—an inquest conducted by a coroner in Oxford, England, near where Lloyd lived. The court heard testimony over two weeks, concluding on October 13, 2006. The verdict: "Unlawful homicide," meaning in English law, in this kind of court, either manslaughter or murder.

The American press, accustomed to coroners' weaker powers, gave the verdict little prominence, but an English inquest (Scotland is slightly different) meets American evidence standards of "beyond a reasonable doubt." Sworn witnesses testify and may be cross-examined; a jury often deliberates; and the coroner's verdict, if it rules that a crime took place, is usually followed with a prosecution. The nearest U.S. equivalent is a preliminary hearing to establish a *prima facie* case to answer before a full trial.

In the Lloyd case, coroner Andrew Walker concluded that the "intention" of the two Marines who fired at him was to "kill or cause serious injury." Walker has written to the British Director of Public Prosecutions and the Attorney General (the government's senior lawyer) to recommend criminal investigation. ITN chief editor David Mannion wrote to the Pentagon. A prosecution decision is awaited.

Coroner Walker expressed severe criticisms of the case, as did the lawyer for Lloyd, one of several participants who described his death as "murder." Apologizing for the three-year delay, Walker said: "I and others made strenuous attempts to secure information from the U.S. forces." Worse, a death scene videotape taken by U.S. personnel and supplied to British military with assurances of its integrity appeared to be missing 15 minutes of deleted material.

Walker found no evidence of careless or improper behavior by ITN or Lloyd. He said:

> I have no doubt that the minibus presented no threat to American forces as, firstly, it was a civilian vehicle, and, secondly, it stopped and turned around to pick up survivors and was facing away from the American forces. It was obvious that wounded persons were getting into the vehicle. If the vehicle was perceived as a threat then it would have been fired on before it did a U-turn. This would have resulted in damage to the front. There is no such damage.
>
> I have no doubt that the fact the vehicle stopped to pick up survivors prompted the Americans to fire at the vehicle. It must be the case that the Americans who opened fire saw people getting into the minibus and must have seen that one of them needed the help of another person and was clearly injured.

The lawyer for Lloyd, Anthony Hudson, also told the court that whoever opened fire on Lloyd did so with the intention of "killing him or causing really serious injury." Hudson added: "If you conclude that U.S. soldiers fired on the civilian minibus containing Lloyd, if those U.S. soldiers had an intention to kill or an intention to cause serious injury, then you can properly conclude that Lloyd was murdered by those U.S. soldiers."

It is important to know that Lloyd, who had covered several wars previously, was working independently, or, in military jargon, was a "unilateral" reporter not officially "embedded" with troops. Although early in Iraq there were only 600 embedded media and over 2,000 independents, evidence suggests the latter are resented by military personnel as more likely to produce unflattering reports. Embedded media, literally dependant on soldiers for survival, are more pliable.

Stewart Purvis, former ITN chief executive, told the inquest that British forces had concealed information and delayed the hearing. He added that the military deliberately put at risk independent journalists who were, for instance, not informed of potential dangers. "The military did not wish to take any responsibility for unilaterals, to such an extent that they wouldn't even recognize their existence... It was pretty clear the British government did not want [independent] news correspondents in Baghdad." The same applied to the U.S.A.

While further Lloyd developments are awaited, a Spanish case has been abandoned. It arose from the deeply suspicious U.S. tank missile attack on the Palestine Hotel in Baghdad in April 2003 that killed Spanish cameraman José Couso and a Ukrainian reporter. The judge, who issued arrest warrants for two American soldiers and an officer, could not proceed, he said, because of U.S. refusal to cooperate.

Although an American inquiry exonerated the tank crew, saying they mistook "glinting light" from a camera as an Iraqi sniper's binoculars, this was widely disbelieved. Tanks have powerful magnifying sights, it was bright daylight, and the hotel, the highest building there, was well known as a journalist headquarters, housing more than 100 reporters. The U.S. official version of events kept changing so it soon became apparent that lies were being told. At one point, a senior U.S. officer had to withdraw his statement. Repeated IFJ's requests for an open accounting have been ignored.

As an obvious murder, the worst case is the U.S. tank shooting of the veteran cameraman Mazen Dana, 43, outside the notorious Abu Ghraib prison in Baghdad, also in daylight. The crew said they mistook his camera for a weapon, but Dana's colleagues told a different and damning version. They said they had been at the spot for 30 minutes or more, clearly visible to the military and that Dana had been filming the tank as it approached over 50 meters. If his camera was a weapon, why did he not fire? Stephan Breitner of France 2 Television said: "They knew we were journalists. After they shot Mazen, they aimed their guns at us. I don't think it was an accident... They are crazy."

In a grim irony Dana, a Palestinian, had been beaten and shot so many times by Israeli soldiers, mainly by rubber bullets but not always, he was transferred to Iraq because it was "safer." The New York-based Committee to Protect Journalists, which honored Dana with a Press Freedom Award in 2001 for coverage of the West Bank, wrote to Rumsfeld asking for an inquiry. Weeks later the Pentagon exonerated the American troops but did not publish full findings.

Several of the 20 dead were killed by a single shot from an American weapon, suggesting a deliberate act or even a sniper, as their deaths did not involve a skirmish. But as the military continues to hide the facts, nothing can be ascertained precisely— except that as numbers mount, so does the evidence in general. "It is time for the U.S. to abandon its policy of cover-up and tell the whole truth about all the cases where media died in unexplained circumstances at the hands of American soldiers," said the IFJ General Secretary Aidan White after the Lloyd verdict. Nothing has come of that.

Yet some may say: journalists know the risks. Horror happens. Mistakes are made. It's war. So?

Well, as the American trades union coalition, the AFL-CIO, wrote to the Pentagon on April 19, 2003, such suspicious killings "easily inflame anti-American sentiments in the foreign press. They also raise serious questions for us about safety of our own [American] members on the ground in Iraq." And elsewhere. The letter asked the defense secretary for an independent investigation of journalist killings. Nothing happened.

Meanwhile there have been plenty of inflammatory incidents to goad foreigners into slaughtering Americans. And they have been slaughtering plenty. There will be more.

Christopher Reed is a freelance journalist and regular contributor to CounterPunch, living in Japan. He can be contacted at christopherreed@earthlink.net

2006

The Press and the Patriot Act: Where Were They When It Counted?

Alexander Cockburn and Jeffrey St. Clair

T HE WEEKEND BEFORE THANKSGIVING 2001, AS THE TALIBAN fled into the Hindu Kush and America's children flocked to *Harry Potter*, the nation's opinion formers discovered that the Bush administration had hijacked the Constitution with the Patriot Act and the military tribunals. *Time* magazine burst out that "war is hell on your civil liberties." The *New York Times* suddenly began to run big news stories about John Ashcroft as if the Attorney General was running an off-the-shelf operation, clandestinely consummating all those dreams of Oliver North back in Reagan time about suspending the Constitution.

On November 15, the *Washington Post*'s Richard Cohen discarded his earlier defenses of Ashcroft, and declared the U.S. attorney general to be "the scariest man in government." Five days earlier, the *New York Times'* editorial was particularly incensed about suspension of client-attorney privileges in federal jails, with monitoring of all conversations. For the Hearst papers Helen Thomas reported on November 17 that Attorney General Ashcroft "is riding roughshod over the Bill of Rights and cited Ben Franklin to the effect that 'if we give up our essential rights for some security, we are in danger of losing both.'"

In this outburst of urgent barks from the watchdogs of the fourth estate, the first yelp came on November 15, from William Safire. In a fine fury, Safire burst out in his first paragraph that "misadvised by a frustrated and panic-stricken attorney general, a president of the United States has just assumed what amounts to dictatorial power." Safire lashed out at "military kangaroo courts" and flayed Bush as a proto-Julius Caesar.

On the same November day, from Britain, whose traditionally appalling emergency laws are now being rendered even more faithful to the vicious tradition of the Star Chamber, the *Economist* chimed in that the Patriot Act and Ashcroft's new rules for federal prosecutors are "drastic," "unnecessary," and "not the way to fight terrorism." Infringements of civil rights, the *Economist* declared, "if genuinely required, should be open to scrutiny and considered a painful sacrifice, or a purely tactical retreat, not as the mere brushing aside of irritating legal technicalities. Those who criticized such measures should be given a careful hearing, even if their views must sometimes be overridden."

Even mainstream politicians began to wail about the theft of liberty. Vermont's independent Senator Jim Jeffords proclaimed on November 19, "I am very concerned about my good friend John Ashcroft. Having 1,000 people locked up with no right to *habeas corpus* is a deep concern." Jeffords said that he felt that his own role in swinging the Senate to Democratic control was particularly vindicated because it had permitted his fellow senator from Vermont, Democrat Patrick Leahy, to battle the White House's increase of police powers, as made legal in the Patriot Act.

Speak memory! It was not as though publication on November 13 of Bush's presidential order on military courts for al-Qaeda members and sympathizers launched the onslaught on civil liberties. Recall that the Patriot Act was sent to Congress on September 19. Nor were the contents of that proposed legislation unfamiliar since in large part they had been offered by the Clinton administration as portions of the Counter-Terrorism and Effective Death Penalty Act of 1996. Well before the end of September, Ashcroft's proposals to trash the Bill of Rights were available for inspection and debate.

At the time when it counted, when a volley of barks from the watchdogs might have provoked resistance in Congress to the

Patriot Act and warned Bush not to try his luck with military tribunals, there was mostly decorum from the opinion makers, aside from amiable discussions of the propriety of torture. Taken as a whole, the U.S. press did not raise adequate alarums about legislation that was going to give the FBI full snoop powers on the Internet; to deny *habeas corpus* to non-citizens; to expand even further warrantless searches unleashed in the Clinton era with new powers given in 1995 to secret courts. These courts operated under the terms of the Foreign Intelligence Surveillance Act passed in the Carter years, in 1978.

In the run-up to Bush's signing of the Patriot Act on October 25, the major papers were spiritless about the provisions in the bill that were horrifying to civil libertarians. It would have only have taken a few fierce columns or editorials, such as were profuse after November 15, to have given frightened politicians cover to join the only bold soul in the U.S. Senate, Russell Feingold of Wisconsin. Now it was Feingold, remember, whose vote back in the spring let Ashcroft's nomination out of the Judiciary Committee, at a time when most of his Democratic colleagues were roaring to the news cameras about Ashcroft's racism and contempt for due process. The *Times* and the *Post* both editorialized against Ashcroft's nomination.

But then, when the rubber met the road, and Ashcroft sent up the Patriot Act which vindicated every dire prediction of the spring, all fell silent except for Feingold, who made a magnificent speech in the U.S. Senate on October 25, citing assaults on liberty going back to the Alien and Sedition Acts of John Adams, the suspension of *habeas corpus* sanctioned by the U.S. Supreme Court in World War I, the internments of World War II (along with 110,00 Japanese-Americans there were 11,000 German-Americans, and 3,000 Italian-Americans put behind barbed wire), the McCarthyite black lists of the 1950s, and the spying on antiwar protesters in the 1960s. Under the terms of the bill, Feingold warned, the Fourth Amendment as it applies to electronic communications, would be effectively eliminated. He flayed the Patriot Act as an assault on "the basic rights that make us who we are." It represented, he warned, "a truly breath-taking expansion of police power."

Feingold was trying to win time for challenges in Congress to specific provisions in Ashcroft's bill. Those were the days in which sustained uproar from Safire or Anthony Lewis or kindred commentators would have made a difference. So the Patriot Act passed into law and Feingold's was the sole vote against it in the Senate. Just like Wayne Morse and Ernest Gruening in their lonely opposition to the Gulf of Tonkin Resolution in 1964, he'll receive his due and be hailed as a hero by the same people who held their tongue in the crucial hours. Instead, as Murray Kempton used to say of editorial writers, they waited till after the battle to come down from the hills to shoot the wounded.

2001

Don't You Dare Call It Treason

Alexander Cockburn and Jeffrey St. Clair

REASON, NO LESS! A LEADING DEMOCRAT, REP. HENRY Waxman, howls in Congress that "the intentional disclosure of a covert CIA agent's identity would be an act of treason. If Rove was part of a conspiracy and intentionally disclosed the name—then that jeopardizes national security."

Liberal columnists like Robert Scheer of the *Los Angeles Times* join the Waxman chorus. Of White House political adviser Karl Rove's efforts to discredit Joe Wilson by outing his wife Valerie Plame as a covert CIA employee, Scheer bellows furiously that Rove might have even endangered Plame's life and that "this partisan game jeopardizes national security. This is the most important issue raised by the Plame scandal."

But suppose one of Valerie Plame's covert CIA missions, until outed by Karl Rove, had been to liaise with Venezuelan right-wingers planning to assassinate president Hugo Chavez, possibly masquerading as a journalist and using her attractions to secure an audience with the populist president and then poison him, just as the CIA tried to poison Castro. In an earlier incarnation Scheer would surely have been eager to jeopardize national security by exposing Plame's employer.

Thirty-eight years ago Scheer was one of the editors of *Ramparts* and in February of 1967 that magazine ran an exposé of covert CIA funding of the National Student Association, prompting furious charges that it had endangered national security which, from the foreign policy establishment's point of view, it most certainly had. Of course *Ramparts*, and the left in general, derided the very phrase "national security" as a phony rationale for covering up years of covert CIA operations entirely inimical to any decent definition of what "national security" should properly mean.

The CIA's covert wing is not in the business of advancing world peace and general prosperity. The record of almost 60 years is one of uninterrupted evil. So we should drop all this nonsense about treason and clap Rove warmly on the back for his courageous onslaughts on the cult of secrecy. By all means delight in the White House's discomfiture, but spare us the claptrap about national security and treason.

To thread one's way through coverage of the Plame affair, the jailing of Judith Miller, the contempt citations of four journalists (though not, alas, of Jeff Gerth of the *New York Times*), and the AIPAC/Franklin spy case is like strolling past distorting mirrors in a fun house. Go from one to the next and the swollen giant of "treason" in the west wing of the White House shrinks to the dwarf-like status of a "leak," which is how AIPAC's defenders like to categorize the transmission of a top secret Presidential Directive on Iran from Larry Franklin in the Pentagon to AIPAC officials and thence to a spymaster, Naor Gilon, in the Israeli embassy in Washington.

Judith Miller too has had an image make-over, from the warmongering fabricator of yesterday to today's martyr to the First Amendment, with years of profitable speaking tours beckoning after she is released from the incarceration she surely hoped would winch her reputation out of the mud.

But why is prosecutor Patrick Fitzgerald going after her? She wrote no story about Plame.

Now, as a prime propagandist of the war faction, Miller had every reason to be as keen to discredit Wilson as was Rove. Suppose it was she who relayed from her pal and prime disinformer, Ahmed Chalabi, the news that it was CIA employee Plame who assigned her husband the Niger mission to assay the veracity of charges that Iraq had bought uranium yellowcake there. Relayed to whom? Maybe to one of the State Department's neocon warmongers, like John Bolton or Eliott Abrams, who duly passed the news on to Scooter Libby and Rove in the White House. Remember, Rove told the prosecutor that he learned about Plame from two journalists. What a joke it would have been to have him behind bars for refusing to disclose his sources.

Stroll on to the next set of mirrors, apropos Wen Ho Lee's suit to discover who leaked the false accusations about his supposed acts of treason at Los Alamos, allegedly transmitting nuclear secrets to China. Four journalists, including James Risen of the *New York Times* and Bob Drogin of the *Los Angeles Times*, may join Miller behind bars for refusing to divulge their sources.

One can understand why Wen Ho Lee is unmoved by charges that he is sabotaging the First Amendment. His case displayed the FBI and the press which smeared him—primarily Risen and Gerth in the *New York Times*—in a disgusting light. He spent nearly a year in solitary confinement, with FBI agents telling him he might face the death penalty for being a traitor.

Who in fact was the betrayer of secrets, if one has to be found? On July 7, Steve Terrell reported in the *New Mexican* that the leaker so eager to disclose a top secret government probe of Wen Ho Lee at Los Alamos may well be the current governor of New Mexico and possible White House aspirant, Bill Richardson, who was Clinton's energy secretary at the time and who had spent a large portion of his political career nurturing the interests of Los Alamos as a nuclear research lab.

We doubt Waxman will start calling for Richardson's blood as a compromiser of national security, leaking secrets as part of a political maneuver to shift blame for the appalling mess at Los Alamos to a person of Chinese origin whom he falsely accused of being a spy, then denied he had done any such thing. This guy wants to be president of the United States.

If you want to start waving words like "treason" around, the AIPAC spy case is surely a better target than Karl Rove. Here we have a four-year FBI probe of possible treachery by senior U.S. government officials, as well as by Israel's premier lobbying outfit in the United States, AIPAC. Yet compared with the mileage given to the Plame affair, coverage of the AIPAC spy case in the press has been sparse, and the commentary very demure, until you get to Justin Raimondo's pugnacious columns on Antiwar.com.

Raimondo's been comparing the AIPAC spy case to the indictment of State Department official, Alger Hiss, back in the 1940s, claiming that just as the foreign policy apparatus was allegedly riddled with Communist spies in the 1940s, the same apparatus is now riddled with Israel's agents today. We reckon that when it comes to agents of influence, the USSR back then couldn't hold a candle to Israel today (or then, for that matter, though in that distant time Zionist and Communist were often hats on the same head).

One answer in the McCarthyite era to accusations of spying was that the Soviet Union was an ally and the supposed transmission of "secrets" was just a routine exchange of information on such matters as the schedule for the 1944 Dumbarton Oaks conference laying the groundwork for the U.N., in which Hiss was involved.

Similar talk about "allies" and "routine exchanges" pops from the mouths of Israel's supporters here, denouncing the FBI probe as some latter-day equivalent of the persecution of Dreyfus.

It's perfectly obvious that Israel exerts huge influence on U.S. policy. Men and women working in Israel's interest throng Washington. But on the left, in the spy case just as in the Plame affair, we should be leery of words like traitor and "national security." They cut both ways.

Here's a useful parable on the fetishization of secrecy from Ernie Fitzgerald's *The Pentagonists*, essential reading for anyone interested in how U.S. politics really works.

In 1973, Nixon fired Pentagon auditor Ernie Fitzgerald for exposing the tidal wave of cost overruns associated with Lockheed's useless C-5A cargo plane. One of the accusations hurled against Ernie at the time was that he had "leaked" to a congressional committee "classified information" about the scandal.

The charge was made by Robert Seamons, Nixon's secretary of the Air Force. When Fitzgerald sued (and won his job back and a major settlement, which he used in part to found the Fund for Constitutional Government), his lawyers deposed Seamons, who retreated a little.

Here's how Ernie describes it:

> Later, after I was fired, Senator William Proxmire forced Seamons to retract this accusation. In his *apologia pro vita sua* to the official tape, he produced this wonderful waffle: "At the time I was testifying, I really thought that Ernie had given them classified material, marked 'Confidential.' Later on, when we still had the opportunity of going over the testimony, it wasn't so clear as to whether any of the material was classified or not. So we changed the word from Confidential with a capital 'C' to confidential with a small 'c.'"

2005

The Military & CNN

Alexander Cockburn

AHANDFUL OF MILITARY PERSONNEL FROM THE 4TH PSYCHO-logical Operations Group (i.e., PSYOPS) based at Fort Bragg in North Carolina have until recently been working in CNN's headquarters in Atlanta. An enterprising Dutch journalist named Abe De Vries came up with this important story in mid-February 2000, and he remains properly astounded that no mainstream news medium in the United States has evinced any interest in the scandal. I came across translations of De Vries' stories on the matter, after they had appeared in late-February 2000 in *Trouw*, the foremost quality newspaper in Holland.

De Vries later told me he'd originally come upon the story via an article in the French *Intelligence* newsletter (available on a pay-per-story basis on the Internet) February 17, which described a military symposium in Arlington, Va., held at the beginning of that same month, discussing use of the press in military operations.

Col. Christopher St. John, commander of the U.S. Army's 4th PSYOPS Group, was quoted by an *Intelligence* correspondent, present at the symposium, as (in the correspondent's words) having "called for greater cooperation between the armed forces and media giants. He [St. John] pointed out that some Army PSYOPS personnel had worked for CNN for several weeks, and helped in the production of some news stories for the network."

Reading this in Belgrade, where he's *Trouw*'s correspondent, De Vries saw a good story, picked up the phone, and finally reached Maj. Thomas Collins of the U.S. Army Information Service, who duly confirmed the presence of these Army PSYOPS experts at

CNN. "PSYOPS personnel, soldiers and officers," De Vries quoted Collins as telling him, "have been working in CNN's headquarters in Atlanta through our program 'Training with Industry.' They worked as regular employees of CNN. Conceivably, they would have worked on stories during the Kosovo war. They helped in the production of news."

I reported this interesting disclosure in our newsletter, *CounterPunch*, and made it the topic of my regular weekly broadcast to *AM Live*, a program of the South Africa Broadcasting Company in Johannesburg. Among the audience of this broadcast was CNN's bureau in South Africa, which lost no time in relaying news of it to CNN headquarters in Atlanta, and I duly received an angry phone call from Eason Jordan*, who identified himself as CNN's president of news gathering and international networks.

Jordan was full of indignation that I had somehow compromised the reputation of CNN. But in the course of our conversation, it turned out that, yes, CNN had hosted a total of five interns from U.S. Army PSYOPS, two in television, two in radio, and one in satellite operations. Jordan said the program had begun on June 7 (just before the end of the war against Serbia), and only recently terminated—I would guess at about the time CNN's higher management read Abe De Vries' stories.

Naturally enough, Eason Jordan and other executives at CNN now describe the Army PSYOPS intern tours at CNN as having been insignificant. Maybe so. Col. St. John, the commanding officer of the PSYOPS group, certainly thought them of sufficient significance to mention at that high-level Pentagon pow-wow in Arlington about propaganda and psychological warfare. Maybe CNN was the target of a PSYOPS penetration and is still too naive to figure out what was going on.

*Paradoxically, in 2005 Eason Jordan was forced to resign as CNN's chief news executive after seeming to suggest in a forum in Davos, Switzerland that it was U.S. official military policy to kill troublesome journalists.

It's hard not to laugh when CNN executives like Eason Jordan start spouting high-toned stuff about CNN's principles of objectivity and refusal to relay government or Pentagon propaganda. The relationship is most vividly summed up by the fact that Christiane Amanpour, CNN's leading foreign correspondent, and a woman whose reports about the fate of Kosovan refugees did much to fan the public appetite for NATO's war, is literally and figuratively in bed with spokesman for the U.S. State Department, and a leading propagandist for NATO during that war, her husband Jamie Rubin. If CNN truly wanted to maintain the appearance of objectivity, it would have taken Amanpour off the story. Amanpour, by the way, remains a passionate advocate for NATO's crusade, most recently on the Charlie Rose show.

In the first two weeks of the war in Kosovo CNN produced thirty articles for the Internet, according to de Vries, who looked them up for his first story. An average CNN article had seven mentions of Tony Blair, NATO spokesmen like Jamie Shea and David Wilby, or other NATO officials. Words like refugees, ethnic cleansing, mass killings, and expulsions were used nine times on the average. But the so-called Kosovo Liberation Army (0.2 mentions) and the Yugoslav civilian victims (0.3 mentions) barely existed for CNN.

During the war on Serbia, as with other recent conflicts involving the U.S. wars, CNN's screen was filled with an interminable procession of U.S. military officers. On April 27, 1999, Amy Goodman of the Pacifica Radio network put the following question to Frank Sesno, who is CNN's senior vice president for political coverage.

> GOODMAN: If you support the practice of putting ex-military men—generals—on the payroll to share their opinion during a time of war, would you also support putting peace activists on the payroll to give a different opinion during a time of war?

> SESNO: We bring the generals in because of their expertise in a particular area. We call them analysts. We don't bring them in as advocates. In fact, we actually talk to them about that—they're not there as advocates.

Exactly a week before Sesno said this, CNN had featured as one of its military analysts, Lt. Gen. Dan Benton, U.S. Army Retired.

> BENTON: I don't know what our countrymen that are questioning why we're involved in this conflict are thinking about. As I listened to this press conference this morning, with reports of rapes, villages being burned, and this particularly incredible report of blood banks, of blood being harvested from young boys for the use of Yugoslav forces, I just got madder and madder. The United States has a responsibility as the only superpower in the world, and when we learn about these things, somebody has got to stand up and say, "That's enough, stop it, we aren't going to put up with this."

Please note what CNN's supposedly non-advocatory analyst Benton was ranting about: a particularly preposterous NATO propaganda item about 700 Albanian boys being used as human blood banks for Serb fighters.

Let's give the last word to the enterprising Abe De Vries. "Of course, CNN says these PSYOPS personnel didn't decide anything, write news reports, etc. What else can they say? Maybe it's true, maybe not. The point is that these kind of close ties with the Army are, in my view, completely unacceptable for any serious news organization. Maybe even more astonishing is the complete silence about the story from the big media. To my knowledge, my story was not mentioned by leading American or British newspapers, nor by Reuters or AP."

2000

Saddam, Osama, and the Man Who Married Them

Alexander Cockburn

BACK IN 1898, WILLIAM RANDOLPH HEARST WAS TRYING TO fan war fever between the United States and Spain. He dispatched a reporter and the artist Frederic Remington to Cuba to send back blood-roiling depictions of Spanish beastliness to Cuban insurgents. Remington wired to say he could find nothing sensational to draw and could he come home. Famously, Hearst wired him: "Please remain. You furnish the pictures and I'll furnish the war." Remington duly did so.

I wouldn't set the *New Yorker*'s editor, David Remnick, in the shoes of a Kong-sized monster like Hearst. Remnick is a third-tier talent who has always got ahead by singing the correct career enhancing tunes, as witness his awful reporting from Russia in the 1990s. Art Spiegelman recently quit the *New Yorker*, remarking that these dangerous times require courage and the ability to be provocative, but alas, "Remnick does not feel up to the challenge."

That's putting it far too politely. Remnick's watch has been lackluster and cowardly. He is also the current sponsor (Marty Peretz of the *New Republic* was an earlier one) of Jeffrey Goldberg, whose first major chunk of agitprop for the *New Yorker* was published on March 25, 2002. Titled "The Great Terror," it was billed as containing disclosures of "Saddam Hussein's possible ties to al-Qaeda."

This was at a moment when the FBI and CIA had just shot down the war party's claim of a meeting between Mohammed Atta and an Iraqi intelligence agent in Prague before the 9/11 attacks. Goldberg saved the day for the Bush crowd. At the core of his rambling, 16,000-word piece was an interview in the Kurdish-held Iraqi town of Sulaimaniya with Mohammed Mansour Shahab, who offered the eager Goldberg a wealth of detail about his activities as a link between Osama bin Laden and the Iraqis, shuttling arms and other equipment.

The piece was gratefully seized upon by the administration as proof of the link. The *coup de grâce* to Goldberg's credibility fell on February 9, 2003, in the London *Observer*, administered by Jason Burke, its chief reporter. Burke visited the same prison in Sulaimaniya, talked to Shahab, and established beyond doubt that Goldberg's great source is a clumsy liar, not even knowing the physical appearance of Kandahar, whither he had claimed to have journeyed to deal with bin Laden, and confecting his fantasies in the hope of a shorter prison sentence.

Another experienced European journalist, whom I reached on the Continent at the end of this week and who visited the prison last year, agrees with Burke's findings. "I talked to prisoners without someone present. The director of the prison seemed surprised at my request. With a prison authority present the interview would be worthless. As soon as we talked to this particular one a colleague said after 30 seconds, 'this is worthless. The guy was just a story teller.'"

The European journalist, who doesn't want to be identified, said to me charitably that Goldberg's credulity about Shab "could have been a matter of misjudgment but my even stronger criticism is that if you talked, as we did and as I gather Goldberg did, to anybody in the Patriotic Union of Kurdistan [the Kurdish group controlling this area of northern Iraq] about this particular Islamic group all of them would tell you they are backed by Iran, as common sense would tell you. Look where they are located. It's 200 meters across one river to Iran. That's what I find upsetting. Misjudging a source can happen to all of us, but Goldberg did talk to generals in the PUK. I think it's outrageous that *New Yorker* ran that story."

An American with a lot of experience in interviewing in prisons adds, "It's tricky interviewing prisoners in the first place—their vulnerability, etc.—and responsible journalists make some sort of minimal credibility assessment before they report someone's statements. But the prisoner said exactly what Jeffrey Goldberg wanted to hear, so Goldberg didn't feel that he needed to mention that the prisoner was nuts." On February 10, amid widespread cynicism about the Administration's rationales for war, Remnick published another Goldberg special, "The Unknown: The C.I.A. and the Pentagon take another look at Al Qaeda and Iraq." This 6,000-word screed had no pretensions to being anything other than a servile rendition of Donald Rumsfeld's theory of intelligence: "Build a hypothesis, and then see if the data supported the hypothesis, rather than the reverse." In other words, decide what you want to hear, then torture the data until the data confess.

This last piece of Goldberg's was a truly disgraceful piece of brown-nosing (of Rumsfeld, Tenet, et al.), devoid of even the pretensions of independent journalism. "Reporter at Large?" Remnick should retire the rubric, at least for Goldberg, and advertise his work as "White House Handout." I should note that Goldberg once served in Israel's armed forces, which may or may not be a guide to his political agenda.

2003

The Making of a Neo-Con: Poddy and Jackie O

Alexander Cockburn

WE HAD SUPPOSED HE WAS DEAD, BUT THERE WAS THE OLD neocon blusterer himself, Norman Podhoretz, in the *National Review* for January 26, 2003, writing about heroism. Poddy had been invited to talk on this theme at a conference honoring Margaret Thatcher, so he dutifully turned in a speech lashing away at that shagged-out old stalking horse: "The Sixties."

Those days are long gone of course, but somehow Poddy can't forgive or forget. It's all the more strange because, back then, he still had liberal pretensions. We were once told that he became a right-winger when Jackie turned him down. On this account, Poddy fiercely admired the Mistress of Camelot and, after Kennedy's death, began to suppose that she reciprocated his passion. Finding her alone in a room at some Manhattan party, he pressed his suit. She gazed at him as if at a slug in the rose garden at Middleburg and said in chill tones: "Why Mr. Podhoretz, just who do you think you are?" Next thing you knew, Poddy had joined the neocons and was rumbling away like Vesuvius about the terrible "antinomian" pass our culture had come to.

In Poddy's view, dreaded "antinomianism"—i.e., rejection of the moral law—began when the Sodomites deified God's law by "inverting the sexual act itself by directing it into the channel of excretion and waste" (which is, when you think about it, not a bad description of the transition of Poddy himself from the path of life to that of editing *Commentary*). As he puts it laconically, "Antinomianism has had its ups and downs throughout history," but never did better than in the Sixties when someone he misspells as Allen "Ginsburg," along with Norman Mailer and Norman O. Brown, "preached the pursuit of instant gratification as the road to individual and social salvation."

One can imagine that Baroness Thatcher beginning to snooze somewhat at this point while keeping one ear cocked for mention of her own dear name. As if sensing her impatience, Poddy slides into his main point, which is what when antinomianism creeps in the window, heroism flies out the door. There's some tricky footwork involved here, because the Devil—quintessential antinomian—is heroic in a beastly sort of way, as John Milton recognized, but Poddy finesses the difficulty by saying that now we no longer even have antinomian heroes, but merely antiheroes "playing games of Trivial Pursuit."

At this point, Poddy repeats for Thatcher what he may have said all those years ago to Jackie: What you need is a real man!

> Other women, desperate to marry before their biological clocks run down, can more and more be heard complaining that all the men out there are either wimps, or gays. It has been said that men are born aggressive and predatory and that only women can tame and civilize them, which is true. But it is also true that if women fail to demand that men be strong, and courageous, and honorable—if, that is, they fail to live by the dictum that only the brave deserve the fair—then they will find no one worth bestowing their favors upon. No doubt they will—human nature being what it is—perforce bestow their favors upon, or at least resignedly decide to marry, the wimps they secretly despise.

Poddy's basic argument is that homosexuals can't be heroes, because they don't want children thus defying God's injunction in the book of Genesis 1, verses 26-28: "Let us make man in our image, after our likeness: and let him have dominion... over all the earth, and over every creeping thing that creepeth upon the earth... Be fruitful and multiply, and replenish the earth and subdue it."

Here's Poddy lashing at the Sixties again. In a famous 1967 essay, "The Historic Roots of Our Ecological Crisis," Lynn White Jr. interpreted this Genesis text as meaning, "God planned and fashioned all the natural world explicitly for man's benefit and rule: no item in the physical creation had any purpose save to serve man's purposes." White concluded that "we shall continue to have a worsening ecologic crisis until we reject the Christian axiom that nature has no reason for existence save to serve man."

So it's Poddy Agonistes, bowed between the pillars of the temple, straining to bring the whole structure crashing down on the gays and greens below. And to think how different everything might have been if only Jackie had said "yes."

2005

Torture as Normalcy:
As American as Apple Pie

Alexander Cockburn and Jeffrey St. Clair

ORTURE'S BACK IN THE NEWS, COURTESY OF THOSE LURID pictures of exultant Americans laughing as they torture their Iraqi captives in Abu Ghraib prison run by the U.S. military outside Baghdad. Apparently it takes electrodes and naked bodies piled in a simulated orgy to tickle America's moral nerve ends. Kids maimed by cluster bombs just don't do it any more. But torture's nothing new. One of the darkest threads in postwar U.S. imperial history has been the CIA's involvement with torture, as instructor, practitioner, or contractor. Since its inception the CIA has taken a keen interest in torture, avidly studying Nazi techniques and protecting their exponents such as Klaus Barbie. The CIA's official line is that torture is wrong and is ineffective. It is indeed wrong. On countless occasions it has been appallingly effective.

Remember Dan Mitrione, kidnapped and killed by Uruguay's Tupamaros and portrayed by Yves Montand in Costa-Gavras' film *State of Siege*? In the late 1960s Mitrione worked for the U.S. Office of Public Safety, part of the Agency for International Development. In Brazil, so A.J. Langguth (a former *New York Times'* bureau chief in Saigon) related in his book *Hidden Terrors*, Mitrione was among the U.S. advisers teaching Brazilian police how much electric shock to apply to prisoners without killing them. In Uruguay, according to the former chief of police intelligence, Mitrione helped "professionalize" torture as a routine measure and advised on psychological techniques such as playing tapes of women and children screaming, to create the impression that the prisoner's family was being tortured.

In the months after the 9/11 attacks on the World Trade Center and Pentagon, "truth drugs" were hailed by some columnists such as *Newsweek*'s Jonathan Alter for use in the war against al-Qaeda. This was an enthusiasm shared by the U.S. Navy after the war against Hitler, when its intelligence officers got on the trail of Dr. Kurt Plotner's research into "truth serums" at Dachau. Plotner gave Jewish and Russian prisoners high doses of mescaline and then observed their behavior, in which they expressed hatred for their guards and made confessional statements about their own psychological makeup.

As part of its larger MK-ULTRA project the CIA gave money to Dr. Ewen Cameron, at McGill University. Cameron was a pioneer in the sensory-deprivation techniques. Cameron once locked up a woman in a small white box for thirty-five days, deprived of light, smell, and sound. The CIA doctors were amazed at this dose, knowing that their own experiments with a sensory-deprivation tank in 1955 had induced severe psychological reactions in less than forty hours. Start torturing, and it's easy to get carried away.

Torture destroys the tortured and corrupts the society that sanctions it. Just like the FBI after 9/11, the CIA in 1968 got frustrated by its inability to break suspected leaders of Vietnam's National Liberation Front by its usual methods of interrogation and torture. So the agency began more advanced experiments, in one of which it anesthetized three prisoners, opened their skulls and planted electrodes in their brains. They were revived, put in a room and given knives. The CIA psychologists then activated the electrodes, hoping the prisoners would attack one another. They didn't. The electrodes were removed, the prisoners shot, and their bodies burned. You can read about it in our book, *Whiteout*.

In recent years the United States has been charged by the U.N. and also by human rights organizations such as Human Rights

Watch and Amnesty International with tolerating torture in U.S. prisons, by methods ranging from solitary, twenty-three-hour-a-day confinement in concrete boxes for years on end, to activating 50,000-volt shocks through a mandatory belt worn by prisoners. Many of the Military Police guards now under investigation for abuse of Iraqis earned their stripes working as guards in federal and state prisons, where official abuse is a daily occurrence. Indeed, Charles Granier, one of the abusers at Abu Ghraib and the lover of Lynndie England, the Trailer Park Torturer, worked as a guard at Pennsylvania's notorious Greene Correctional Unit and has since gone back to work there.

And as a practical matter, torture is far from unknown in the interrogation rooms of U.S. law enforcement, with Abner Louima sodomized by a cop using a stick as one notorious recent example. The most infamous disclosure of consistent torture by a police department in recent years concerned cops in Chicago in the mid-70s through early-80s who used electroshock, oxygen deprivation, hanging on hooks, the bastinado, and beatings of the testicles. The torturers were white and their victims black or brown. A prisoner in California's Pelican Bay State Prison was thrown into boiling water. Others get 50,000-volt shocks from stun guns.

Many states have so-called "secure housing units" where prisoners are kept in solitary in tiny concrete cells for years on end, many of them going mad in the process. Amnesty International has denounced U.S. police forces for "a pattern of unchecked excessive force amounting to torture."

In 2000, the U.N. delivered a severe public rebuke to the United States for its record on failure to prevent torture and degrading punishment. A 10-strong panel of experts highlighted what it said were Washington's breaches of the agreement ratified by the United States in 1994. The U.N. Committee Against Torture, which monitors international compliance with the U.N. Convention Against Torture, has called for the abolition of electric-shock stun belts (1,000 in use in the U.S.A.) and restraint chairs on prisoners, as well as an end to holding children in adult jails.

It also said female detainees are "very often held in humiliating and degrading circumstances" and expressed concern over alleged cases of sexual assault by police and prison officers. The panel criticized the excessively harsh regime in maximum-security prisons, the use of chain gangs in which prisoners perform manual labor while shackled together, and the number of cases of police brutality against racial minorities.

So far as rape is concerned, because of the rape factories more conventionally known as the U.S. prison system, there are estimates that twice as many men as women are raped in the U.S. each year. A Human Rights Watch report in April of 2001 cited a December 2000 *Prison Journal* study based on a survey of inmates in seven men's prison facilities in four states. The results showed that 21 per cent of the inmates had experienced at least one episode of pressured or forced sexual contact since being incarcerated, and at least 7 per cent had been raped in their facilities.

A 1996 study of the Nebraska prison system produced similar findings, with 22 per cent of male inmates reporting that they had been pressured or forced to have sexual contact against their will while incarcerated. Of these, more than 50 per cent had submitted to forced anal sex at least once. Extrapolating these findings to the national level gives a total of at least 140,000 inmates who have been raped.

2005

Part 5

Faking It: Why Does the Press Mostly Believe Prosecutors?

The FBI and the Myth of Fingerprints

Alexander Cockburn and Jeffrey St. Clair

F EW LAW ENFORCEMENT INSTITUTIONS HAVE BEEN SO THOR-
oughly discredited in recent years as the FBI's forensic lab.
In 1997 the Bureau's inspector general of the time issued
a devastating report, stigmatizing one instance after another of
mishandled and contaminated evidence, inept technicians, and
outright fabrication. The IG concluded that there were "serious
and credible allegations of incompetence" and perjured courtroom testimony.

CounterPunch's view is that taken as a whole, forensic evidence
as used by prosecutors is inherently untrustworthy. For example,
for years many people went to prison on the basis of the claims
of a North Carolina anthropologist, Louise Robbins. She helped
send people to prison or to Death Row with her self-proclaimed
power to identify criminals through shoe prints. As an excellent 2004 *Chicago Tribune* series on forensic humbug recalled, on
occasion she even said she could use the method to determine a
person's height, sex, and race. Robbins died in 1987, her memory
compromised by the conclusion of many appeals courts that her
methodology was bosh. There have been similarly hollow claims
for lip prints and ear prints, all of them invoked by their supporters as "100 per cent reliable" and believed by juries, too easily
impressed by passionate invocations to 100 per cent reliable scientific data.

Of course the apex forensic hero of prosecutors, long promoted as the bottom line in reliability—at least until the arrival
of DNA matching—has been the fingerprint.

Fingerprints entered the arsenal of police and prosecutors in the late-nineteenth century, touted as "scientific" in the manner of other fashionable methods of that time in the identification of supposed criminals, such as phrenology. A prime salesman was Ernest Galton, Charles Darwin's cousin and a founding huckster for the bogus "science" of eugenics. Actually fingerprints, at least in modern times, found their original use in the efforts of a British colonial administrator to intimidate his Indian laborers (whose faces he could not distinguish) from turning up more than once to get paid. He'd make a great show of scrutinizing the fingerprints he insisted they daub on his ledger book. Then, as now, the use of the so-called "unique fingerprint" has been histrionic, not scientific. In 1995, so the *Chicago Tribune* series discovered, "one of the only independent proficiency tests of fingerprint examiners in U.S. crime labs found that nearly a quarter reported false positives, meaning they declared prints identical even though they were not—the sort of mistakes that can lead to wrongful convictions or arrests."

Decade after decade people have been sent to prison for years or dispatched to the death cell, solely on the basis of a single, even a partial print. So great is the resonance of the phrase "a perfect match" that defense lawyers throw in the towel, as judge and jury listen to the assured conclusions of the FBI analysts who virtually monopolize the fingerprint industry in the U.S.A. Overseas, in London's Scotland Yard for example, the same mesmerizing "certainty" held sway, and still does. In the U.S.A., part of the mystique stems from the "one discrepancy rule" which has supposedly governed the FBI's fingerprint analysis. The rule says that identifications are subject to a standard of "100 per cent certainty" where a single difference in appearance is supposed to preclude identification.

The 1997 lab scandals threw a shadow over the FBI's forensic procedures as a whole and the criminal defense bar began to raise protests against prosecutorial use of latent fingerprint identification evidence, as produced by FBI's procedures. In

2002 Judge Louis Pollak, in a case in Pennsylvania, initially ruled that the FBI's fingerprint matching criteria fell below new standards of forensic reliability (the Daubert standards) stipulated by the U.S. Supreme Court. Ultimately he was persuaded that the FBI's fingerprint lab had never made a mistake. In 2004, in *U.S. v. Mitchell*, the Third Circuit Court of Appeals upheld these same procedures.

Now at last, in 2006, the FBI's current inspector general, Glenn Fine, has grudgingly administered what should properly be regarded as the deathblow to fingerprint evidence as used by the FBI and indeed by law enforcement generally.

The case reviewed by Inspector General Fine, at the request of U.S. Rep. John Conyers and U.S. Senator Russell Feingold, concerns the false arrest by the FBI of Brandon Mayfield, a lawyer from Beaverton, Oregon.

On March 11, 2004, several bombs exploded in Madrid's subway system, with 191 killed and 1,460 injured. Shortly thereafter the Spanish police discovered a blue plastic bag filled with detonators in a van parked near the Acala de Heres train station in Madrid, whence all of the trains involved in the bombing had originated on the fatal day.

The Spanish police were able to lift a number of latent prints off the bag. On March 17 they transmitted digital images of these fingerprints to the FBI's crime lab in Virginia. The lab ran the images through its prized IAFIS, otherwise known as the Integrated, Automated, Fingerprint Identification System, containing a database of some 20 million fingerprints.

The IAFIS computer spat out twenty "candidate prints," with the warning that these 20 candidates were "close non-match." Then the FBI examiners went to work with their magnifying glasses, assessing ridges and forks between the sample of 20 and the images from Spain. In a trice the doubts of the IAFIS computer were thrust aside, and senior fingerprint examiner Terry Green determined that he had found "a 100 per cent match" with one of the Spanish prints of the fourth-ranked print in the IAFIS batch of 20 close non-matches. Green said this fourth-ranked print came from the left index finger of Brandon Mayfield. Mayfield's prints were in the FBI's master file, not because he had been arrested or charged with any crime, but because he was a former U.S. Army lieutenant.

Green submitted his conclusions to two other FBI examiners who duly confirmed his conclusions. But as the inspector general later noted, these examiners were not directed to inspect a set of prints without knowing that a match had already been asserted by one of their colleagues. They were simply given the pair of supposedly matched prints and asked to confirm the finding. (These two examiners later refused to talk to the FBI's inspector general.)

The FBI lost no time in alerting the U.S. Prosecutor's office in Portland, which began surveillance of Mayfield with a request to the secret FISA court (i.e., created by the Foreign Intelligence Surveillance Act) which issued a warrant for Mayfield's phone to be tapped on the grounds, laid out in the Patriot Act, that he was a terrorist, and therefore by definition a foreign agent.

Surreptitious tapping and surveillance of Mayfield began. On April 2, 2004, the FBI sent a letter to the Spanish police informing them that they had made a big break in the case, with a positive identification of the print on the bag of detonators.

Ten days later the forensic science division of the Spanish national police sent the FBI its own analysis. It held that the purported match of Mayfield's print was "conclusively negative." (The inspector general refers to this as the "negativo.")

The next day, April 14, the U.S. prosecutor in Portland became aware of the fact that the Spanish authorities were vigorously disputing the match with Mayfield's left forefinger. But by now the prosecutor and his team were smelling blood. Through covert surveillance they had learned that Mayfield was married to an Egyptian woman, had recently converted to Islam, was a regular attendee at the Bailal mosque in Portland, and had as one of his clients in a child custody dispute an American Muslim called

Jeffrey Battle. Battle, a black man, had just been convicted of trying to go to Afghanistan to fight for the Taliban.

Armed, so they thought, with this arsenal of compromising details, the U.S. prosecutor and the FBI had no patience with the pettifogging negativism of the Spanish police. So confident were the Americans of the guilt of their prey that they never went back to take another look at the supposedly matching prints. Instead, on April 21, they flew a member of the FBI's latent print unit to Spain for on-the-spot refutation of the impertinent Madrid constabulary.

The inspector general's report makes it clear that the FBI man returned from Spain with a false account of his reception, alleging that the Spanish fingerprint team had bowed to his superior analytic skills. The head of the Spanish team, Pedro Luis Melida-Weda, insists that his team remained entirely unconvinced: "At no time did we give our approval. We refused to validate the FBI's conclusions. We kept working on the identification."

By now either the U.S. Attorney's Office or, more likely, the FBI was leaking to the press news of the pursuit of a U.S. suspect in the Madrid bombing. But they knew that the actual evidence they had on Mayfield was virtually non-existent, aside from the dubious fingerprint. On May 6, the U.S. prosecutor in Portland told U.S. District Court Judge Robert Jones that the Spanish police had ultimately accepted the FBI's match, that Mayfield, alerted by the stories in the press about an unnamed suspect, might start destroying evidence, and that, therefore, they wanted to seize Mayfield, using the now favored charge *du jour* of the war on terror, claiming him to be a "material witness." Judge Jones okayed an arrest warrant.

Mayfield had no idea that the FBI had been tapping his phones and secretly rummaging through his office. The first time he became aware that he was a citizen under suspicion was on the afternoon of May 6. On that day eight FBI agents showed up at his law office, seized him, cuffed his hands behind his back and ridiculed his protestations. As they approached the door,

Mayfield implored them to take the handcuffs off, saying he didn't want his clients or staff to see him in this condition. The FBI agents said derisively, "Don't worry about it. The media is right behind us." And they were.

Mayfield ended up with two federal public defenders, Steven Wax and Christopher Schatz. Like many such, these two were dedicated to the interests of their client, tireless and resourceful. Their first concern was to get Mayfield out of the Multnomah Federal Detention Center in downtown Portland. Though jailed under an alias chosen for him by the U.S. prosecutor, the feds had immediately leaked this alias—Randy Barker—to the *Oregonian* newspaper, and a guard at the jail had promptly roughed up Mayfield.

The two public defenders went before Judge Jones and asked that as a material witness he be kept under house arrest, there being scant apparent evidence against him. Judge Jones finally compelled the prosecutor to disclose what evidence he had against Mayfield. A fingerprint, said the U.S. prosecutor, withholding from the court the fact that this fingerprint was highly controversial and had been explicitly disqualified by the Spanish police.

The federal defenders questioned the imprisonment of their client, who faced penalties of the utmost gravity, on the basis of a fingerprint. Judge Jones allowed as how he had sent people to prison for life on the basis of a single fingerprint. Mayfield's attorneys asked to see a copy of the allegedly matched fingerprints and have them evaluated by their own expert witness. Knowing he was on thin ice the U.S. prosecutor refused, claiming it was an issue of national security. Under pressure from Judge Jones, himself pressured by the assiduous federal defenders, the U.S. prosecutor finally agreed he would give the prints to an independent evaluator selected by Judge Jones.

The prints were given to Kenneth R. Moses of San Francisco, an SFPD veteran who runs a company called Forensic Identification Services which, among other things, proclaims its skills in "computer enhancement of fingerprints." It was "quite difficult," Moses said, because of "blurring and some blotting out," but yes, the FBI had it right, and there was "100 per cent certainty" that one of the prints on the blue bag in Madrid derived from the left index finger of Brandon Mayfield.

Moses transmitted this confident opinion by phone to Judge Jones on the morning of May 19. Immediately following Moses' assertion, the U.S. attorney stepped forward to confide to Judge Jones dismaying news from Madrid communicated by the Spanish police that very morning. The news "cast some doubt on the identification." This information, he added, "was classified or potentially classified."

The prosecutors then huddled with the judge in his chambers. After 20 minutes, Judge Jones stormed back out and announced that the prosecutors needed to tell the defense lawyers what they had just told him. The prosecutor duly informed the courtroom that the Spanish police had identified the fingerprint as belonging to the right middle finger of Ouhnane Daoud, an Algerian national living in Spain. Daoud was under arrest as a suspect in the bombing. Judge Jones ordered Mayfield to be freed. The U.S. prosecutor said he should be placed under electronic monitoring, a request which the judge turned down.

Four days later, on May 24, the warrant for his detention was dismissed.

The FBI sent two of their senor fingerprint analysts to Spain on a mission to salvage the Bureau from humiliation. The two analysts did their best, returning with the claim that the fingerprint sent to the FBI by the Spanish police was of "no value for identification purposes," a claim which the inspector general later shot down by pointing out that only a few weeks thereafter the FBI's latent fingerprint unit concurred with the Spanish national police lab's determination that the print on the bag matched the right middle finger of Ouhnane Daoud.

The FBI lab fought an increasingly desperate rearguard battle, eventually claiming that it had been the victim of an excessive reliance on technology. The inspector general points out that the only investigator in the FBI's lab to emerge with any credit is in fact the IAFIS computer that had stated clearly, "close, no match."

The inspector general writes the bottom line on the "science" of fingerprint-matching. He gets the FBI's top examiner to admit that if Mayfield had "been like the Maytag repair man" and not a Muslim convert married to an Egyptian, "the laboratory might have revisited the identification with more skepticism."

And what about Daoud's fingerprint match? We don't know, but if he was convicted on the basis of fingerprints alone, we would say there is grounds for an appeal.

2006

The Portland Six, the Patriot Act, and a Black Bag Job on the Constitution
Jeffrey St. Clair

A FEW WEEKS AFTER THE ATTACKS OF 9/11, A VIGILANT CITIZEN in rural Skamania County, Washington, noticed something strange: four black men dressed in turbans and robes taking target practice in a local rock quarry. Skamania County, known throughout the Pacific Northwest for the ripeness of its xenophobia, doesn't have many Muslims and it has even fewer blacks. Phone calls were made to the local sheriff's office. Soon a patrol car was dispatched to the gravel pit. The lawman's eyeballs must have bulged at the sight: turbans, blacks, and guns. Here was a trifecta in the terrorist profiling sweepstakes. The sheriff rang up the FBI and within hours the insidious new machinery of the Patriot Act was put into stealthy motion.

And although the Patriot Act authorizes the convening of secret tribunals and covert investigations, the FBI quickly leaked all of this information to favored reporters at the *Oregonian* and *Seattle Post-Intelligencer*, including the names of the suspected terrorists. Jeffrey Battle, brothers Ahmed and Muhammed Bilal, and Patrice Lumumba Ford was soon vilified on the front pages of the region's papers as the leaders of an al-Qaeda cell in the heart of the Cascadia. Editorials ladled praise on the diligence of the FBI and the local sheriff's department without sparing a paragraph to question whether the men's rights had been trampled. The second front in the war on terror had been opened, and the press went along for the ride.

In the FBI men's eyes Ford, a gifted student of Chinese languages and a former intern for Portland Mayor Vera Katz, was born with three strikes against him: he was black, his father was a former Black Panther, and he was named after the leader of the Democratic Republic of the Congo, who was assassinated at the behest of the CIA. The G-men must have wondered how Ford had escaped their clutches to this point in his young life.

All of the men lived in Portland, Oregon, and attended the same mosque. All are American citizens.

With this faint scent of evidence, the FBI rushed to the nation's top spy court with a demand to begin a covert investigation of the men, who they alleged were would-be terrorists. The covert court swiftly gave the feds all they wanted: 36 warrants for wiretaps of phones and computers and secret searches of their homes.

Over the next year the men were put under 24-hour-a-day surveillance. Their every move was watched, their friends identified, each conversation tapped into and recorded. The FBI also sent a wired informant named Khalid Ibrahim Mostafa into their inner circle. Mostafa is an Egyptian-born auto mechanic, who coaxed Battle and others into inflammatory conversations and even recorded prayer services inside a Portland mosque.

In late October of 2001, the men traveled to Hong Kong, crossed into China, and eventually landed in Bangladesh. There Battle supposedly approached a representative of Tabligh Jamaat, an evangelical Islamic sect started in India in 1923. The FBI alleges that this was the fatal moment when Battle crossed a treasonous boundary from which there could be no safe return. Tabligh Jamaat, the FBI charges, is a front for Osama bin Laden, a recruiting station for potential soldiers heading to al-Qaeda training camps in Afghanistan.

Most Islamic scholars dispute the connection as being more tenuous than the alleged links between al-Qaeda and Saddam Hussein. They say that Tabligh Jamaat is a largely apolitical sect far removed from bin Laden's brand of jihad-happy Wahhabism. Indeed, Jeffrey Battle's relatives say he was on a religious quest, made all the more vivid by the events of 9/11 and the vicious backlash against Muslims in the United States. Battle is a former U.S. Army reservist, who had lately worked as a security guard in Portland.

"He was looking to find the straight path," says Abdullah Muhammad, Battle's uncle. "People travel to Asia and live in mosques, visit Muslims in the home, study and teach, and invite 'slackers' in the religion to come back. That's what Jeffrey was doing. My nephew never stepped foot in Afghanistan."

But the FBI claims something more sinister was afoot. They charge that the men were trying to get into Afghanistan to join up with the Taliban and fight against U.S. troops and the U.S.-backed Northern Alliance. Whatever their intent, the FBI agrees that the men never made it to Afghanistan. Nevertheless on October 4, 2002, the Justice Department, armed with secret evidence gained through secret warrants, indicted Battle, Ford, and the Bilal brothers, charging them conspiring to wage war against the United States. Also indicted was Habis Abu al Saoub, a Jordanian native, whom the FBI fingers as the leader of the group.

Another unfortunate soul caught in the FBI's driftnet was October Martinique Lewis, a Portland nurse's assistant, who was charged under the Patriot Act with providing aid to terrorists. Lewis is Battle's ex-wife and allegedly sent him $2,130 while he was traveling in Asia. Lewis says she had no idea that Battle was planning to enlist in the Taliban and merely thought she was helping underwrite his spiritual journey. Under the expansive trawl of the Patriot Act, Lewis didn't even have to be aware the money might be spent on terrorist activities. Indeed, the law allows her to be prosecuted even if the money was used to buy innocuous items such as food, cab fare, or cigarettes. Once Battle was labeled a terrorist (or a terrorist's associate) by the FBI, any money that came his way was considered criminally tainted.

Ford, Battle, and Lewis were arrested in their apartments in Portland. Muhammad Bilal was arrested in his sister's Detroit home. A few days later, his brother Ahmed surrendered to police in Mayalasia. Al Saoub remains at large.

Ashcroft and his underlings were anxious to leak malicious information about the defendants, referring to the bumbling group as "a terrorist cell." His deputies spoke of plots to machine-gun synagogues and schoolyards. Neighbors came forward to tell of suspicious late night meetings in the parking lot of Battle's apartment complex. It was said that Battle's 5-year-old son lectured kids on the playground on the merits of the 9/11 attacks. The fear factor was fiercely fanned. "The enemy recruits in this country, it trains in this country and acts in this country," warned Charles Matthews, the head of the FBI's office in Portland.

But Ashcroft and his prosecutors balked at allowing the defendants to see the affidavits the FBI filed with FISA court showing the reasons for granting the secret warrants. This is no trifling matter. It's a stab at the heart of the Fourth Amendment's protection against unreasonable searches and seizures. The Fourth Amendment has been rudely battered by the drug war; but it seems likely to be euthanized by Bush's anti-terror crusade.

"While all citizens should certainly be cognizant of the need for national security, we must not abrogate the need for a fair trial and the due process clause of the Constitution," says Jack Ransom, October Lewis' lawyer. "The court must disclose these materials to the accused where such disclosure is necessary to make an accurate determination of the legality of the surveillance. How do you attack applications for surveillance that you haven't and won't see? We're shooting in the dark."

But it gets worse. Not only did the Justice Department object to the defendants seeing the applications for the warrants, they also objected to allowing a federal judge to examine them *in camera* to determine if they could be turned over without compromising national security. Even stranger, Federal Judge Robert Jones agreed with the feds in a ruling that amounts to a kind of judicial self-emasculation. These day's judges are so cowed by the rhetoric of terror that they are willing to surrender the last real check the Republic has against the legal depredations of prosecutorial zealots.

"This is a very troubling development," writes Anita Ramasastry, a law professor at the University of Washington. "Unless this ruling is overturned on appeal, it will mean that a U.S. citizen can now be convicted of a crime without ever knowing the reasons why the government was given permission to spy on them in first place."

Judge Jones' ruling places a judicial hood over the defendants and their lawyers, as blinding as those on the heads of the prisoners at Camp X-Ray. The Portland Six don't know the basis of the charges against them. They haven't even been allowed to see much of the evidence collected on the basis of those secret warrants. In the future, American school children won't need to worry about suspending their disbelief when compelled to read Kafka's literary mind games. It'll be seem as pedestrian as Hemingway.

Over the course of a year, the feds amassed 271 different wiretapped conversations by the defendants. To date, only 86 tapes have been turned over to the defense teams. From the snippets released to date, the banter between Battle and his cohorts is pretty tame fare as jihad talk goes. You'll find much more incendiary religious rhetoric streaming out of the Rev. Pat Robertson's daily broadcasts than what was caught on these tapes.

The Portland Six case will most likely be the first direct challenge of the Patriot Act's provision giving the FBI the right to get secret warrants to snoop on American citizens from the clandestine court set up under the Foreign Intelligence Surveillance Act or FISA.

FISA was a well-intentioned law that has now run amok. It was created in 1978 by reformists in the Congress following the revelations made by the Church Committee of widespread domestic spying on political dissidents by the FBI and CIA. FISA's spy courts were meant to insure that the use of secret wiretaps and searches by the FBI was limited to counterintelligence investigations meant to uncover spies for foreign governments. In practice, the courts served as little more than rubber stamps, rarely rebuking any request brought to it by the Justice Department.

Even so, the Patriot Act grossly expanded the power of the FBI to use the FISA court to get secret warrants to launch criminal investigations of U.S. citizens. The original language of FISA required that the sole purpose of a request for secret search and wiretap warrants must be counterintelligence. The Patriot Act amended this pivotal phrase to "a significant purpose" must be intelligence gathering. The gate opened. This subtle edit creates a kind of black bag job provision in the law, which slashes right at the heart of the Bill of Rights. It is now clear that only a handful of members of Congress read this provision before voting to enact it into law and even fewer had any idea of its implications—not that that would have changed many minds in this paranoid climate.

But in a rational environment, it should have sent chills down their spine. Because the FBI now enjoys the kind of unrestrained investigative power that J. Edgar Hoover only dreamed about. Not just the power to snoop into every private corner without any hint of wrongdoing, but the power to use whatever they find as evidence for future prosecutions. "The question is whether it's constitutional to tap a suspect's phone in a criminal investigation, without probable cause of criminal activity," says David Cole, a professor of constitutional law at Georgetown University and author of the very useful book, *Terrorism and the Constitution.*

There was certainly no showing of probable cause in the Portland Six case and no evidence to believe that the FBI could have prevailed on a federal judge to issue even a normal search warrant. So Ashcroft's men retreated to offering ominous homilies about might-have-beens. One of the prosecutors called it a case of "preventive arrest." Here we get to the rotten core of the matter. The Portland Six aren't charged for anything they did. There's no evidence that they planned to carry out any attacks on the U.S. military or on American citizens. No evidence they met with al-Qaeda or the Taliban. They're charged with acting on an impulse to go to Afghanistan, an impulse they never realized. So what we're left with is the prosecution of a thought crime and anyone who crossed these men's path and befriended them in any way could find themselves labeled as being part of this inept conspiracy. We've entered an era of preventive arrests and pre-emptive wars.

This prosecutorial strategy is not new. For the past couple of decades, Department of Justice lawyers have sharpened their teeth on similar tactics, using the RICO conspiracy statutes and other conspiracy laws like legal cluster bombs to take down as many bystanders as possible, even though their connection to criminal activity is remote at best. These days it's all about conviction rates, the body count of the Justice Department. As in Vietnam, it's all about numbers, not about who was taken down or how.

But the Patriot Act gives the feds sweeping new powers that go far beyond a mere fishing expedition into the lives of U.S. citizens. Under Ashcroft, the Justice Department has become a factory trawler, casting legal driftnets into the populace that can ensnare anyone in its wake.

One of the first casualties of the Portland Six case was Sheik Mohammed Abdirahman Kariye, the prayer leader at the Islamic Center of Portland, where the Portland Six attended services. Kariye was arrested on September 8, 2002, at the Portland International Airport. He was charged with Social Security Fraud, and the FBI leaked information to the press that airport security had found traces of TNT in his luggage. This turned out to be a lie. But the damage was done. Kariye was smeared as a would-be terrorist.

It gets more unsavory. Kariye became a target of the FBI in part because of the illicit recordings made in the mosque by FBI informant Khalid Mustafa under the auspices of the FISA court-recordings that flatly violate an Oregon law prohibiting wiretaps inside houses of worship.

"The government has this script," says Stanley Cohen, Kariye's lawyer. "They've got all these little pieces and they're trying to fit them together. But it's like a John Candy movie. It looks hot. It looks sexy. But there's nothing there."

These raids have rightly left the Muslim community living in a state of perpetual anxiety: fearful that their most private conversations and prayers are being tapped into by America's secret police; fearful that they face deportation merely because of their religious practices; fearful that they may be rounded up, placed in an interrogation camp, and no one will ever know what has happened to them. "The feeling that someone could knock on your door at night and you could be taken away—that's a feeling I thought I left behind when I left Baghdad in 1979," says Abul Haider, spokesman for the Islamic Center of Beaverton, Oregon.

John Ashcroft, our minister of fear, craves even more power and he is using the arrest of the Portland Six as a cudgel to convince a cowering Congress to give him all he demands. In a speech before Congress, Ashcroft said the Portland Six were proof that there were sleeper cells embedded within the American heartland just waiting to strike. He said recordings revealed that the group "was amazingly aware of the impact of the Patriot Act" and changed their plans because of it. But that's not good enough for the crowd now in charge of the administration of justice in this country.

A few days after Ashcroft's speech, someone in the Justice Department leaked a draft of Ashcroft's scheme to upgrade the Patriot Act to the Center for Public Integrity, run by Charles Lewis. Lewis immediately posted it on his website, where the plan generated howls of protest from defense lawyers and civil libertarians, but elicited mainly yawns from the mainstream press.

The 86-page draft bill is titled the Domestic Security Enhancement Act of 2003 and reads like marching orders from Savak, the notorious Iranian security agency from the days of the Shah.

Among other intrusions into basic liberties, Ashcroft's new snooping law:

- offers blanket immunity to snitches who knowingly provide false information;
- restricts access to information about toxic chemicals produced by American factories;
- permits personal information about U.S. citizens to be shared with local law enforcement, even without any connection to terrorism;
- authorizes collection and cataloguing of DNA databases on Americans without court orders;
- allows for illegal surveillance without court orders and permits the Justice Department to strip Americans of their citizenship.

Give Ashcroft an inch and he'll take the entire Bill of Rights.

Is it any wonder that Ashcroft and his retinue of fundamentalist prosecutors vow to defend the Pledge of Allegiance at all costs, while they pillage the Constitution? It is after all the nature of senescent empires to demand allegiance and criminalize dissent, even as they undermine the very foundations for the legitimacy of their rule. We are becoming a nation of snitches and paranoids. Even our judges have buried their heads in the sand as wraith-like prosecutors swarm unfettered across the land.

It took a revolution to secure the Bill of Rights and a Civil War and century-long struggles for women, labor, civil rights, and environmental justice to transfuse those guarantees with meaning. If they're lost in the name of Bush's war on terror, it'll take another revolution to get them back. But Ashcroft and his allies are now putting in place measures of domestic repression that will make that prospect a very remote fantasy indeed.

2003

Polygraphs, the Press and Gary Condit

Alexander Cockburn and Jeffrey St. Clair

WE'RE NO FANS OF THE MAN FROM MODESTO, GARY CONDIT. But it was troubling to see him being hounded by the cable news shows into taking a polygraph test, and then trashed for using his own polygrapher. Even J. Edgar Hoover knew that the polygraph wasn't any good for detecting deception. He dropped the test for analysis of his own men—but used it to coerce confessions out of civilian suspects.

The press is almost always reverential about the results yielded by polygraph-based interrogation. In fact it should be the rule in every newsroom to deride it.

The polygraph was invented in 1915 by a Harvard man called William Moulton Marston, who crowed that his clunky little gizmo could detect lies by measuring blood pressure. Marston's main claim to fame derives not from his machine, but from a doodle he came up with: the cartoon character Wonder Woman.

In the past 85 years, the polygraph hasn't changed much from the Marston prototype. "The secret of the polygraph is that their machine is no more capable of telling the truth than were the priests of ancient Rome standing knee-deep in chicken parts," says Alan Zelicoff, a physician and senior scientist at the Center for National Security and Arms Control at the Sandia Labs in Albuquerque, New Mexico. Zelicoff presented this view in an article in the July–August 2001 edition of *The Skeptical Inquirer*.

Zelicoff writes that the polygraph administer is a kind of confidence artist or modern-day mesmerist who tries to seduce (or scare) his subjects into believing in the power of the machine to catch them in the most minute inconsistency. "The subject, nervously strapped in a chair, is often convinced by the aura surrounding this cheap parlor trick, and is then putty in the hands of the polygrapher, who then launches into an intrusive, illegal and wide-ranging inquisition," Zelicoff writes. "The subject is told from time to time that the machine is indicating deception. It isn't, of course. And he is continuously urged to clarify his answers, by providing more and more personal information." At an arbitrary point, the polygrapher calls off the testing, consults the spools of graph paper and makes an entirely subjective rendering on whether the subject has given a "deceptive response."

Connoisseurs of the Wen Ho Lee affair will remember that at one point the FBI falsely told the Taiwanese nuclear physicist (accused of spying for the Chinese in Los Alamos) that polygraph tests showed he was lying. Cops play these sorts of tricks all the time, faking forensic reports and then shoving them under the noses of their suspects, shouting that they're proven liars and that they'd best sign a confession right away.

The most comprehensive review of the polygraph was conducted in 1983 by the Office of Technology Assessment, a research branch of Congress. The OTA concluded, "There is no known physiological response that is unique to deception." The report did note that the CIA and its companions "believe that the polygraph is a useful screening tool."

There are numerous ghastly stories of federal employees abused by the machine and its operators. A few years ago FBI agent Mark Mallah was given a routine polygraph. The polygrapher, who had only 80 hours experience with the machine, concluded that Mallah had lied. (Zelicoff notes that even barbers must have 1,000 hours of training before getting a license to cut hair.) His life soon transformed into a Kafka story. He was stripped of his badge; subjected to midnight searches of his house; his diary and appointment book seized and scrutinized; his neighbors, friends, and relatives interrogated; his every move outside monitored by helicopters. In the end, Mallah's life was pretty much destroyed, but nothing was ever proved against him. The FBI finally apologized, and Congress outlawed the use of the polygraph for civilian employees in 1988.

It's worth noting that the Walker brothers and Aldrich Ames both beat the polygraph with no sweat. Kim Philby settled himself with a dollop of Valium before breezing through his polygraph exams.

One investigator (and CounterPuncher) for a defense lawyer in California's Bay Area tells us that while the polygraph isn't admissible in most courts it's used all the time by prosecutors, mostly to seal plea bargains. "It's a perilous option, because the utility of the polygraph is almost totally up to the operator. There are good polygraphers, but many who work for the district attorneys have only minimal training."

The investigator described a recent case where a defense witness in a homicide case, who had passed a polygraph given by a former FBI polygrapher with 20 years experience, was sent to the DA for another test given by their examiner, a relative novice with the device. Defense lawyers can't be in the room while the test is given, even when their clients are being examined. The prosecutors videotape the session, and while the results of the polygraph can't be used at trial, the videotape can become evidence. In this case, the defense lawyer waited in the hall until the witness emerged from the room "with his face red as a beet." The lawyer heard the DA's investigator threaten the witness: "You little slime bag, I know you're lying. We're going to revoke your parole." The DA's examiner had interpreted the readings from one of his answers as being "deceptive."

2001

The Hoof Prints of Lucifer

Alexander Cockburn

THE HOOF PRINTS OF LUCIFER ARE EVERYWHERE. AND SINCE this is America, eternally at war with the darker forces, the foremost Enemy Within is sex, no quarter given. For the accused sex offender, no mercy, no quarter can be expected from the press, which has helped doom many an unfortunate to years, even lifetimes, behind bars after unfounded pillorying on the front page or news headline. It is one of the greatest blots on the Fourth Estate.

Here are some bulletins from the battlefront, drawn from a smart essay on "Sex & Empire" in the March issue of *The Guide*, a Boston-based monthly travel magazine, whose features and editorials have "about the best gay sex politics around," according to Bill Dobbs of queerwatch, whom *CounterPunch* takes as its advisor in these matters.

In February 2000, 18-year-old Matthew Limon had oral sex with a 14-year-old male schoolmate. A Kansas court sentenced him to 17 years in prison, a punishment upheld by a federal court in February.

Last July, Ohio sentenced 22-year-old Brian Dalton to seven years in prison because of sex fantasies he wrote in his diary. A woman teacher in Arizona up on trial last month for a relationship with a 17-year-old boy faces 100 years in prison.

Apropos the triumph of identity politics across the last thirty years Bill Andriette, the author of "Sex & Empire," remarks wittily that "in America, your clout as identity group depends how much of an enhanced sentence someone gets for dissing you" and then observes that "the same PR machinery that produces all these feel-good identities naturally segues into manu-facturing demonic ones—indeed, creates a demand for them. The ascription of demonic sexual identities onto people helps drive repression, from attacks on Internet freedom to sex-predator laws. Identity politics works gear-in-gear with a fetishization of children, because the young represent one class of persons free of identity, the last stand of unbranded humanity, precious and rare as virgin prairie."

This brings us into an Olympian quadruple axel of evil: sexu-ally violent predators (familiarly known as SVPs) preying on minors of the same sex. There's no quarrelling between prosecu-tor and judge, jury and governor, Supreme Court and shrinks. Lock 'em up and throw away the key.

I went to a Bar Mitzvah in Berkeley the other day, and after listening to passages from the Torah transmitting Yahweh's extremely rigorous prescriptions for his temple, right down to the use of acacia wood and dolphin skins, listened to Marita Mayer, an attorney in the public defender's office in Contra Costa County, describe the truly harrowing business of trying to save her clients—SVPs—from indeterminate confinement in Atascadero, the state's prime psychiatric bin within its prison system.

Among Mayer's clients are men who pleaded guilty to sex crimes in the mid-1980s, mostly rape of an adult woman, getting a fixed term of anywhere from 10 to 15 years. In the good old days, if you worked and behaved yourself, you'd be up for parole after serving half the sentence.

In California, as in many other states, SVP laws kicked in the mid-1990s, the crest of the repressive wave by hysteria over child sex abuse and crime generally: mandatory minimum sentences, reduction or elimination of statutes of limitation, erosion of the right to confront witnesses, community notification of released sex offenders, surgical and chemical castration, prohibition of mere possession of certain printed materials, this last an indig-nity previously only accorded to atomic energy secrets.

So California passes its SVP law in January of 1996, decreeing that those falling into the category of SVP have a sickness that requires treatment and cannot be freed, until a jury agrees unanimously that they are no longer a danger to the community. (The adjudicators vary from state to state. Sometimes it's a jury, or merely a majority of jurors, sometimes a judge, sometimes a panel, sometimes an unlicensed "multidisciplinary team.")

Mayer's clients, serving out their years in Pelican Bay or Vacaville or San Quentin, counting the months down to parole date, suddenly find themselves back to jail in Contra Costa County, told they've got a mental disorder and can't be released till a jury decides they're no danger to the community. Off to Atascadero they go for a two-year term, at the end of which they get a hearing, and almost always another two-year term.

"Many of them refuse treatment," Mayer says. "They refuse to sign a piece of paper saying they have a mental disease." Of course they refuse. Why sign a document saying that for all practical purposes you may well be beyond reform or redemption, that you are Evil by nature, not just a guy who did something bad and paid the penalty?

It's the AA model of boozing as sin, having to say you are an alcoholic and will always be in that condition, one lurch away from perdition. Soon everything begins to hinge on someone's assessment of your state of mind, your future intentions. As with the damnable liberal obsession with hate crime laws, it's a nosedive into the category of "thought crimes."

There the SVPs sit in Atascadero, surrounded by psych techs eager to test all sort of statistical and behavioral models, phallometric devices designed to assist in the persuasion of judge and jury that yes, the prisoner has a more than 50 per cent likelihood of exercising his criminal sexual impulses, should he be released.

Thus, by the circuitous route of "civil commitment" (confining persons deemed to be a danger to themselves or others) we have ended up with a situation that, from the constitutional point of view, is indeed absolutely Evil: held in preventive detention or being locked up twice for the same crime. Mayer concludes:

> It's using psychiatry, like religion, to put people away. Why not hire an astrologer or a goat-entrail reader to predict what the person might do? Why not the same for robbers as for rapists? What's happening is double jeopardy. If we don't watch it, it will come back to haunt us. People don't care about child rapists, but the Constitution is about protections. I think it's shredding the Constitution. I get into trouble because they say I'm into jury nullification and that's not allowed.
>
> Most of my clients tell me it's worse in Atascadero than in the regular prisons. How do I feel about these guys? When I talk to my clients I don't presume to think what they'll do in future. I believe in redemption. I don't look at them as sexually violent predators, I see them as sad sacks. They have to register. They could be hounded from county to county. Even for a tiny crime they'll be put away. Their lives are in ruins. I pity them.

But not goat entrails, surely. The animal rights crowd would never stand for it.

2002

Waco and the Press

Alexander Cockburn and Jeffrey St. Clair

T HE ASHES OF THE MURDERED BRANCH DAVIDIANS AND THEIR children—all 74 of them—were still smoldering as the nation's major news institutions rousingly endorsed the decision of Janet Reno and her boss, Bill Clinton, to give the FBI (and, as it turned out, the Delta Force) the go-ahead for an operation that ensured massacre. *Newsweek*, we particularly remember, rushed out its cover of David Koresh swathed in flames like one of the damned in a medieval painting. It was one of the great failures of American journalism, one of the most sickening, one of the most predictable, and one of the most revealing. To this day one can meet progressive types who devote many of their waking hours to activities designed to save Mumia abu Jamal who didn't give a toss about the Branch Davidians and their terrible slaughter by the federal government, and who still don't. Use the word "cult" and both reason and moral judgment enter recess.

So now comes further proof of the lies, deceptions and cover-ups of the FBI, and how do the big press pooh-bahs react? Do they make confession that they bought a cover-up and tried to sell it to the American people, the vast majority of whom steadfastly continued to believe that the government was lying and that an infamy had been perpetrated? Here's Ted Koppel, the night of September 1, 1999, discussing the seizure by federal marshals of tapes of FBI hostage "negotiators," discussing the use of pyrotechnic grenades the morning of the Waco raid:

> ... The credibility of the FBI, which probably did tell the truth about most of what happened, that credibility is badly damaged,

> while the credibility of conspiracy theorists, who tend to be
> wrong about most of what they've spun together about Waco,
> their credibility is newly enhanced. It is on these two fronts that
> the greatest damage has been done.

In this disgusting paragraph Koppel defines his career role
as flack for state power. For him the issue is not that an agency
of government planned mass murder, just as the so-called conspiracy nuts first surmised, then proved. For him the issue is
the credibility of the state. For the liberal elite—in whose ranks
most so-called conservatives can be numbered—this is always the
issue.

In the Koppel program that night was Henry Ruth, a former
Watergate prosecutor who was appointed in the aftermath of
Waco to investigate the federal raid. "The real issue," Ruth said,
"was whether any military force was actually used in the raid,
separate and apart from just military advisors, and my guess is
that such force is so dangerous, so controversial, that it probably
did not happen, but it's certainly worth looking at in this environment where the whole credibility of the investigation is now
at stake." Note here Ruth's desperate eagerness to let the government off the hook, and preserve the cover-up (code-named
"credibility") intact.

Koppel was scarcely alone. Here's a CBS broadcast of
September 2:

> For years now the disaster near Waco has been exhibit number
> one for many who have deep distrust of the American govern-
> ment. From conspiracy sites on the Internet to documentary
> films, Waco has provided a focus for those who see the gov-
> ernment as the enemy. And now they say there is proof the
> government has been lying, reports CBS News Correspondent
> John Blackstone. "This is just fodder for the conspiracy theo-
> rists," says psychologist Margaret Singer. She says this is just
> what the militia movement needs to say we told you so.... Many
> are certain to see this as government out of control. "The anti-
> government movement, the militia, hate groups are absolutely
> going to get a boost out of this and I think it's really a tragedy

for that reason," said Mark Potok of the Southern Poverty Law Center. At one time conspiracy theorists may have been viewed as eccentrics far out on the fringe, but then Timothy McVeigh drove a truck full of explosives to Oklahoma City and we all discovered just how dangerous it can be when people stop trusting the government.

As with Koppel, the problem for these CBS broadcasters, and for the shrink, Singer, and for Potok, from the Morris Dees money-raising machine, is not one of overweening and murderous government, but of potential sedition. Anything that disturbs popular torpor is tactically inept. Accomplices in the great and ongoing Cover-up of Everything that Really Matters—the central mission of the Fourth Estate—they tremble for Power, whenever Power is displayed in an undignified or unappetizing light. The film *Waco: A New Revelation*, whose disclosures about the pyrotechnic devices *CounterPunch* reported many weeks ago, has had the benign effect of discrediting the FBI and the Department of Justice and its chieftain, but in the end it may permit the FBI to recoup, by saying that the target of the pyrotechnic devices was just an outhouse and that these same projectiles never struck the main building in which the Branch Davidians were sheltered.

As Dan Gifford, executive producer of the earlier *Waco: The Rules of Engagement*, asserted on September 3, "No national news organization is saying anything at all about the government's careful prepping of the Davidian building to burn nor its machine-gunning of the Davidians in the burning building that is so clearly shown in the FBI's own aerial surveillance video that is included in *Waco: The Rules of Engagement*."

One riposte of the state to the Waco disclosures is to emphasize, as did the CBS man, that those who mistrust government are by definition subversive, dangerous, and possibly homicidal and, therefore, presumptively deserving of incineration. A Reuters story by Jim Wolf, put out on August 31, 1999, sets the stage. "The U.S. government is preparing for possible violence from cults, guerrillas, hate groups and end-of-world-fearing zealots as 2000 approaches," the report began. "The Federal Bureau of Investigation 'expects to see increased and possibly violent activities among certain groups related to the millennium,' a top official warned Congress in July." The official in question was Michael Vatis, head of a new FBI-led interagency center "to protect critical U.S. infrastructure." According to Reuters, Jim Wolf, "Vatis did not cite possible targets but FBI director Louis Freeh has said they include Jews, non-whites and their 'establishment allies,' i.e. the federal government."

So we can see the stage being set for the next Waco. Maybe the Bureau of Alchohol, Tobacco and Firearms, whose agents launched the first unprovoked assault on the Branch Davidian compound, should plan a pre-emptive strike on the residence of former President Ronald Reagan. After all, Reagan more than once affirmed his confidence in impending Apocalypse, citing Holy Scripture as his source. Reagan even identified Megiddo as ground zero for the apocalyptic finale. Here's just the sort of dangerous extremist the FBI is concerned about.

Among upcoming Koppel's broadcasts: "Wounded Knee: the bitter legacy:" Koppel explains that "in many ways the saddest consequence of this infamous massacre of American Indians was that it served to buttress the position of extremist native Americans who have long argued that the white man was intent on exterminating Indians altogether."

"Tuskegee: the tragic fallout:" Koppel explains that "in many ways the saddest consequence of this infamous medical experiment in which federal scientists and doctors deliberately failed to treat 600 black men suffering from syphilis (while pretending that they were) is that it served to buttress the position of extremist advocates of 'Black Power' who have long argued that the white man is intent on exterminating Native blacks altogether."

"Vietnam: The..." Enough. You get the idea.

1999

Part 6

CounterPunch's Side of The Story

The Great Communicator

Alexander Cockburn

THEY KEEP TALKING ABOUT REAGAN BEING A "BIG PICTURE" man, indifferent to petty detail. The phrase gives a false impression, as though Reagan looked out at the world as at some Cinemascope epic, a vast battlefield where, through those famous spectacles (one lens close-up, for speech reading, the other long distance) he could assess the global balance of forces. Wrong. Reagan stayed awake only for the cartoons, where the global balance of forces were set forth in simple terms, in the tiffs between Tom and Jerry or Mickey Mouse and Donald Duck.

When he became president, and thus "commander in chief," the Joint Chiefs of Staffs mounted their traditional show-and-tell briefings for him, replete with simple charts and a senior general explicating them in simple terms. Reagan found these briefings way too complicated and dozed off. The Joint Chiefs then set up a secret unit, staffed by cartoonists. The balance of forces were set forth in easily accessible caricature, with Soviet missiles the size of upended Zeppelins, pulsing on their launch pads, with the miniscule U.S. ICBMs shriveled in their bunkers. Little cartoon bubbles would contain the points the Joint Chiefs wanted to hammer into Reagan's brain, most of them no doubt to the effect that "we need more money." Reagan really enjoyed the shows and sometimes even asked for encores.

I have boundless faith in the American people, but it was startling to see the lines of people sweating under a hot sun waiting to see Reagan's casket. How could any of them take the dreadful old faker seriously? The nearest thing to it I can think of is the hysteria over Princess Di. In its way, the "outpouring" reminds me of what, nearly 20 years ago, I termed "news spasms," expertly fuelled by the imagineers in the Reagan White House. These spasms—Nuremberg rallies really—were totalitarian in structure and intent, obsessively monopolistic of newsprint and the airwaves, forcing a "national mood" of consensus, with Reagan (in this reprise, his casket) as master of ceremonies. Particularly memorable spasm events included the downing of KAL 007, the destruction of the U.S. Marine barracks outside Beirut, the commandeering of the Achille Lauro, and the explosion of the Challenger space shuttle on January 28, 1986, which disaster prompted one of the peak kitsch moments in a presidency that was kitsch from start to finish. Reagan ended his address to the nation thus: "We will never forget them, nor the last time we saw them, this morning, as they prepared for their journey and waved good-bye and 'slipped the surly bonds of earth' to 'touch the face of God.'"

In fact it was the White House that had doomed Christa McAuliffe and her companions to be burned alive in the plummeting Challenger. The news event required the Challenger to go into orbit and be flying over Congress while Reagan was delivering his State of the Union address. He was to tilt his head upward and, presumably gazing through the long-distance half of his spectacles, send a presidential greeting to the astronauts. A CounterPuncher living in Florida remembers that fatal morning well: "I was working on my open air porch that morning, before sunrise, and in Florida that morning it was freezing. Frost was on everything. I had CNN on (they were the only channel following the launch, as I recall), and the talk nonstop was about Reagan talking to the astronauts that coming night on the State of the Union speech. Now I'm an engineer, and though I knew nothing about the details of launch condition protocol, I did know enough from prior launch news to know that temperatures in the 30s F° threatened a safe launch. I recall scoffing at the Challenger going up that a.m., and turning off the set."

But NASA was having its arm twisted by the White House to stay on schedule. The Challenger was launched with that notorious O-ring fatally compromised by the cold. The day after the crash there was one brief news item in, I think, the *Washington Post*, about the possibility of pressure on NASA, then silence. The White House news managers successfully iced the story. It wasn't until October 5, 1986, the day of the crash in Nicaragua of Eugene Hasenfus' plane, carrying documents linking him to officials including Vice President George Bush and to an arms smuggling operation, that the press gave Reagan any sort of a hard time.

Back at the start of 1983 Reagan authorized a disinformation campaign, calling for a "public diplomacy" campaign superintended by the NSC and "designed to generate support for our national security objectives." This secret propaganda program surfaced eight days after Hasenfus crashed, by Alfonso Chardy, a terrific reporter working for the *Miami Herald*, who got many scoops around that time. The public diplomacy campaign seems to have consisted mostly of leaking anti-Nicaraguan material to journalists who leaked it to their readers without saying where it came from. The usefulness of this operation, subsequently transferred to the State Department, was best demonstrated by the great disinformation coup of election night 1984, when television reporters—Bernard Kalb in the lead—breathlessly cited White House tips of a shipload of Soviet MIG fighters nearing Nicaragua. With this tremendous Reaganite bluster about worrisome escalation filling the airwaves, any remote possibility of benign or even objective coverage of Nicaragua's first elections in history was successfully averted.

The press would buy any threat from the Reaganites, no matter how preposterous. Grenada "lay athwart vital U.S. sea lanes," thus threatening all trans-Atlantic trade. Libya, the press trumpeted on cue from the White House in late 1981, had sent a team of assassins south across the Canadian border to murder Reagan. The "Libyan Assassination Plot" received wide coverage.

There were anywhere from three to thirteen hit men, armed with missiles, depending on which channel you were watching. They were coming from Canada, or from Mexico. The hit squads were variously made up of three Libyans, three Iranians, and three Syrians. Imagine the ethnic jokes they swapped. But the networks all agreed that there was one Palestinian, one Lebanese, and one East German. During the Iran-Contra hearings it came out that the disseminator of these fairy tales was an Israeli agent and the CIA had known all along the story was false. A federal customs agent working the tunnel from Detroit to Windsor, Canada, told me later that no word had ever come through to watch out for this supposed Libyan hit team even though the tunnel was an obvious point of entry.

It was all part of the long effort to demonize Qaddafi, which culminated in the bombing raid on Libya by F-111s on April 14, 1986. The raid was timed to coincide with the TV evening newscasts, with a Pentagon press release readied to announce Qaddafi's accidental death. The missiles aimed at his living quarters killed his 18-month-old adopted daughter, Hana.

Reagan loved to trumpet the threat of the "Soviet-supplied and trained" Nicaraguan army rampaging north through Honduras, Guatemala, and Mexico before descending like a wolf on the fold, in this case Harlingen, Texas, with Corpus Christi prostrate in its path a few score miles north up State Highway 77. These were the glory days of the "Threat Inflaters," practitioners of the tumid art like Robert Moss, Clare Sterling and Arnaud de Borchgrave, along with the dragoons in Paul Nitze's Committee on the President Danger.

The press dutifully relayed their fantasies, even the very mad one about a Nicaraguan invasion. In 1987, ABC ran a solemn and much discussed series, called "Amerika," about a Soviet takeover of the Midwest. The Pentagon wasn't too worried about the Reds landing in Iowa (where they would presumably run the small kulak farmers out of business and force consumers to do their shopping in warehouses filled with cheap goods piled up on pallets), but they were actively discussing how to fight and win a nuclear war with the Soviet Union, right down to nuclear "decapitation" of the Soviet high command.

"Amerika" tied into another rich fantasy of the Threat Inflaters, that there was a vast "civil defense gap," to the advantage of the Soviet Union. At a given signal from the Kremlin, a large proportion of the Soviet population would vanish like moles into subterranean shelters and emerge in the post-Holocaust world, presumably to cross the sea and till the irradiated acres of the Midwest on which they might live, until they moved into beach front property in Southern California, welcomed by such film quislings as had survived the McCarthy years.

The problem for the press was that Reagan didn't really care that he'd been caught out with another set of phony statistics or a bogus anecdote about him liberating Auschwitz or fighting on the Normandy beaches. Truth, for him, was what he happened to be saying at the time. He went one better than George Washington in that he couldn't tell a lie and he couldn't tell the truth, since he couldn't tell the difference between the two.

His mind was a wastebasket of old clippings from *Popular Science*, SF magazines (the origin of Star Wars), lines from movies, and homely saws from the *Reader's Digest* and the Sunday supplements. He had a stout belief in astrology, the stars being the twinkling penumbra of his incandescent belief in the "free market," with whose motions it was blasphemous to tamper. Astrologers exulted when they saw his visit to Bitburg was timed to coincide with a concurrence of a full moon while at its perigee with the earth, along with a total eclipse of the moon. Elsewhere in the heavens Saturn, Uranus, Neptune, and Pluto appeared to move retrograde. The same four planets appeared retrograde a year later when Reagan bombed Libya. This being said, Dame Quigley, the Reagans' preferred astrologer, was a benign counterweight in her policy advice to Jeane Kirkpatrick and the other berserkers.

Of course Reagan believed Armageddon was right around the corner, and would probably arrive "in our lifetime." He also believed tomato ketchup could be classified as a vegetable for school lunches, striking back at the nose-candy crowd who, as Stevie Earle once said, spent the Seventies trying to get cocaine classified as a vegetable.

Hearing all the warm and fuzzy talk about the Gipper, young people spared the experience of his awful sojourn in office, probably imagine him as a kindly, avuncular figure. He was a vicious man, with a breezy indifference to suffering and the consequences of decisions. This indifference was so profound that Dante would surely have consigned him to one of the lowest circles of hell, to roast for all eternity in front of a malfunctioning TV set and a dinner tray swinging out of reach like the elusive fruits that tortured Tantalus. And talking of torture, there wasn't a torturer in Latin America who didn't raise a cheer when Reagan was elected, even though Carter hadn't cramped their style particularly. They were right to exult. In Guatemala, Rios Montt plunged into his butchery of 200,000 Mayans. David Rockefeller made haste to Buenos Aires to tell the generals that with Reagan's election a new era of understanding had been launched. A CIA-inspired torture manual surfaced from El Salvador, though the U.S. press made little of it at the time. RENAMO perpetrated ghastly massacres in Mozambique, as did Savimbi's UNITA in Angola, spurred on and paid for by Reagan's men.

Reagan hailed the Contra murderers attacking Nicaragua as the "moral equivalent of the founding fathers" (an assessment with which the Iroquois would have readily agreed). Fresh from honoring the SS men buried in Bitburg, he went two days later to Spain where he declared that the Lincoln Brigaders and the defenders of the Republic had fought on the wrong side. He was surrounded by scoundrels large and small. Probably the worst was William Casey, head of the CIA, and an out-and-out crook, who stood at the head of a vast cavalcade of fringe players, all the way down to the neocons who flocked to his standard.

I pulled Reagan's hair once, in the company of the late Murray Kempton. It was in 1976 when Reagan was running for the Republican nomination. There was unkind talk in the press about him dying his hair, possibly even wearing a toupee. His handlers made him and his hair available for inspection in New York, and we stood in line to take a close look for traces of dye or a hairpiece. I gave his thick thatch of apparently genuine hair a tug to make sure. He took it calmly, as placid as a cow in a country fair. I'm sure that if I'd asked to check his teeth he'd have opened up, right on cue.

I last saw him at the Republican convention in New Orleans in August of 1988, where he sat in his presidential box entirely immobile, with the kind of somber passivity one associates with the shrouded figure in some newly opened Egyptian tomb before oxygen commences its mission of decay. I never saw him being "sunny," a favorite adjective of the hagiographers. As an orator or "communicator" he was terrible, with one turgid cliché following another, delivered in a folksy drone. His range of rhetorical artifice was terribly limited.

He was an awful president, never as popular as the press pretended, presiding over a carnival of corruption and greed. On March 23, 1983, a friend of mine watched as a naval officer and a defense contractor in the Fort Myer Officers' Club in Virginia listened impatiently as Reagan churned his way through a longish overture to his excited launch of Star Wars. Then, as Reagan began to token forth the billion-dollar feeding trough of the Strategic Defense Initiative, they screamed to each other in incredulous delight: "He's going to do it... he's doing it... he's done it! We're rich, we're rich!" With these words, they both made a rush to the telephones.

The blue-collars who thought Reagan was their guy didn't do well in his two terms, any more than the poor did, despite oceans of drivel last week about the Reagan boom lifting all boats. So far as individual wage earners are concerned, the real median wage for the bottom 20 per cent of earners was $7.20 an hour in

1981 when he entered the White House and $7.14 an hour when he left in 1989. (By 2001, after the Clinton boom it was at $8.07.) Reagan's rhetoric was anti-government, but in fact he was pressing programmatically for a different use of government power, in which the major corporations would occupy a much stronger position. The tendencies he presided over were probably inevitable, given the balance of political forces after the postwar boom hit the ceiling in the late 1960s. Then it was a matter of triage, as the rich made haste to consolidate their position. It was a straight line from Reagan's crude attacks on welfare queens to Clinton's compassionate chewing of the lip (same head wag as RR's) as he swore to "end welfare as we know it." As a PR man, it was Reagan's role, as it was Thatcher's, to reassure the wealthy and the privileged that not only might but right was on their side. He installed fantasy as the motor of national consciousness, and it's still pumping disastrously along.

2004

When Billy Graham Planned To Kill One Million People

Alexander Cockburn

THERE'S A PIQUANT CONTRAST IN THE PRESS COVERAGE ACROSS the decades of Billy Graham's various private dealings with Nixon, as displayed on the tapes gradually released from the National Archive or disclosed from Nixon's papers. I'll come shortly to the recent flap over Graham and Nixon's closet palaverings about the Jews, but first let's visit another interaction between the great evangelist and his commander in chief. Back in April 1989, a Graham memo to Nixon was made public. It took the form of a secret letter from Graham, dated April 15, 1969, drafted after Graham met in Bangkok with missionaries from Vietnam. These men of God said that if the peace talks in Paris were to fail, Nixon should step up the war and bomb the dikes. Such an act, Graham wrote excitedly, "could overnight destroy the economy of North Vietnam."

Graham lent his imprimatur to this recommendation. Thus the preacher was advocating a policy to the U.S. commander in chief that on Nixon's own estimate would have killed a million people. The German high commissioner in occupied Holland, Seyss-Inquart, was sentenced to death at Nuremberg for breaching dikes in Holland in World War II. (His execution did not deter the U.S. Air Force from destroying the Toksan dam in North Korea, in 1953, thus deliberately wrecking the system that irrigated 75 per cent of North Korea's rice farms.)

This disclosure of Graham as an aspirant war criminal did not excite any commotion when it became public in 1989, twenty years after it was written. I recall finding a small story in the

Syracuse Herald-Journal. No one thought to chide Graham or even question him on the matter. Very different has been the reception of a new tape revealing Graham, Nixon, and Haldeman palavering about Jewish domination of the media and Graham invoking the "stranglehold" Jews have on the media.

On the account of James Warren in the *Chicago Tribune*, who has filed excellent stories down the years on Nixon's tapes, in this 1972 Oval Office session between Nixon, Haldeman, and Graham, the president raises a topic about which "we can't talk about it publicly," namely Jewish influence in Hollywood and the media.

Nixon cites Paul Keyes, a political conservative who is executive producer of the NBC hit, *Rowan and Martin's Laugh-In*, as telling him that "11 of the 12 writers are Jewish." "That right?" says Graham, prompting Nixon to claim that *Life* magazine, *Newsweek*, the *New York Times*, the *Los Angeles Times*, and others, are "totally dominated by the Jews." Nixon says network TV anchors Howard K. Smith, David Brinkley, and Walter Cronkite are "front men who may not be of that persuasion," but that their writers are "95 per cent Jewish."

"This stranglehold has got to be broken or the country's going down the drain," the nation's best-known preacher declares. "You believe that?" Nixon says. "Yes, sir," Graham says. "Oh, boy," replies Nixon. "So do I. I can't ever say that but I believe it." "No, but if you get elected a second time, then we might be able to do something," Graham replies.

Magnanimously Nixon concedes that this does not mean "that all the Jews are bad" but that most are left-wing radicals who want "peace at any price except where support for Israel is concerned. The best Jews are actually the Israeli Jews." "That's right," agrees Graham, who later concurs with a Nixon assertion that a "powerful bloc" of Jews confronts Nixon in the media. "And they're the ones putting out the pornographic stuff," Graham adds.

Later Graham says that "a lot of the Jews are great friends of mine. They swarm around me and are friendly to me. Because they know I am friendly to Israel and so forth. They don't know how I really feel about what they're doing to this country." After Graham's departure Nixon says to Haldeman, "You know it was good we got this point about the Jews across." "It's a shocking point," Haldeman replies. "Well," says Nixon, "it's also, the Jews are an irreligious, atheistic, immoral bunch of bastards."

Within days of these exchanges becoming public, the 83-year old Graham was hauled from his semi-dotage and impelled to express public contrition. "Experts" on Graham were duly cited as expressing their "shock" at Graham's White House table talk.

Why the shock? Don't they know that this sort of stuff is consonant with the standard conversational bill of fare at 75 per cent of the country clubs in America, not to mention many a Baptist soiree? Nixon thought American Jews were lefty peaceniks who dominated the Democratic Party and were behind the attacks on him. Graham reckoned it was Hollywood Jews who had sunk the nation in porn. Haldeman agreed with both of them. At whatever level of fantasy, they were all acknowledging power. But they didn't say they wanted to kill a million Jews. That's what Graham said about the Vietnamese, and no one raised a bleat.

It's supposedly the third rail in journalism even to have a discussion of how much the Jews do control the media. Since three of the prime founders of Hollywood were Polish Jews who grew up within fifty miles of each other in Galicia, it's reckoned as not so utterly beyond the bounds of propriety to talk about Jewish power in Hollywood, though people still stir uneasily. The economic and political commentator Jude Wanniski remarked in his web newsletter that even if the Jews don't control the media overall, it is certainly true to say that they control discussion of Israel in the media here.

Certainly, there are a number of stories sloshing around the news now that have raised discussion of Israel and of the posture of American Jews to an acrid level. Rocketing around the web and spilling into the press are many stories about Israeli spies in America at the time of 9/11. On various accounts, they were trailing Atta and his associates, knew what was going to happen but did nothing about it, or were simply spying on U.S. facilities. Some, posing as art students, have been expelled, according to AP. There were the substantiated accounts of the Israelis in a van in New Jersey arrested after being spotted cheering as the Towers fell. To the fury of FBI agents, they were deported to Israel after high-level intervention. The cheering men with the van obviously knew that these were terror assaults on the Towers, not accidental collisions. There's Sharon's bloody repression of the Palestinians, and Israel's apparently powerful role in Bush's foreign policy, urging him into action against at least two of the axes of evil, Iraq and Iran.

2002

Al Gore, Narc

Alexander Cockburn and Jeffrey St. Clair

NOW IT'S AL GORE, CRIME FIGHTER, OUTLINING HIS PLANS IN a recent speech in Atlanta. The erstwhile dope smoker from Tennessee fears the erstwhile cocaine user from Texas has the edge on the crime issue. Hence his dash for the low ground. Among the Atlanta pledges: The minute he's settled into the Oval Office and signed a pardon for the former incumbent, President Gore will be calling for 50,000 more cops (more half-trained recruits like the ones who shot Amadou Diallo) and for allowing off-duty cops to carry concealed weapons (which almost all of them do anyway).

No, it's unlikely Gore will endorse medical marijuana, despite his erstwhile post-Vietnam therapy with opium-laced marijuana in the days when he worked for the *Tennessean*. In the words of his friend John Warnecke (who imported the Thai sticks from the West Coast), Al "smoked as much as anybody I knew down there, and loved it."

Gore is promising prisoners "a simple deal: before you get out of jail, you have to get clean. And if you want to stay out, then you'd better stay clean." Not only does he want to test prisoners for drugs while they're in jail, he wants to test parolees twice a week and return them to jail if they fail. Other features of Al's war on crime: he wants to put Tommy Hilfiger out of business. How else can we interpret Gore's call for gang-free zones, banning "gang-related" clothing? What about gang-related music? Hmmm, Tipper tried that last one, and it didn't work out too well.

Among Gore's other big plans to combat crime: he wants to target telemarketers who prey on seniors. What about telemarketers who prey on people sitting down to dinner? George W. says he'll put them on Death Row. Where are you on that one, Al?

Here we are in a time when a sizable chunk of the population thinks there are some serious flaws in the justice system. Governor of Illinois George Ryan, a believer in capital punishment, suspends the death penalty in his state because he no longer believes it can be fairly administered. New York and Los Angeles are in an uproar over trigger-happy and corrupt cops. That AP photo of the INS snatch of Elián Gonzalez stirs Republicans in the House to start talking about federal goons. Sphinx-like silence from Gore on most of these matters, except of course a tip of his hat to the Miami Cubans. The only difference between Gore and George W. on the death penalty is that George W. actually laughs when he's quizzed about state poisoning in the Texas death house outside Huntsville.

As for Al's favored drug of the early Seventies, last year about 700,000 were arrested for marijuana offenses, about 87 per cent for possession. That's more than double the equivalent number for the early Nineties. Of the federal prison population of 118,000, about 60 per cent are in for drug-law violations, the largest proportion for marijuana. So Al should feel a special kinship with these inmates. Drug offenders constitute about a quarter of the 1.2 million in state prisons and the 600,000 in local jails. Most state drug prisoners are in for heroin or cocaine-related offenses, so maybe George, the coke snorter, should save his tiny reserves of compassion for them.

The other day we were at a meeting in Berkeley organized by people who want cities to shift gears on the drug war. One of the other speakers was Ethan Nadelmann of the Lindesmith Center, which pushes for drug-policy reform.

Nadelmann made some good points at the event and later, when we asked him about Gore's crime proposals. "The idea that when people relapse the punishment should be prison is both antiscientific and fundamentally inhumane," Nadelmann said. "The whole motto of twelve-step is 'one step at a time.' Relapse is part of the recovery process. The notion that people should be reincarcerated based on dirty urine, even when they are getting the rest of their life together, is bad public policy, costly, inefficient and, again, inhumane."

America is so hooked on prisons that right now, as Nadelmann points out, the easiest way to get treatment for drug addiction is to commit a crime and get yourself arrested. Of course, it's the worst place to get drug treatment, but finding it outside the criminal justice system is very tough, unless you have plenty of money. Someone should tell Al that the surest place to get drugs is prison, where it's brought in by the guards, the very folks who are supposed to be supervising punishment and cleanup. Gore won't have anything to say about that. He's far too chicken to take on the correctional officers' associations.

Is there a way out of the insane drug war, which is debauching the Bill of Rights, filling our prisons and failing in all its professed aims (though not its tacit one, of social control)? Nadelmann is thinking along the right lines: "an alternative drug-control regime, based on individual sovereignty—control of your body and what you put into it—plus a public health program. People should not be punished for what they put into their bodies but for the harm they do to others."

Gore knows all about addiction. His sister Nancy, as he reminds us from time to time, was killed by cigarettes, unable to kick the habit even as she was breathing with one cancerous lung. He also knows about congenital dispositions. His wife, Tipper, is a depressive. He knows about therapy too, having communed with shrinks when he was having the midlife sag that partly prompted his 1992 book *Earth in the Balance.*

Suppose tobacco someday becomes a criminalized drug. Booze too. Suppose sister Nancy were still around and got put in prison for manslaughter while driving under the influence of alcohol. How would brother Al feel if she were given more jail time because she couldn't quit smoking? How would he feel if she were out on parole, then put back in jail because nicotine or alcohol showed up in her blood in a routine test when she applied for a job? How would he like it if someone told Tipper that she should just "snap out of" her depression?

We doubt Al will connect the dots between Nancy's smoking habit and his stupid anticrime proposals. He's slow to see connections. After all, he stayed addicted to subsidies for his own tobacco farm and to tobacco-industry cash for seven years after Nancy died, before finally claiming that he'd tested clean.

2000

Clinton Comes to Harlem

Alexander Cockburn and Jeffrey St. Clair

BILL CLINTON NOW PROPOSES TO ESTABLISH AN OFFICE IN Harlem, on 125th street, scarce more than a few stone throws away from where Gore delivers homilies to journalism students in Columbia University. Each has found his appropriate setting: the defeated veep pouring earnest banalities about journalism and politics into the eager ears of ambitious high fliers already sending their resumes and worthy clips to the *New York Times*; Clinton, the moral reprobate, fleeing a blizzard of criticism for auctioning a pardon to a billionaire crook by setting up shop among the poorer folk.

Sneering at Bill, the press corps has nothing much to be proud of. How come not a single one of those high-flying, White House-connected newshounds managed to get hold of the sensational fact, finally disclosed a couple of weeks ago, that Bill Clinton and Al Gore hadn't had a significant conversational encounter in a full year? They finally had a meltdown gripe session not long before the 2000 election. As always, it turns out we know nothing about what really goes on in the White House. George W. could be tossing back dry martinis, partying till dawn, and four years down the road we'll still be reading about him and Laura saying their prayers and tucked up by 10:30 p.m.

We can look forward to months, if not years of civil war between the Clinton and Gore factions. Late last week, a very senior pollster in Clinton's inner circle spotted a journalistic acquaintance in a Georgetown supermarket and pinned him against his shopping cart with a vibrant diatribe against Gore. How, the pollster hissed, can we explain that Gore was unable to run on the Clinton economy, unable to mention millions of jobs created through the Clinton 90s? She answered her own question. Because to do so would have meant mentioning Clinton's name and Gore couldn't bring himself to do that.

Why not? The answer, the pollster said, went far back before the Lewinsky affair that so troubled Al and Tipper. It seems that Al has always felt that it was he who actually won the 1992 election, bailing Bill out of all his problems over draft dodging and Gennifer Flowers. Through Clinton's two terms, Al's conviction that he rather than Bill should by rights be sitting in the Oval Office throbbed painfully in his psyche. Result: he never spoke to the boss and couldn't bear to ask him to help in those last desperate campaign days.

Even as Bill and Al joust across the great moral divide, we find the Democrats failing to rediscover a social conscience. As the prospect of a Bush tax cut looks more and more as though it will come to pass, the air is filled with righteous passion about how the Republicans are about to steal dollars from the little people. Democratic pundit Mark Shields howls that under Bush the super rich are stealing from the rich, and the class war is over; the super rich won.

It's true. The rich are winning. But don't forget. They won all through Clinton time too. In the Spring of 2000 Robert Pollin, an economist at the University of Massachusetts, Amherst, published an "Anatomy of Clintonomics," concluding his survey thus: "The core of Clinton's economic program has been global economic integration, with minimum interventions to promote equity in labor markets or stability in financial markets. Gestures to the least well-off have been slight and back-handed, while wages for the majority have either stagnated or declined. Wealth at the top, meanwhile, has exploded."

Clinton did very little to advance the interests of working people or organized labor. Take the two-step rise in the minimum wage. The overall rise from $4.25 to the current $5.15, set in September 1997, hardly offset the plunge in the real value of the minimum wage. That $5.15 is 30 per cent below its real value in 1968, even though the economy has become 50 per cent more productive across that those thirty years.

The combination of a low minimum wage and a widening of the earned income tax credit, Pollin went on, "have allowed business to offer rock-bottom wages, while shifting onto tax payers the cost of alleviating the poverty of even those holding full-time jobs."

Now the economy is contracting rapidly, and soon we'll be finding out what the rending of the social safety nets in Clinton time will mean in harder times ahead. Now that he proposes to work north of Central Park, Bill Clinton won't have to stroll very far to find out.

2001

What Kerry Really Did in Vietnam

Alexander Cockburn and Jeffrey St. Clair

N HIS SENIOR YEAR AT YALE IN 1966 JOHN KERRY ENLISTED IN the U.S. Navy, with his actual induction scheduled for the summer, after his graduation. Already notorious among his contemporaries for his political ambition, he'd maneuvered himself into the top slot at the Yale political union, while also winning admission to the Skull and Bones secret society.

While Bush, two years behind Kerry, was seeking commercial opportunity at Yale by selling ounce bags of cocaine (so one contemporary has recalled), Kerry was keeping a vigilant eye on the political temperature and duly noted a contradiction between his personal commitment to go to war and the growing antiwar sentiment among the masses, some of whom he hoped would vote for him at a not too distant time.

It was a season for important decisions, and Kerry pondered his options amid the delights of a Skull and Bones retreat on an island in the St. Lawrence River. He duly decided to junk his speech on the theme of "life after graduation" and opted for a fiery denunciation of the war and of an LBJ. The speech was well received by the students and some professors. Most parents were aghast, though not Kerry's own mother and father.

Unlike Bill Clinton and George Bush, Kerry duly presented himself for military service. After a year's training he was assigned to the USS Gridley, deployed to the Pacific, probably carrying nuclear missiles. Beset by boredom, Kerry received the news that once of his best friends, Dickie Pershing, grandson of "Black Jack" Pershing had been killed in Vietnam. Kerry seethed with rage and yearned, as he put it years later to his biographer

Douglas Brinkley, for vengeance. (Brinkley's recently published and highly admiring bio, *A Tour of Duty: John Kerry and the Vietnam War*, offers many telling vignettes to an assiduous reader. It's based almost entirely on Kerry's diaries and letters of the time.)

Kerry engineered reassignment to the Swift boat patrol. In Vietnam, the Tet offensive had prompted a terrible series of search-and-destroy missions by the U.S.A., plus the assassination program known as Phoenix. As part of the U.S. Navy's slice of the action, Admiral Elmo Zumwalt and his sidekick Captain Roy "Latch" Hoffman had devised Operation Sea Lords in which the Swift boats would patrol the canals and secondary streams of the Mekong Delta, with particular emphasis on the areas near the Cambodian border. The basic plan, explicitly acknowledged by many Swift boat veterans, was to terrorize the peasants into turning against the National Liberation Front, a.k.a. Viet Cong. The entire area, except for certain designated "friendly villages," was a free fire zone, meaning the Americans could shoot at will and count anyone they killed as VC.

Arriving in Vietnam on November 17, 1968, Kerry chafed at patrols around Cam Ranh Bay and pushed successfully for assignment to the forward, killing patrols. He was no Al Gore, peaceably smoking dope and shooting hoops on his Army base in Vietnam and writing home fierce moral critiques of the war. "I was more opposed to the war than ever," Kerry told Brinkley in 2003, "yet more compelled by patriotism to fight it. I guess until you're in it, you still want to try it."

Day after day, night after night, the Swift boats plied the waters, harassing and often killing villagers, fishermen, and farmers. In this program, aimed at intimidating the peasants into submission, Kerry was notoriously zealous. One of his fellow lieutenants, James R. Wasser, described him admiringly in these words: "Kerry was an extremely aggressive officer and so was I. I liked that he took the fight to the enemy, that he was tough and gutsy—not afraid to spill blood for his country."

On December 2, Kerry went on his first patrol up one of the canals. It was near midnight when the crew caught sight of a sampan. Rules of engagement required no challenge, no effort to see who was on board the small boat. Kerry sent up a flare, signal for his crew to start blazing away with the boat's two machine guns and M-16 rifles. Kerry described the fishermen "running away like gazelles."

Kerry sustained a very minor wound to his arm, probably caused by debris from his own boat's salvoes. The scratch earned him his first Purple Heart, a medal awarded for those wounded in combat. Actually there's no evidence that anyone had fired back, or that Kerry had been in combat, as becomes obvious when we read an entry from his diary about a subsequent excursion, written on December 11, 1968, nine days after the incident that got Kerry his medal. "A cocky air of invincibility accompanied us up the Long Tau shipping channel, because we hadn't been shot at yet, and Americans at war who haven't been shot at are allowed to be cocky."

He got two more Purple Hearts, both for relatively minor injuries. Indeed, Kerry never missed a day of duty for any of the medal-earning wounds.

Craving more action, Kerry got himself deployed to An Thoi, at Vietnam's southern tip, one of the centers for the lethal Phoenix sweeps and the location of an infamous interrogation camp which held as many as 30,000 prisoners.

Kerry's first mission as part of the Phoenix program was to ferry a Provincial Reconnaissance Unit of South Vietnamese soldiers, which would have been led by either a Green Beret or CIA officer. After off-loading the unit, Kerry hid his Swift boat in a mangrove backwater. Two hours later a red flare told them that the PRU wanted an emergency "extraction." Kerry's boat picked up the PRU team, plus two prisoners. The leader of the PRU team told Kerry that while they were kidnapping the two villagers (one of them a young woman) from their hut, they'd seen four people in a sampan and promptly killed them. The two prisoners were "body-snatched" as part of a regular schedule of such seizures in the victims would be taken to An Thoi for interrogation and torture.

Kerry's term to Brinkley for such outings—and there were many in his brief—is "accidental atrocities."

On daylight missions, the Swift boats were accompanied by Cobra attack helicopters that would strafe the riverbanks and the skeletal forests, already ravaged by napalm and Agent Orange. "Helos upset the VC [sic, meaning anyone on the ground] more than anything else that we had to offer," Kerry tells Brinkley, "and any chance we had to have them with us was more than welcome."

An example of these Cobras in action: It's daylight, so the population is not under curfew. Kerry's boat is working its way up a canal, with a Cobra above it. They encounter a sampan with several people in it. The helicopter hovers right above the sampan, then empties its machine guns into it, killing everyone and sinking the sampan. Kerry, in his war diary, doesn't lament the deaths but does deplore the senselessness of the Cobra's crew in using all of its ammunition, since the chopper pilot "requested permission to leave in order to rearm, an operation that left us uncovered for more than 45 minutes in an area where cover was essential."

Christmas Eve, 1968, finds Kerry leading a patrol up a canal along the Cambodian border. The Christmas ceasefire has just come into effect. So what the boat was doing there is a question in and of itself. They spot two sampans and chase them to a small fishing village. The boat takes some sniper fire (or at least Kerry says it did). Kerry orders his machine-gunner, James Wasser, to open up a barrage. At last a note of contrition, but not from Kerry. Wasser describes to Brinkley how he saw that he'd killed an old man leading a water buffalo. "I'm haunted by that old man's face. He was just doing his daily farming, hurting nobody. He got hit in the chest with an M-60 machine-gun round. It may have been Christmas Eve, but I was real somber after that... to see the old man blown away sticks with you." It turned out that Kerry's boat had shot up one of the few "friendly" villages, with a garrison of South Vietnamese ARV soldiers, two of whom were wounded.

Contrast Wasser's sad reflections with Kerry's self-righteous account in his diary of such salvoes, often aimed into Cambodian territory. "On occasion we had shot towards the border when provoked by sniper or ambush, but without fail this led to a formal reprimand by the Cambodian government and accusations of civilian slaughters and random killings by American 'aggressors.' I have no doubt that on occasion some innocents were hit by bullets that were aimed in self-defense at the enemy, but of all the cases in Vietnam that could be labeled massacres, this was certainly the most spurious."

It's very striking how we never find, in any of Kerry's diaries or letters, the slightest expression of contrition or remorse—and Brinkley would surely have cited them had Kerry ever written such words. Nor did Kerry, in his later career as a self-promoting star of the antiwar movement, ever go beyond generalized verbiage about accidents of war, even as many vets were baring their souls about the horrors they had perpetrated.

It's not that he couldn't have summoned up for his audiences back then some awful episodes. For example, a few weeks after the incident on the Cambodian border Kerry's boat was heading up the Cua Lon River toward Square Bay, when one of the crew yelled "sampan off port bow." Kerry ordered the machine guns to fire on the fishing boat. The sampan stopped and Kerry and his crew boarded it. They found a woman holding an infant, and near her the body of her young child riddled with machine gun bullets, lying face down among bags of rice. Kerry tells Brinkley he refused to look at the dead child, saying, "the face would stay with me for the rest of my life and it was better not to know whether it was a smile or grimace or whether it was a girl or boy." Kerry's preferred mode is the usual one. "Our orders," he tells

Brinkley a few pages later, "were to destroy all the hooches [i.e., huts] and sampans we could find."

As part of Operation Sea Lords Kerry would ferry Nung tribesmen on assassination missions. The Nung were paid by the kill, and Kerry contrasts them favorably to the South Vietnamese PF guardsmen, derisively terming the latter "Cream Puffs." On one occasion, Kerry tells Brinkley, he ferried Nung to a village where they seized an old man and forced him to act as a human mine detector, walking ahead of them along the trail. There were no mines and the Nung encountered no enemy. But for the old man it was a one-way trip. The Nung slit his throat, disemboweled him, and left a warning note on his body.

When Kerry was awarded his Silver Star, he had it pinned on by Admiral Elmo Zumwalt and at the ceremony had the opportunity to meet Commander Adrian Lonsdale, the operational commander of Sea Lords. Kerry seized the chance to criticize the conduct of the war: "It's not that the men are afraid or chicken to go into the rivers," he says he told Lonsdale. "It's not that they're not willing to risk their lives, or that they don't agree with the principle of what's being done over here. It's just that they want to have a fair chance to do something that brings results and what they're doing now isn't bringing them anything. If we were to have some support, something that would guarantee that we were gaining something, but for a country with all the power that we have, we're making men fight in a fashion that defies reason.... What we need, Sir, are some troops to sweep through the areas and secure them after we leave; otherwise we're just going to be shot to hell after we go through, and there'll be nothing gained."

Yes, this is the same Kerry who today is calling for 40,000 more U.S. troops to be deployed to Iraq.

The incident that won U.S. Navy Lieutenant John Kerry his Silver Star, thus lofting him to the useful status of "war hero," occurred on February 28, 1969. His Swift boat was ferrying U.S. "explosives experts" and some South Vietnamese soldiers up the

Dong Cung River. After dropping them off, Kerry's boat came under small arms fire. Kerry turned the boat toward the source of the shots, beached the boat and opened up fire at the forest with the boat's .50 and .60 caliber machine guns.

By beaching the boat Kerry was disobeying standard orders forbidding this maneuver on the grounds that it made the craft and its crew a sitting duck. Kerry's motive? As crew member Michael "Duke" Medeiros explained it to Kerry's biographer, Douglas Brinkley, it was a matter of verifying kills. "We never knew whether we killed any VC or not. When fired upon, he [Kerry] wanted to beach the boat and go get the enemy."

The boat's machine guns had in fact killed a Vietnamese, described as "a VC guerilla," and they took evidence from the body.

The boat continued downstream and was fired on once more, by a rocket-propelled grenade launcher. Here's where accounts of the event diverge markedly, depending on the interests of the various narrators. The citation for Kerry's Silver Star describes the event this way: "With utter disregard for his own safety and the enemy rockets, he again ordered a charge on the enemy, beached his boat only ten feet from the VC rocket position, and personally led a landing party ashore in pursuit of the enemy. Upon sweeping the area, an immediate search uncovered an enemy rest and supply area which was destroyed. The extraordinary daring and personal courage of Lieutenant (junior grade) Kerry in attacking the numerically superior force in the face of intense fire were responsible for the highly successful mission."

This citation, issued by Admiral Elmo Zumwalt, was based on the incident report written by, yes, John Kerry. Missing from the Zumwalt version was a dramatic confrontation described by Kerry 27 years later in 1996, in the heat of a nasty re-election fight against Republican William Weld, when Kerry was seeking a third senate term. Kerry imparted to Jonathan Carroll, writing for the *New Yorker*, a story which went as follows: he had faced down a Viet Cong standing a few feet from him with a B-40 rocket launcher. "It was either going to be him or it was going to be us," Kerry told Carroll. "It was that simple. I don't know why it wasn't us—I mean, to this day. He had a rocket pointed right at our boat. He stood up out of that hole, and none of us saw him until he was standing in front of us, aiming a rocket right at us, and, for whatever reason, he didn't pull the trigger—he turned and ran. He was shocked to see our boat right in front him. If he'd pulled the trigger, we'd all be dead. I just won't talk about all of it. I don't and I can't. The things that probably really turn me I've never told anybody. Nobody would understand."

Kerry may not have wanted to talk but he certainly liked to screen. The first time Kerry took Hollywood star Dana Delany to his home in the Eighties, she says his big move was showing her video clips taken of him in the Navy when he was in Vietnam. She never went out with him again. (As he prepared to make his grand entry to the Democratic convention in Boston, stories circulated that Kerry had reenacted his skirmishes, filming them with an 8mm camera for later political use.)

Two of Kerry's crew members, Medeiros and machine-gunner Tommy Belodeau, found no mystery in why the VC soldier didn't fire his B-40 RPG launcher. The Vietnamese was effectively unarmed. He hadn't reloaded the RPG after the first shot at Kerry's boat as it headed down the river.

Later in that year of 1996 Belodeau described the full scope of the incident to the *Boston Globe*'s David Warsh. Belodeau told Warsh that he opened fire with his M-60 machine gun on the Vietnamese man at a range of ten feet after they'd beached the boat. The machine gun bullets caught the Vietnamese in the legs, and the wounded man crawled behind a nearby hooch. At this point, Belodeau said, Kerry had seized an M-16 rifle, jumped out of the boat, gone up to the man who Belodeau says was near death, and finished him off.

When the *Globe* published Warsh's account of Belodeau's recollection, essentially accusing Kerry of a war crime, the Kerry campaign quickly led Madeiros to the press and he described how the Vietnamese, felled by Belodeau's machine-gun fire, got up, grabbed the rocket launcher, and ran off down a trail through the forest and a disappeared around a bend. As Kerry set off after him, Medeiros followed. They came round the corner to find the Vietnamese once again pointing the RPG at them ten feet away. He didn't fire, and Kerry shot him dead with his rifle.

Circulating around veterans' websites in early February of 2004 was an email written by Mike Morrison who, like Kerry, won a Bronze Star in Vietnam. Morrison, who later went on to write speeches for Lee Iacocca, was highly suspicious of Kerry's claims to martial glory. In a letter to his brother Ed he wrote as follows:

> I've long thought that John Kerry's war record was phony. We talked about it when you were here. It's mainly been instinct because, as you know, nobody who claims to have seen the action he does would so shamelessly flaunt it for political gain.
>
> I was in the Delta shortly after he left. I know that area well. I know the operations he was involved in well. I know the tactics and the doctrine used. I know the equipment. Although I was attached to CTF-116 (PBRs) I spent a fair amount of time with CTF-115 (swift boats), Kerry's command.
>
> Here are my problems and suspicions:
>
> (1) Kerry was in-country less than four months and collected a Bronze Star, a Silver Star, and three Purple Hearts. I never heard of anybody with any outfit I worked with (including SEAL One, the Sea Wolves, Riverines and the River Patrol Force) collecting that much hardware so fast, and for such pedestrian actions. The Swifts did a commendable job. But that duty wasn't the worst you could draw. They operated only along the coast and in the major rivers (Bassac and Mekong). The rough stuff in the hot areas was mainly handled by the smaller, faster PBRs. Fishy.
>
> (2) Three Purple Hearts but no limp. All injuries so minor that no time lost from duty. Amazing luck. Or he was putting himself in for medals every time he bumped his head on the wheel house hatch? Combat on the boats was almost always at close range. You didn't have minor wounds. At least not often. Not three times in a row. Then he used the three Purple Hearts

to request a trip home eight months before the end of his tour. Fishy.

(3) The details of the event for which he was given the Silver Star make no sense at all. Supposedly, a B-40 (rocket-propelled grenade) was fired at the boat and missed. Charlie jumps up with the launcher in his hand, the bow gunner knocks him down with the twin .50 (caliber machine guns), Kerry beaches the boat, jumps off, shoots Charlie, and retrieves the launcher. If true, he did everything wrong. (a) Standard procedure when you took rocket fire was to put your stern to the action and go (away) balls to the wall. A B-40 has the ballistic integrity of a Frisbee after about 25 yards, so you put 50 yards or so between you and the beach and begin raking it with your .50s. (Did you ever see anybody get knocked down with a .50 caliber round and get up? The guy was dead or dying. The rocket launcher was empty. There was no reason to go after him (except if you knew he was no danger to you—just flopping around in the dust during his last few seconds on earth, and you wanted some derring-do in your after-action report). And we didn't shoot wounded people. We had rules against that, too.

Kerry got off the boat. This was a major breach of standing procedures. Nobody on a boat crew ever got off a boat in a hot area. EVER! The reason was simple. If you had somebody on the beach, your boat was defenseless. It couldn't run and it couldn't return fire. It was stupid and it put his crew in danger. He should have been relieved and reprimanded. I never heard of any boat crewman ever leaving a boat during or after a firefight.

Something is very fishy.

The account that makes sense to us is Belodeau's. There were three high-powered machine guns on the boat and one Vietnamese at close range on the land, and Belodeau says his machine gun knocked him down. Even if the Vietnamese fighter miraculously got up and started running away down that trail, is it likely that the two would have pursued him down an unknown path on foot? Wouldn't it be more likely that the boat would have used its machine guns again, blazing away as on Kerry's own account they did, day and day and night after night?

On March 13, 1969, two weeks after the episode that yielded the Silver Star, Kerry saw his last slice of action. It got him his

Bronze Star and his third Purple Heart, which meant he could file a request to be transferred out of Vietnam.

Kerry earned the Bronze Star by pulling another lieutenant out of the water after the latter's Swift boat had hit a mine. That same mine's detonation caused enough wake to throw Kerry against a bulkhead, bruising his arm. This was classed as a wound, which meant the third Purple Heart. Then, amid rifle fire, Kerry maneuvered his boat toward Lieutenant James Rassman and hoisted him onto the deck.

Both boats had been on yet another mission ferrying Green Berets, U.S. Navy SEALs, and Nung assassins to a village. Once again they had mistakenly targeted a friendly village, where they opened fire on South Vietnamese troops who were interrogating a group of women and children lined up against a wall.

When the Green Berets and SEALs opened fire, the South Vietnamese soldiers jumped the wall and at least ten of the women and children were killed. Meanwhile, against orders, Kerry had again left his boat and attached himself to the Nung and was, by his own words, "shooting and blowing things up." One of the Nung threw a grenade into a hut, which turned out to be filled with sacks of rice. Kerry got grains of rice and some bits of metal debris embedded in his ass, the most severe wounds he sustained in Vietnam.

With three Purple Hearts, the Silver and Bronze stars, Kerry now applied for reassignment as a personal aide to a senior officer in either Boston, New York, or Washington, D.C. He ended up in New York working for Admiral Walter F. Schlech. In January 1970 he applied for early discharge to run for office. As he put it, he'd decided not to join the antiwar movement but work within the system and try and win a seat in Congress from the Third District in Massachusetts.

A former assistant secretary of defense and Fletcher School of Diplomacy professor, W. Scott Thompson, recalled a conversation with the late Admiral Elmo R. Zumwalt Jr. that clearly had a slightly different take on Kerry's recollection of their discussions: "[T]he fabled and distinguished chief of naval operations, Admiral Elmo Zumwalt, told me—30 years ago when he was still CNO [chief naval officer in Vietnam] that during his own command of U.S. naval forces in Vietnam, just prior to his anointment as CNO, young Kerry had created great problems for him and the other top brass, by killing so many non-combatant civilians and going after other non-military targets. 'We had virtually to straitjacket him to keep him under control,' the admiral said. 'Bud' Zumwalt got it right when he assessed Kerry as having large ambitions—but promised that his career in Vietnam would haunt him if he were ever on the national stage."

2004

Murdoch's Game

Alexander Cockburn

"I have done the state some service, and they know't"—Othello.

I
T HAS BEEN ASTOUNDING THAT A WORLD-SCALE MONSTER SUCH
as Rupert Murdoch has thus far fared well at the hands of
his various profilists and biographers. Criticisms of him have
either been too broad-brush to be useful, or too tempered with
Waugh-derived facetiousness about press barons. Murdoch is
far too fearsome an affront to any civilized values to escape with
mere facetiousness.

Now, at last, Murdoch is properly burdened with the chroni-
cler he deserves. *The Murdoch Archipelago* (just published by
Simon and Schuster in the U.K.) is written by Bruce Page, a
distinguished, Australian-raised journalist who has lived and
worked in England for many years, perhaps best known for his
work in leading one of the great investigative enterprises of twentieth century journalism, the Insight team at the (pre-Murdoch)
London Sunday Times.

As an essay in understanding what the function of the press
should be in a democratic society, Page's book is an important
one, focused on one of the world's leading villains who controls
such properties as Fox in the U.S.A., huge slices of the press in
the U.K. and Australia, a TV operation in the Chinese Peoples
Republic. Most recently he's been in the news, because the
Federal Communications Commission, chaired by Colin Powell's
son Michael, rewarded Murdoch's tub-thumping for Bush by
voting 3-2 to allow his News Corp. to buy control of Hughes
Electronics and its DirecTV satellite operation from General

Motors in a deal valued at $6.6 billion. The FCC's green light will give Rupert Murdoch even more power in determining what material gets beamed to television sets across U.S.A. and how much consumers pay for them.

I had some brief and vivid personal encounters with Murdoch in the late 1970s at the *Village Voice* and I've known Page for many years. In the late 1960s I shared billing with him as one of the four helmsmen of the London-based Free Communications Group, whose manifesto about the media and democracy was set forth in the first issue of our very occasional periodical, *The Open Secret*. The other two helmsmen were Gus McDonald, latterly a Blair-ennobled Labor enforcer in the House of Lords, and Neal Ascherson, most recently the author of an interesting book, *Stone Voices: The Search for Scotland*.

I talked to Page about his book in London in mid-November in the midst of twin invasions of Bush and Murdoch, the latter briefly alighting in London to crush a rising by some shareholders in British Sky Broadcasting who had been claiming that the company was being run by Murdoch as a private fiefdom in a manner injurious to their interests.

It was a characteristic Murdoch performance, marked by his usual arrogance, thuggery, and deception. In one particularly spectacular act of corporate contempt, he first told the shareholders at the annual general meeting that Tony Ball moved over to make way for Murdoch's son James, had received no severance payment, and then revealed briefly thereafter that £10 million was being paid to Ball to make sure he would not compete with Sky's now non-existent rivals. The true function of the £10 million is more likely to ensure Ball's future discretion since the latter knows the whereabouts of many bodies whose disinterment might inconvenience Murdoch, throwing an unpleasing light on Sky's unfettered (by Blair's regulators) use of its Thatcher-derived monopoly.

Amid his rampages at BSkyB Murdoch gave an interview to the BBC in which he placed Tony Blair on notice that the loyalty of Murdoch's newspapers was not to be taken for granted.

Referring to himself respectfully in the first person plural, Murdoch was kind enough to intimate that "we will not quickly forget the courage of Tony Blair" but then made haste to emphasize that he also enjoys friendly relations with the new Tory leader Michael Howard.

On the mind of this global pirate is a topic in which one would have thought he would have had scant interest, namely, national sovereignty. Murdoch professed himself exercised by the matter of the EU constitution. Slipping on the mantle of Britishness, Murdoch pronounced, "I don't like the idea of any more abdication of our sovereignty in economic affairs or anything else."

The *Guardian* found this altogether too brazen and editorialized the following Monday that "Rupert Murdoch is no more British than George W. Bush. Once upon a time, it's true, he was an Australian with Scottish antecedents. But some time ago he came to the view that his citizenship was an inconvenience and resolved to change it for an American passport. He does not live in this country and it is not clear that he is entitled to use 'we' in any meaningful sense of shared endeavor. To be lectured on sovereignty by someone who junked his own citizenship for commercial advantage is an irony to which Mr. Murdoch is evidently blind."

Then the *Guardian* got a bit rougher: "Readers have to be put on notice that the view expressed in Murdoch titles have not been freely arrived at on the basis of normal journalistic considerations."

This brings me back to Page's book, whose core thesis is that Murdoch offers his target governments a privatized version of a state propaganda service, manipulated without scruple and with no regard for truth. His price takes the form of vast government favors such as tax breaks, regulatory relief (as with the recent FCC ruling on the acquisition of DirecTV), monopoly markets and so forth. The propaganda is undertaken with the utmost cynicism, whether it's the stentorian fake populism and soft porn in the U.K.'s *Sun* and *News of the World*, or shameless bootlicking of the butchers of Tiananmen Square.

I asked Page if he thought this a fair summary.

Page: "Your précis of my argument is exact. It may be worth noting that reviewers of *Archipelago* drawn from the still-persist-ent Old Fleetstrasse culture have (in the words of my old col-league Lew Chester) produced 'innumerable contortions devised to miss its main argument.' Peter Preston stated that 'Bruce' (we are *not* on first-name terms) failed to offer any thesis of how it was all done. Similarly Anthony Howard, who of course has worked many years under the Murdoch banner. You may recall the first three paragraphs of the book:

> Rupert Murdoch denies quite flatly that he seeks or deals in political favors 'Give me an example!' he cried in 1999 when William Shawcross interviewed him for *Vanity Fair*. 'When have we ever asked for anything?'
>
> Shawcross didn't take up the challenge. Rather, he endorsed Murdoch's denial, by saying that Rupert had never lied to him.
>
> We can show that Murdoch was untruthful—and Shawcross far too tolerant, both in the interview and in his weighty biog-raphy of Murdoch. Not only has Murdoch sought and received political favors: most of the critical steps in the transmuta-tion of News Limited, his inherited business, into present-day Newscorp were dependent on such things. Nor is there essential change in his operations as the new century gets under way, and he prepares his sons to extend the dynasty.

"I worked quite hard with the Simon & Schuster lawyers to make this so blunt as to show that anyone missing the point was practicing voluntary astigmatism.

"On sovereignty: my belief is that Murdoch and his like deeply fear every kind of collaboration between effective demo-cratic entities. They can exist only in an offshore domain from which they truck and barter with comprador elites. Sadly for them, there is an antagonistic tendency which every now and then makes crucial advances: if and when the OECD countries organize a viable tax system, Newscorp is toast. The U.S. and the EC have made more progress in that direction than is generally realized. Only crooks really like offshore, and crooks have no guaranteed monopoly over the world.

"Murdoch's ludicrous remarks on the BBC are a reminder that the whole brood constitutes a black hole for irony: as does the coronation of his son James. Murdoch rarely takes part in open democratic processes, as the results are too chancy for him. But the Australian referendum on the monarchy struck him as a sure thing, so he plunged in taking his boys with him. Now the failure of that campaign involved many complexities, but its root cause was that while the Oz working-class tradition (color it Irish) has no great love for Mrs. Windsor, it also doesn't think she has done much harm. But these same traditionalists noted that many riders on the republican bandwagon were practiced class malefactors, Rupert conspicuously so. In wonderful evidence of this, another of Murdoch's sons, Lachlan, stated that he could not see the justice of a system (i.e., monarchy) in which you got a job through inheritance alone.

"The Oz character has flaws like any other, but it is nearly impossible to be an Australian and have so devastating an incapacity for self-mockery.

"When I was asked in various TV and radio spots for comments on the James/BSkyB business, there was usually some question of whether there was abuse of power involved. My answer was to say, of course this is pure abuse of power. But such abuse is Newscorp's product: it's what the company sells. The purchasers, of course, are deluded politicians. It's absurd to fancy that Newscorp's internal affairs would be conducted on any other lines.

"On one radio show I was put up with a certain Teresa Wise of Accenture (formerly Andersen Consulting, limb of Rupert's defunct auditors). She purported to knot her brow over the question of Newscorp's governance, and produced one of the true standard lines:

"'It's very easy to demonize Mister Murdoch...' Into the sagacious pause which would clearly have been followed by a *laissez-passer*, I managed to insert: 'Can we have a little less of this? It is actually very difficult, and very hard work, to demonize Rupert. This is because he is in fact demonic, and he frightens a great many people in and around the media industries. Nobody should say how easy it is to demonize unless they have some working experience of the process.'

"We then had a period of silence from her.

"Murdoch often denies he is the world's most powerful media boss. There's a natural discretion in those who have unelected political influence: as their power lacks legitimacy, they prefer it to pass unnoticed. But it goes somewhat further in Murdoch's case. Though his Australian-based News Corporation controls newspapers and broadcasting networks to a unique extent, and the governments of America, Australia, Britain, and China treat him with great solicitude, Murdoch considers himself a simple entrepreneur ringed by relentless opponents.

"He is in reality the man who for whom Margaret Thatcher set aside British monopoly law so that he could buy the *Times* and the *Sunday Times*, and to whom she later handed monopoly control of British satellite television. His newspapers supported Thatcher with ferocious zeal—but switched eagerly to Tony Blair's side once it was clear that New Labour would leave Murdoch in possession of the marketplace advantages bequeathed by conservative predecessors. But Murdoch (who likes a royal plural) says: 'We are... not about protectionism through legislation and cronyism...'

"In similar transactions, Ronald Reagan's right-wing administration let Murdoch dynamite U.S. media laws and set up the Fox network and a left-wing Australian administration let him take monopoly control of the country's newspaper market. But to Murdoch, who thinks himself a victim of 'liberal totalitarians,' this is no less than he deserves. He observes no connection between the business concessions governments award to Newscorp and the support Newscorp affords to such benefactors —deep subservience in the case of China's totalitarian elite: 'We are about daring and doing for ourselves,' he believes."

Cockburn: "But surely he retains some sense of irony, of cynicism, when he professes such nonsense?"

Page: "In *Alice in Wonderland* the White Queen says she can believe 'six impossible things before breakfast,' but Murdoch easily outdoes her. Sigmund Freud's grandson Matthew, a celebrated London public-relations man, is married to Rupert's daughter Elisabeth and has said with surprise that his father-in-law actually believes the stuff in his own newspapers.

"We may be sure Mr. Freud is not so credulous. Nor are most people who know Newscorp's publications. The *London Sun* coins money. But opinion surveys show less than one in seven readers trust what it says (however diverting).

"In legend Murdoch has an infallible popular touch, displayed in escalating circulations. But the legend misleads somewhat: Murdoch is not commercially invincible in areas where governments can't help. The plinth of his British empire, the rigorously prurient *News of the World*, was selling more than six million copies when he bought it: since, half its sales have vanished, while other papers have gained. The *New York Post* consistently loses money, and most companies would close it.

"But central to it is the psychology of the Murdoch family, and the credulousness Matthew Freud diagnosed. Murdoch is the man who promoted the 'diaries' of Adolf Hitler, and today believes in Saddam Hussein's Weapons of Mass Destruction—scarcely more real, though the two dictators indeed share attributes.

"For politicians in Beijing, Washington, and London this psychology makes Mr. Murdoch an ideal media ally. They have illusions to peddle: Murdoch may be relied on to believe, and try to persuade others. Beijing, for instance, asserts that China cannot prosper except by accepting totalitarian Communist rule—ignoring, therefore, the Party's matchless record of criminal incompetence. Rupert's achievements here are notorious, but those of his son James hardly less. James' speech celebrating in Rupert's presence the 'strong stomach' which enables them both to admire Chinese repressive technique shocked even the rugged investors hearing it.

"It appears that Rupert considers James his successor, planning to give him command of BSkyB, the British satellite-TV broadcaster which Newscorp wants to link into a worldwide system. Such an advance in media power will require much political aid—that of the Bush administration particularly—and there is no supporter of Mr. Bush and his wars can outdo Rupert's enthusiasm."

Cockburn: "It's awful to think that we have younger Murdochs on hand to plague the planet for a few more decades."

Page: "Such psychology is a family tradition. Rupert inherited the basis of Newscorp from his Australian father Sir Keith Murdoch, a great propagandist in 1914–18 (the 'golden age of lying'). Purportedly an independent war correspondent, Keith Murdoch acted in fact as political agent to Billy Hughes, his country's wartime prime minister: plotting with him to conscript thousands of young men into a bloodbath supervised by incompetent British generals.

"The plot narrowly failed—as did an anti-Semitic intrigue against the Australian general John Monash, whose volunteer divisions broke the German line. Details are an Australian concern, but we should note the success with which Rupert's father later posed as an heroic rebel rescuing young men from ruthless generals: a pioneer feat of spin-doctoring and truth-inversion. Rupert's media still sustain his father Keith's mythology ('the journalist who stopped a war'). The son, born in 1931, has always lived in the shadow of a spurious hero, uncritically promoted.

"Just such narratives characterize the 'authoritarian personality,' identified by Theodor Adorno, and refined by later psychologists. Growth requires us all to make terms with our parents' real qualities—good or bad—and where that process fails, authoritarian qualities appear: intolerance of relationships other than dominion or submission, and intolerance of the ambiguity which equal standing implies. Such characteristics in Murdoch are shown by the testimony of many Newscorp veterans. Executives—editors specially—are ejected, regardless of quality, at a flicker of independence. Murdoch demands internally the same subservience he offers to outside power.

"Conformity is enforced by mind games like Murdoch's notorious telephone calls—coming to his executives at random moments, and consisting on his own part chiefly of brooding silence. The technique generates fear, and those who rebel against it are swiftly removed.

"Authoritarians often possess charm—or skill in flattery. But a strong component is swift, apparently decisive judgment: 'premature closure,' or jumping to conclusions. This explains the credulousness Adorno found in authoritarians, for penetrating complex truths usually demands some endurance of ambiguity."

Cockburn: "If the authoritarian personality is unsuited to realistic news-gathering, how has Murdoch achieved media pre-eminence?"

Page: "Journalists are insecure, because they must trade in the unknown. Their profession, said the sociologist Max Weber, is uniquely 'accident-prone.' Good management may reduce this insecurity—but the Newscorp style actually uses insecurity as a disciplinary tool. And the seeming assurance of the authoritarian has tactical benefits: Murdoch can swap one attitude for another with zero embarrassment, and it enables him to 'deliver' newspapers to any power he approves of. Readers naturally grow skeptical. But this does not yet harm Newscorp's business model.

"It would have been remarkable for Rupert to develop in nonauthoritarian fashion, given his inheritance. When his father died, he had neither graduated from university, nor gained any real newspaper tradecraft. In order to take control of what was then News Limited, under the trust Sir Keith established, Rupert had to accept his father as a paragon of journalistic integrity: to convince the trustees, believers in that myth, of his desire to emulate it. Exactly when independence is essential for personal and professional development, a spurious parental image descended on him. And he has emulated the political propagandist, not the mythological paragon.

"The outcome attracts today's politicians because a sickness afflicts them. In all developed societies trust in politics has declined: while democracy advances in the developing world, it finds itself ailing in its homelands. Finding themselves distrusted, politicians turn for a cure to tabloid journalism—Murdoch's especially—which they realize is distrusted still more than themselves. They do so just as victims of a slow, fatal disease use quack medicines if the real cure still seems too strenuous.

"The real problem of politics is the increasingly complex, and therefore occult nature of advanced society. We fancy it has become more open, and it somewhat has. But progress has fallen behind the needs of better-educated, less deferential citizens whose problems grow more daunting intellectually. The state for which politicians are responsible cannot explain itself to its citizens. It might change this by opening itself far more freely to scrutiny. But against this the bureaucrats—public and private—on whom politicians rely for administrative convenience conduct relentless guerrilla attack. Should politicians choose to fight back, they will not lack allies, for most Western societies still have some competent, independent news media and the demand exists among citizens. In Britain, real newspapers and broadcasters like the BBC continue to be trusted as Murdoch's tabloids will never be. But quack remedies still appeal to governments: and all Murdoch asks in return is a little help in extending his monopolies.

"Of course if the process goes far enough, only the quack remedy will be available, and democracy's ailment would then be terminal."

2003

Hitchens and The New Yorker

Alexander Cockburn

ODAY, OCTOBER 11, 2006, THE PUBLIC HEALTH DEPARTMENT at Johns Hopkins has released a new study of deaths in Iraq, based on a sample of the population. Around 600,000 have died in Iraq since the U.S. attacked in the spring of 2003. This terrible number won't come as a surprise to readers of the *CounterPunch* website. Back on January 9, 2006, we published a piece by Andrew Cockburn reviewing the first Johns Hopkins study, done last year. With the help of statistics expert Pierre Sprey, Andrew recomputed the raw numbers assembled by the Johns Hopkins team and their researchers and samplers in Iraq. He began thus:

> President Bush's off-hand summation last month (December 2005) of the number of Iraqis who have so far died as a result of our invasion and occupation as "30,000, more or less" was quite certainly an under-estimate. The true number is probably hitting around 180,000 by now, with a possibility, as we shall see, that it has reached as high as half a million.

I turned from headlines about the disintegration of Iraq amid ghastly carnage to a profile of Christopher Hitchens in the current *New Yorker* by Ian Parker. It was fairly obvious from the start that this was going to be a fawning piece of work. David Remnick, the *New Yorker*'s editor, is certainly not going to sponsor any determined unkindness about one of the prime journalistic war-boosters. Back in 2002, the *New Yorker* published a very influential piece of claptrap about Saddam's ties to Osama bin Laden by Jeffrey Goldberg, later exposed as a fraud. The *New Yorker* has never apologized for that.

Here is the entire email traffic—our sole form of communication—between Parker and me, starting in September 20 and ending ten days later. I've put the quotes Parker and his editor ended up using in the *New Yorker* in **bold type**.

Ian Parker to Alexander Cockburn

> Dear Alexander Cockburn
>
> I'm sorry to bother you. I'm writing a profile of Christopher Hitchens for the *New Yorker*, and I was wondering if you might spare me a few minutes, by phone or email.
>
> I do hope to hear from you.
>
> With thanks and best wishes,
>
> Ian Parker
>
> ———

AC to Parker

> Hello there Ian,
>
> I'd be happy to answer your questions. I'm on the road at the moment, about to drive back from South Carolina to the Pacific Northwest. It might be easier to have some email exchanges. I'll be reading email every day (I hope). So fire away.
>
> Best Alexander C
>
> ———

Parker to AC

> Many thanks. It's good to hear from you. Here goes: What happened to Christopher Hitchens?
>
> Thanks, Ian.

——

AC to Parker

Hello Ian, Sorry for pause; there have been a couple of mechanical crises. I write this from southeastern Utah. But what an odd question. Nothing happened to Christopher Hitchens. Best Alex C

——

Parker to AC

Hi. I suppose I meant: You were friends and allies, and now you're not; how would you describe what happened in between?

——

AC to Parker

Okay, I thought you were asking about some supposed change in Hitchens, often presumed to have started in the period he tried to put his friend Blumenthal behind bars for imputed perjury. If that had been the question, as it so often is, my answer is always that CH has been pretty much the same package since the beginning—always allowing for the ravages of entropy as the years pass.

As so often with friends and former friends, it's a matter of what you're prepared to put up with and for how long. I suppose I met him in the early 1980s and all the long-term political and indeed personal traits were visible enough. I never thought of him as at all radical. In basic philosophical take he has always seemed to me to hold as his central premise a profound belief in the therapeutic properties of capitalism and empire. He was an instinctive flagwagger and has remained so. He wrote some disgusting stuff in the early 90s about how indigenous peoples—Indians in the Americas—were inevitably going to be rolled over by the wheels of Progress and should not be mourned. That's when I stopped having much intellectual or moral respect for him, as I told many people and probably him at the time, though our personal relations remained fairly amiable for a few years longer.

On the smaller plane of weekly columns, in the late Eighties and Nineties it mostly seemed to be a matter of what was currently obsessing him: for years in the 80s he wrote scores, maybe hundreds of columns, charging that the Republicans had stolen the 1980s election by the "October surprise," denying Carter the advantage of a hostage release. He got terribly boring. Then in the 90s he got this mad bee in his bonnet about Clinton which developed into full-blown obsessive megalomania: the dream that he, Hitchens, would be the one to seize history's mallet and finish off Bill. Why did Bill—a zealous and fairly efficient executive of Empire—bother Hitchens so much? I'm not sure. He used to hint that Clinton had behaved abominably to some woman he, Hitchens, knew—maybe his wife Carol. I don't know or care. You can't believe anything Hitchens says anyway. He's always been a terrible fibber. Actually, I think **he'd got to that moment in life when he was asking himself if he could Make a Difference. He obviously thought he could, and so he sloshed his way across his own personal Rubicon and tried to topple Clinton via betrayal of his close friendship** with Sid Blumenthal, whom he did his best to ruin financially (lawyers' fees) and get sent to the joint for perjury. That's when I drew the line and said to myself, To hell with him, and wrote harshly about him in a column for *New York Press*.

Since then it's all been pretty predictable, down to his present role as semi-coherent flagwagger for Bush, making a fool of himself on the talk shows. I think he knew long,

long ago that this is where he would end up, as a right-wing codger. He used to go on, back in the 1980s, about sodden old wrecks like John Braine, who'd ended up more or less where Hitchens is now, trumpeting away like a Cheltenham colonel in some ancient *Punch* cartoon. I used to warn my left-wing friends at *New Left Review* and Verso Books in the early 90s who were happy to make money off Hitchens' books on Mother Teresa and the like that they should watch out, but they didn't and then kept asking ten years later, What happened? I've told you my views on that. Anyway, **between the two of them, my sympathies were always with Mother Teresa. If you were sitting in rags in a gutter in Mumbai, who would be more likely to give you a bowl of soup?** You'd get one from Mother Teresa. Hitchens was always tight with beggars, just like the snotty Fabians who used to deprecate charity. That's the basic problem. His moral and intellectual life has been expressed in postures which, on anything more than deeply indulgent inspection, turn out to be either unalluring or deeply disgusting.

Those are some thoughts, on a nice sunny morning, looking at Thousand Lakes Mountain from a 1970 Airstream in southeast Utah. If you have further questions, fire away. Best, Alexander C.

————

Parker to AC

Dear Alexander, Many thanks for this, it's kind of you to take the trouble, and I'm sorry to be slow to get back to you; I'm uncomfortably close to my deadline—and envying you your Utah landscape. Is it ok to quote from this? Maybe your comment about Mother Theresa and soup, and the "Make a Difference" observation, and perhaps more besides? (If I quote you on Mother T, can I move it from Mumbai to Calcutta, just to head off the letter-writers?)

All best wishes, Ian

———

AC to Parker

Ian, Yes you can quote it, but though he recently confirmed publicly that I am right about his long-term consistency, I hope you don't swerve past that basic point about his profound belief in capitalism and empire. Send me what you use. I don't want to end up with one crack about Mother Teresa, in Calcutta or Bombay. Best AC

———

Parker to AC

Yes, I'll check back with you. Sorry to make this seem a bit of a quote-hunt—I'm doing this piece a little too quickly. Best, Ian

———

And finally, AC to Parker, September 30.

I should allude to one more particularly despicable piece of opportunism on Hitchens' part, namely his decision to attack Edward Said just before his death, and then for good measure again in his obituary. That is in some ways even lower than the treachery towards Blumenthal. With his attacks on Edward, especially the final post mortem, Hitchens couldn't even claim the pretense of despising a corrupt presidency, a rapist and liar or any of the other things CH called Clinton. That final attack on Said was purely for attention—which fuels his other attacks but this one most starkly because of the absence of any high principle to invoke. Here he decided both to bask in his former friend's fame, recalling the little moments that made it clear he was intimate with the Great Man, and to put himself at the center of the spotlight by taking his old friend down a few notches. In a career of awful moves, that was one of the worst.

No answer from Parker. Nothing about CH's behavior to Said in the profile.

The profile is servile. Hitchens' modest arsenal of quotations from the Oxford Book of English Poetry becomes "his vast stock of remembered English poetry." Hitchens' brutish misogyny does peek through, in the form of a stream of foul-mouthed abuse during a dinner in San Francisco. The most ludicrous moment is the reverent evocation by Paul Wolfowitz's aide Kevin Kellems of a meeting between Hitchens and Wolfowitz as one in which there were "two giant minds unleashed in the room. They were finishing each other's sentences."

The second most ludicrous moment is Parker's excited quote from Hitchens, portraying himself as a Hemingway of the kitchen garden as he confronts "Jihadism:" "You know, recognizing an enemy—it's not just your mental cortex. Everything in you *physically* conditions you to realize that this means no good, like when you see a copperhead coming towards you. It's basic: it lives or I do."

Parker sees no irony in citing Hitchens as regarding Tom Paine as a prime hero, immediately following this by quoting Hitchens as saying how he wished he had been in Baghdad to join in the exultation over the killing of Saddam Hussein's sons, Uday and Qusay. Paine was a humane man, and nearly lost his head to the guillotine because he had publicly counseled against the execution of Louis XVI.

Being English, Parker has the class obsessions of his race, and does enter a diligent corrective to the notion, promoted with increasing confidence by Hitchens down the years, that he is from the upper classes. I'd been awaiting a retrospective entry into *Burke's Peerage*, but Parker notes carefully that Hitchens' father was from "a working-class family" and his mother "from a lower-middle-class Liverpudlian family."

He doesn't deserve them, but think what Hazlitt or even, from one of the writers in the pre-World War II *New Yorker*, could have done with this seedy character, the last man on the deck of America's Titanic, the war in Iraq.

2006

The Row Over the Israel Lobby

Alexander Cockburn

THIS SPRING OF 2006 A SOMETIMES-COMIC DEBATE HAS SIM-
mering in the American press, focused on the question
of whether there is an Israeli Lobby, and if so, just how
powerful is it?

I would have thought that to ask whether there's an Israeli
Lobby here is a bit like asking whether there's a Statue of
Liberty in New York Harbor and a White House located at 1600
Pennsylvania Avenue, Washington, D.C. For the past sixty years,
the Lobby has been as fixed a part of the American scene as
either of the other two monuments, and not infrequently exercising as much if not more influence on the onward march of
history.

The late Steve Smith, brother-in-law of Teddy Kennedy and a
powerful figure in the Democratic Party for several decades, liked
to tell the story of how a group of four Jewish businessmen got
together two million dollars in cash and gave it to Harry Truman
when he was in desperate need of money amidst his presidential
campaign in 1948. Truman went on to become president and to
express his gratitude to his Zionist backers.

Since those days the Democratic Party has long been hospita-
ble to and supported by rich Zionists. In 2002, for example, Haim
Saban, the Israel-American who funds the Saban Center at the
Brooking Institute and is a big contributor to AIPAC, gave $12.3
million to the Democratic Party. In 2001, the magazine *Mother
Jones* listed on its website the 400 leading contributors to the 2000
national elections. Seven of the first 10 were Jewish, as were 12
of the top 20 and 125 of the top 250. Given this, all prudent can-

didates have gone to amazing lengths to satisfy their demands. There have been famous disputes, as between President Jimmy Carter and Menachem Begin, and famous vendettas, as when the Lobby destroyed the political careers of Representative Paul Findley and of Senator Charles Percy because they were deemed to be anti-Israel.

None of this history is particularly controversial, and there have been plenty of well-documented accounts of the activities of the Israel Lobby down the years, from Alfred Lilienthal's 1978 study, *The Zionist Connection*, to former U.S. Rep. Paul Findley's 1985 book *They Dare To Speak Out* to *Dangerous Liaison: The Inside Story of the U.S.-Israeli Covert Relationship*, written by my brother and sister-in-law, Andrew and Leslie Cockburn, and published in 1991.

Three years ago, the present writer and Jeffrey St. Clair published a collection of 18 essays called *The Politics of Anti-Semitism*, no less than four of which were incisive discussions of the Israel Lobby. Jeffrey St. Clair described how the Lobby had successfully stifled any public uproar after Israeli planes attacked a U.S. Navy ship in the Mediterranean in 1967 and killed 34 U.S. sailors with 174 left injured, many seriously. Kathy and Bill Christison, former CIA analysts, reviewed the matter of dual loyalty, with particular reference to the so-called neocons, alternately advising an Israeli prime minister and an American president. Jeffrey Blankfort offered a detailed historical chronology of the occasions on which the Lobby had thwarted the plans of U.S. presidents including Carter, Reagan, Ford, and Bush Sr.

Most vividly of all in our book, a congressional aide, writing pseudonymously under the name George Sutherland, contributed a savagely funny essay called "Our Vichy Congress." Some extracts:

> For expressions of sheer groveling subservience to a foreign power, the pronouncements of Laval and Petain pale in comparison to the rhetorical devotion with which certain congressmen have bathed the Israel of Ariel Sharon.... Command performanc-

es before AIPAC [the American Israel Public Affairs Committee, a leading organization in the overall Israel Lobby] have become standard features in the life of a Washington elected official... The stylized panegyrics delivered at the annual AIPAC meeting have all the probative value of the Dniepropetrovsk Soviet's birthday greeting to Stalin, because the actual content is unimportant; what is crucial is that the politician in question be seen to be genuflecting before the AIPAC board. In fact, to make things easier, the speeches are sometimes written by an AIPAC employee, with cosmetic changes inserted by a member of the senator's or congressman's own staff.

Of course, there are innumerable lobbies in Washington, from environmental to telecommunications to chiropractic; why is AIPAC different? For one thing, it is a political action committee that lobbies expressly on behalf of a foreign power; the fact that it is exempt from the Foreign Agents' Registration Act is yet another mysterious "Israel exception." For another, it is not just the amount of money it gives, it is the political punishment it can exact... Since the mid-1980s, no member of Congress has even tried to take on the Lobby directly. As a Senate staffer told this writer, it is the "cold fear" of AIPAC's disfavor that keeps the politicians in line.

As year chases year, the Lobby's power to influence Congress on any issue of importance to Israel grows inexorably stronger.... Israel's strategy of using its influence on the American political system to turn the U.S. national security apparatus into its own personal attack dog—or Golem—has alienated the United States from much of the Third World, has worsened U.S. ties to Europe amid rancorous insinuations of anti-Semitism, and makes the United States a hated bully. And by cutting off all diplomatic lines of retreat—as Sharon did when he publicly made President Bush, the leader of the Free World, look like an impotent fool— Israel paradoxically forces the United States to draw closer to Israel because there is no thinkable alternative for American politicians than continuing to invest political capital in Israel.

So it can scarcely be said that there had been silence here about the Israel Lobby until two respectable professors, John J. Mearsheimer and Stephen M. Walt (the former from the University of Chicago and the latter from Harvard) offered their analysis in March of 2006. Their paper, "The Israel Lobby and

U.S. Foreign Policy," being published in longer form by the Kennedy School at Harvard (which has since disowned it) and, after it had been rejected by the *Atlantic Monthly* (which originally commissioned it), in shorter form by the *London Review of Books*.

In fact, the significance of this essay rests mostly on timing (three years' worth of public tumult about the neocons and Israel's role in the attack on Iraq) and on the provenance of the authors, from two of the premier academic institutions of the United States. Neither of them has any tincture of radicalism.

After the paper was published in shortened form in the *London Review of Books*, there was a brief lull, broken by the howls of America's most manic Zionist, Professor Alan Dershowitz of Harvard, who did Mearshseimer and Walt the great favor of thrusting their paper into the headlines. Dershowitz managed this by his usual eruptions of hysterical invective, investing the paper with the fearsome allure of that famous anti-Semitic tract, a forgery of the Czarist police, *The Protocols of the Elders of Zion*. The Mearsheimer-Walt essay was Nazi-like, Dershowitz howled, a classic case of conspiracy mongering, in which a small band of Zionists were accused of steering the Ship of Empire onto the rocks.

In fact, the paper by Mearsheimer and Walt is extremely dull. The long version runs to 81 pages, no less than 40 pages of which are footnotes. I settled down to read it with eager anticipation but soon found myself looking hopefully for the end. There's nothing in the paper that any moderately well-read student of the topic wouldn't have known long ago, but the paper has the merit of stating rather blandly some home truths which are somehow still regarded as too dangerous to state publicly in respectable circles in the United States.

For example, on the topic of what is often called here "America's only democratic ally in the Middle East," Mearsheimer and Walt have this to say:

The 'shared democracy' rationale is also weakened by aspects of Israeli democracy that are at odds with core American values. The United States is a liberal democracy where people of any race, religion, or ethnicity are supposed to enjoy equal rights. By contrast, Israel was explicitly founded as a Jewish state and citizenship is based on the principle of blood kinship. Given this conception of citizenship, it is not surprising that Israel's 1.3 million Arabs are treated as second-class citizens, or that a recent Israeli government commission found that Israel behaves in a neglectful and discriminatory manner towards them. Similarly, Israel does not permit Palestinians who marry Israeli citizens to become citizens themselves, and does not give these spouses the right to live in Israel. The Israeli human rights organization B'Tselem called this restriction a racist law that determines who can live here according to racist criteria. Such laws may be understandable given Israel's founding principles, but they are not consistent with America's image of democracy. Israel's democratic status is also undermined by its refusal to grant the Palestinians a viable state of their own. Israel controls the lives of about 3.8 million Palestinians in Gaza and the West Bank, while colonizing lands on which the Palestinians have long dwelt. Israel is formally democratic, but the millions of Palestinians that it controls are denied full political rights and the "shared democracy" rationale is correspondingly weakened.

After Dershowitz came other vulgar outbursts, such as from Eliot Cohen in the *Washington Post*. These attacks basically reiterated Dershowitz's essential theme: there is no such thing as the Israel Lobby and those asserting its existence are by definition anti-Semitic.

This method of assault at least has the advantage of being funny, because there obviously is a Lobby—as noted above and because Mearsheimer and Walt aren't anti-Semites any more than 99.9 per cent of others identifying the Lobby and criticizing its role. Partly as a reaction to Dershowitz and Cohen, the *Washington Post* and *New York Times* have now run a few pieces politely pointing out that the Israel Lobby has indeed exercised a chilling effect on the rational discussion of U.S. foreign policy. The tide is turning slightly.

Meanwhile, mostly on the left, there has been an altogether different debate, over the actual weight of the Lobby. Here the best known of the debaters is Noam Chomsky, who has reiterated a position he has held for many years, to the general effect that U.S. foreign policy has always hewed to the national self-interest, and that the Lobby's power is greatly overestimated. The debate was rather amusingly summed up by the Israeli writer Yuri Avnery, a former Knesset member:

> I think that both sides are right (and hope to be right, myself, too). The findings of the two professors are right to the last detail. Every senator and congressman knows that criticizing the Israeli government is political suicide.... If the Israeli government wanted a law tomorrow annulling the Ten Commandments, 95 U.S. Senators (at least) would sign the bill forthwith....
>
> The question, therefore, is not whether the two professors are right in their findings. The question is what conclusions can be drawn from them. Let's take the Iraq affair. Who is the dog? Who the tail?...
>
> The lesson of the Iraq affair is that the American-Israeli connection is strongest when it seems that American interests and Israeli interests are one (irrespective of whether that is really the case in the long run). The U.S.A. uses Israel to dominate the Middle East; Israel uses the U.S.A. to dominate Palestine.
>
> But if something exceptional happens, such as the Jonathan Pollard espionage affair or the sale of an Israeli spy plane to China, and a gap opens between the interests of the two sides, America is quite capable of slapping Israel in the face.

Will the debate roused by the Mearsheimer-Walt paper continue? I think so, if only because in the era of George Bush the influence of the Israel lobby and of the Christian Zionists has become so crudely overt.

And as Avnery concludes, far more colorfully than the two professors:

> American-Israeli relations are indeed unique. It seems that they have no precedent in history. It is as if King Herod had given orders to Augustus Caesar and appointed the members of the Roman senate.

I have to say I'm not 100 per cent on board with Chomsky on this one. The Lobby really does have very hefty clout. Ask Gerald Ford, Jimmy Carter, Ronald Reagan, and Bush Sr. In her excellent book, *The One-State Solution*, Virginia Tilley makes a persuasive case that the U.S. strategy and tactics in Iraq have more to do with what Israel wants than any self-interested "realist" U.S. plan.

2006

Palestine Down the Decades

Alexander Cockburn

THE FIRST ITEM I EVER WROTE ABOUT PALESTINIANS WAS around 1973, when I was just starting a press column for a New York weekly called the *Village Voice*. It concerned a story in the *New York Times* about a "retaliatory" raid by the Israeli air force, after a couple of Al Fatah guerillas had fired on an IDF unit. I'm not sure whether there were any fatalities. The Israeli planes flew north and dumped high explosive on a refugee camp in Lebanon, killing a dozen or so men, women, and children.

I wrote a little commentary, noting the usual lack of moral disquiet in the *Times'* story about this lethal retaliation inflicted on innocent refugees. Dan Wolf, the *Voice*'s editor, called me in and suggested I might want to reconsider. I think, that first time, the item got dropped. But Dan's unwonted act of censorship riled me, and I started writing a fair amount about the lot of the Palestinians.

These were the days when Palestinians carried far less news value for editors than Furbish's lousewort, and no politician ever held that this beleaguered plant didn't actually exist as a species, which is what Golda Meir, Israel's prime minister said of Palestinians.

Back then you had to dig a little harder to excavate what Jewish Israelis were actually doing to Palestinians. Lay out the facts about institutionalized racism, land confiscations, torture and a hail of abuse would pour through the mailbox, as when I published a long interview in the *Voice* in 1980 with the late Israel Shahak, the intrepid professor from Hebrew University.

It's slightly eerie now to look at what Shahak was saying back then and at the accuracy of his analysis and predictions: "The basic trends were established in '74 and '75, including settler organizations, mystical ideology, and the great financial support of the United States to Israel. Between summer '74 and summer '75 the key decisions were taken, and from that time it's a straight line." Among these decisions, said Shahak, was "to keep the occupied territories of Palestine," a detailed development of much older designs consummated in 1967.

Gradually, through the 1980s, very often in the translations from the Hebrew language press that Shahak used to send, the contours of the Israeli plan emerged, like the keel and ribs and timbers of an old ship: a road system that would bypass Palestinian towns and villages and link the Jewish settlements and military posts; ever-expanding clusters of settlements; a master plan for control of the whole region's water.

It wasn't hard to get vivid descriptions of the increasingly intolerable conditions of life for Palestinians: the torture of prisoners, the barriers to the simplest trip, the harassment of farmers and school children, the house demolitions. Plenty of people came back from Israel and the occupied territories with harrowing accounts, though few of them ever made the journey into a major newspaper or onto national TV.

And even in the testimonies that did get published here, what was missing was any acknowledgement of the long-term plan to wipe the record clean of all troublesome U.N. resolutions, crush Palestinian national aspirations, steal their land and water, cram them into ever smaller enclaves, ultimately balkanize them with the Wall, which was on the drawing board many years ago. Indeed, to write about any sort of master plan was to incur further torrents of abuse for one's supposedly "paranoid" fantasies about Israel's bad faith, with much pious invocation of the "peace process."

But successive Israeli governments did have a long-term plan. No matter who was in power, the roads got built, the water stolen, the olive and fruit trees cut down (a million), the houses knocked over (12,000), the settlements imposed (300), the shameless protestations of good faith issued to the U.S. press (beyond computation).

As the new millennium shambled forward, surely it became impossible to believe any Israeli claim to be bargaining, or even to wish to bargain in good faith. By now the "facts on the ground" in Israel and the territories were as sharply in focus as one of Dali's surrealist paintings.

In May 2006 the Israeli prime minister, Ehud Olmert, comes to Washington and addresses a joint session of Congress in which he declares: "I believed, and to this day still believe, in our people's eternal and historic right to this entire land." In other words he doesn't recognize the right of Palestinians to even the wretched cantons currently envisaged in his "realignment." Why should Hamas believe a syllable of Olmert's poppycock? When Arafat and the PLO gave worrisome signs of being eager for an accommodation, Israel's reply was to invade Lebanon.

In Olmert's "realignment plan," the "Separation Barrier," now scheduled to be Israel's permanent "demographic border," annexes 10 per cent of the West Bank, while melding into Israel vast settlements and half a million settlers. The Palestinians lose their best agricultural land and the water. Israel's greater Jerusalem finishes off all possible viability for a viable, separate Palestinian state. This Palestinian mini-archipelago of cantons is shuttered to the east by Israel's security border in the Jordan Valley.

The press here, timid and ignorant, greets Olmert's "realignment" with tranquil respect. In the meantime a frightful historical tragedy is in its final chapters. With the connivance of what is sometimes laughably referred to as the "world community"—notably the U.S. and EU, Israel is deliberately starving Palestinians into submission as the reward for having democratically elected the party of their choice. Whole communities are on the edge of starvation, cut off by Israel from food and medicines.

The World Bank predicts a poverty rate of over 67 per cent later this year. A U.N. Report issued in Geneva on May 30, 2006, says that four out of 10 Palestinians in the territories live under the official poverty line of less than $2.10 a day. The ILO estimates the jobless rate to be 40.7 per cent of the Palestinian labor force.

The end of the story? I'd say the basic Israeli strategy is what it was in 1948: population transfer, to be achieved by making life so awful for Palestinians that most of them will depart, leaving a few bankrupt ghettoes behind as memorials to all those foolish hopes of a sovereign Palestinian state. But of course no population would thus voluntarily annul its national existence, however hard the Israelis may try to persuade the Palestinians to do just that.

2006

The Left and the Blathersphere

Alexander Cockburn

THE WAR GRINDS ON, BUT THE DEMOCRATS PREFER TO TALK about other matters, such as the fact that Karl Rove is not going to be indicted. Thank God the left will have to talk about something else for a change. As a worthy hobbyhorse for the left, the whole Plame scandal has never made any sense. What was it all about in the first analysis? Outing a CIA employee. What's wrong with that? Many years ago a man came into the offices of the *New Left Review* in London where I was manning the portcullis at the time and said his name was Philip Agee and he wanted to write a book about the CIA. Did we call for a special prosecutor to have this fellow hauled over the coals? No, we did not.

Rove has swollen in the left's imagination like a descendant of Pere Ubu, Jarry's surreal monster. There was no scheme so deviously diabolical but that the hand of Rove could not be detected at work. Actually the man has always been of middling competence. He makes Dickie Morris look like Cardinal Richelieu.

Since 9/11 where has been the good news for the administration? It's been a sequence of catastrophes of unexampled protraction. Under Rove's deft hand, George Bush has been maneuvered into one catastrophe after another. Count the tombstones: "Bring it on," "Mission Accomplished," the sale of U.S. port management to Arabs. It was Rove who single-handedly rescued the antiwar movement last July by advising Bush not to give Cindy Sheehan fifteen minutes of face time at his ranch in Crawford.

And when Rove's disastrous hand is wrenched from the steering wheel, it passes to another bugaboo of the left, in the form of Dick Cheney. It was the imbecilic vice president who gave Jack Murtha traction last October when the Democrats were trying cold shoulder him for calling for instant withdrawal from Iraq. In his wisdom, the draft-dodging Cheney insulted the bemedaled former drill instructor as a clone of Michael Moore, and had to apologize three days later.

Rove and Cheney, the White House's answer to Bouvard and Pecuchet, are counselors who have driven George Bush into the lowest ratings of any American president. Yet the left remains obsessed with their evil powers. Is there any better testimony to the vacuity and impotence of the endlessly touted "blogosphere" which in mid June had twin deb balls in the form of the Yearly Kos convention in Las Vegas and the "Take America Back" folk-moot of "progressive" MoveOn Democrats in Washington, D.C.?

In political terms the blogosphere is like white noise, insistent and meaningless, like the wash of Pacific surf I can hear most days. But MoveOn.Org and Daily Kos have been hailed as the emergent form of modern politics, the target of excited articles in the *New York Review of Books*.

Beyond raising money swiftly handed over to the gratified veterans of the election industry, both MoveOn and Daily Kos have had zero political effect, except as a demobilizing force.

The effect on writers is horrifying. Talented people feel they have produce 400 words of commentary every day and you can see the lethal consequences on their minds and style, both of which turn rapidly to mush. They glance at the *New York Times* and rush to their laptops to rewrite what they just read. Hawsers to reality soon fray and they float off, drifting zeppelins of inanity. (In December 2006, the president of Google disclosed that the average readership of a blog is 1.3 people a day. In other words, the blogger daily and one other person every three days.)

Take Truthout, the site identified with William Rivers Pitt and Mark Ash. After months and months of obsessive bloggings about the Plame scandal, Truthout contributor Jason Leopold declared on May 13, 2006, that Karl Rove had been indicted on charges of perjury and lying to investigators. Leopold cited "sources" averring that prosecutor Fitzgerald had met for 15 hours with Rove's lawyer, Robert Luskind, that Rove had told Bush and his chief of staff Joshua Bolton that he was about to be indicted.

"Details of Rove's discussions with the President and Bolton," Leopold confided, "have spread through the corridors of the White House, where low-level staffers and senior officials were trying to determine how the indictment would impact an administration that has been mired in a number of high profile political scandals for nearly a year." As his secret confidantes the apparently omniscient Leopold invoked "a half dozen White House aides and two senor officials who work at the Republican National Committee."

In the days that followed, came immediate, categorical denials from Rove's lawyer and the White House. The week progressed with no indictment. It looked as though Truthout would have to sponge the egg off its face. Truthout did nothing of the sort, insisting as vehemently as any lunatic claiming abduction by aliens that it stuck by its story.

On June 12, Leopold even raised the ante: "Four weeks ago, during the time when we reported that White House political advisor Karl Rove was indicted for crimes related to his role in the leak of CIA operative Valerie Plame Wilson, the grand jury empanelled in the case returned an indictment that was filed under seal in U.S. District Court for the District of Columbia under the curious heading of Sealed versus Sealed." This, Leopold wrote, could be well mean the Rove indictment.

Rarely has a story been more swiftly and conclusively undercut. Later that same day Prosecutor Fitzgerald formally advised Rove's lawyer that he did not anticipate seeking charges against Rove. Truthout's reaction? On June 13, Truthout's chief editor, Mark Ash, told a reporter that they were sticking by their story and that Rove's non-indictment was "directly contradicted by the information we have."

Only two days later did Ash reluctantly strike his colors, confiding to Truthout's punch drunk audience, "Obviously there is a major contradiction between our version of the story and what was reported yesterday. As such, we are going to stand down on the Rove matter at this time. We defer instead to the nation's leading publications."

Game to the end, Ash added defiantly, "In that Mr. Luskin has chosen the commercial press as his oracle—and they have accepted—we call upon those publications to make known the contents of the communiqué which Luskin holds at the center of his assertions. Quoting only those snippets that Mr. Luskin chooses to characterize in his statements is not enough. If Special Counsel Patrick Fitzgerald has chosen to exonerate Mr. Rove, let his words—in their entirety—be made public."

Welcome to blog world. These people are going to stop a war, change the direction of our politics? They make Barbra Streisand sound like Che Guevara.

2006

New Orleans After Katrina

Alexander Cockburn and Jeffrey St. Clair

TUESDAY NIGHT, AS WATER ROSE TO 20 FEET THROUGH MOST of New Orleans, CNN relayed an advisory that food in refrigerators would last only four hours, and would have to be thrown out. The next news item from CNN was an indignant bellow about "looters" of 7/11s and a Wal-Mart. Making no attempt to conceal the racist flavor of the coverage, the press openly describes white survivors as "getting food from a flooded store," while blacks engaged in the same struggle for survival are smeared as "looters."

The reverence for property is now the underlying theme of many newscasts, with defense of The Gap being almost the first order of duty for the forces of law and order. But the citizens looking for clothes to wear and food to eat are made of tougher fiber and are more desperate than the polite demonstrators who guarded The Gap and kindred chains in Seattle in 1999 during the WTO protests. The police in New Orleans are only patrolling in large armed groups. One spoke of "meeting some resistance," as if the desperate citizens of New Orleans were Iraqi insurgents.

Also on Tuesday night the newscasts were reporting that in a city whose desperate state is akin to the Dacca in Bangladesh a few years ago, there were precisely seven Coast Guard helicopters in operation. Where are the National Guard helicopters? Presumably strafing Iraqi citizens on the roads outside Baghdad and Fallujah.

As the war's unpopularity soars, there will be millions asking, why is the National Guard in Iraq, instead of helping the afflicted along the Gulf in the first crucial hours, before New Orleans,

Biloxi, and Mobile turn into toxic toilet bowls with thousands marooned on the tops of houses.

As trapped residents face the real prospect of perishing for lack of a way out of the flooding city, Bush's first response was to open the spigots of the Strategic Petroleum Reserve at the request of oil companies and to order the EPA to eliminate Clean Air standards at power plants and oil refineries across the nation, supposedly to increase fuel supplies—a goal long sought by his cronies at the big oil companies.

In his skittish Rose Garden press conference, Bush told the imperiled people of the Gulf Coast not to worry, the Corps of Engineers was on the way to begin the reconstruction of the Southland. But these are the same cadre of engineers who, after three years of work, have yet to get water and electrical power running in Baghdad for more than three hours a day.

It didn't have to be this bad. Much of New Orleans need not have been lost. Hundreds of people need not have perished. Yet, it now seems clear that the Bush administration sacrificed New Orleans to pursue its mad war on Iraq.

As the New Orleans *Times-Picayune* has reported in a devastating series of articles over the last two years, city and state officials and the Corps of Engineers had repeatedly requested funding to strengthen the levees along Lake Pontchartrain that breached in the wake of the flood. But the Bush administration rebuffed the requests repeatedly, reprogramming the funding from levee enhancement to Homeland Security and the war on Iraq.

This year the Bush administration slashed funding for the New Orleans Corps of Engineers by $71.2 million, a stunning 44.2 per cent reduction from its 2001 levels. A Corps' report noted at the time that "major hurricane and flood protection projects will not be awarded to local engineering firms.... Also, a study to determine ways to protect the region from a Category 5 hurricane has been shelved for now."

Work on the 17th Street levee, which breached on Monday night, came to a halt earlier this summer for the lack of $2 million.

"It appears that the money has been moved in the president's budget to handle Homeland Security and the war in Iraq, and I suppose that's the price we pay," Walter Maestri, emergency management chief for Jefferson Parish, Louisiana, told the *Times-Picayune* in June of last year. "Nobody locally is happy that the levees can't be finished, and we are doing everything we can to make the case that this is a security issue for us."

These are damning revelations that should fuel calls from both parties for Bush's resignation or impeachment.

The greatest concern for poor people in these days has come from President Hugo Chavez of Venezuela, who—fresh from a chat with Fidel Castro—has announced that Venezuela will be offering America's poor discounted gas through its Citgo chain. He says his price will knock out the predatory pricing at every American pump. Citgo should issue to purchasers of each tankful of gas vouchers for free medical consultations via the Internet with the Cuban doctors in Venezuela.

No politician in America has raised the issue of predatory pricing as gasoline soars above $3 a gallon. The last time there was any critical talk about the oil companies was thirty years ago.

Maybe the terrible disaster along the Gulf Coast will awaken people to the unjust ways in which our society works. That's often the effect of natural disasters, as with the Mexican earthquake, where the laggardly efforts of the police prompted ordinary citizens to take matters into their own hands.

2006

The Attack on Micro-Radio

Alexander Cockburn and Jeffrey St. Clair

RUST THE BROADCASTING INDUSTRY TO RECOIL IN HORROR at the prospect of more choice for the American people, who—be it never forgotten—actually own the airwaves this same broadcasting industry claims as its own. In a shameful vote on April 13, 2000, just before the Easter recess and after furious lobbying by the National Association of Broadcasters (NAB), the House of Representatives voted 274 to 110 to scuttle one of the few creditable rulings issued in recent years by the Federal Communications Commission. Congress has issued a stark "No" to free speech and democratic communications, just as ruthlessly as any dictator sending troops into a broadcasting station.

The broadcasting lobby has been on a rampage ever since the FCC voted on January 20, 2000, to authorize license applications for noncommercial FM stations to begin low-power broadcasting to their communities. Such stations, with a range of up to ten miles, would be able to get on the air for as little as $1,000.

The FCC's January ruling came as a welcome surprise amid the pell-mell concentration of station ownership prompted by the 1996 Telecommunications Act. The FCC acted partly to show it's not an industry serf, partly to head off the possibility of court rulings endorsing low-watt radio on free-speech grounds. The very same day as the House vote, April 13, 2000, the Court of Appeals for the Ninth Circuit gave a friendly hearing to low-watt pioneer Steve Dunifer, who has been battling the FCC in court for many years.

Even so, the FCC did bow to industry pressure on a technical question of enormous importance, the issue of "separation requirements." Old FCC rules required three separations between one FM station and another. This meant that if a station is broadcasting on, say, 91.1, another broadcaster couldn't grab 91.3, 91.5 or 91.7. The next available frequency would be 91.9. This effectively meant that the only FM frequencies available to new low-power stations were in virtually uninhabited regions of the country, mostly desert.

Technology has changed greatly since those old rules were made, and by the new millennium the FCC was prepared to move to a separation requirement of one, regarded by independent communications engineers as quite sufficient to preserve the integrity of existing FM signals. But finally the FCC flinched in the face of fierce NAB pressure, and its January 20 ruling called for a separation requirement of two, meaning that there would be no new low-watt stations operating legally in cities like New York, Los Angeles, or San Francisco.

But this still wasn't enough for the broadcasting industry. Even as the FCC ruling prompted hundreds of excited nonprofit groups to ready their license applications, NAB lobbyists began to deploy across Capitol Hill. To befuddled lawmakers, these lobbyists played an utterly fraudulent CD purporting to show the chaos on the airwaves that would be caused by the new two-separation requirement. Engineers from the FCC and from legal, church, and community groups came to hearings and demonstrated the fraudulence of the NAB's claims.

But by now lawmakers were being pressed by an NAB ally, formerly furtive but now brazen in its stance: National Public Radio. Kevin Klose, president of NPR, stated flatly in a recent Radio World broadcast that "the American public would not be well served by an FCC ruling that creates LPFM [low-power FM] at the expense of the existing public radio services." Klose has good reason to be afraid. Ever since NPR forced its affiliates to accept nationally syndicated NPR programming, the proportion of locally originated and community-oriented programming on these public radio stations has plummeted, and many listeners are discontented. Low-power FM is a threat to the NPR empire.

There's another, more sinister factor in NPR's opposition. Both Klose and the boss of the Corporation for Public Broadcasting, Robert Coonrod, come from careers in U.S. government propaganda abroad. Klose ran Radio Free Europe and Radio Liberty, long a stamping ground for the CIA. Coonrod oversaw the Voice of America and both Radio and TV Martí. As Peter Franck of the National Lawyers Guild's Committee on Democratic Communications puts it, "Klose and Coonrod come out of the national security state. Their instinct is to see federally-funded public radio as an actual or potential propaganda arm of government, and they're terrified of independent voices." Indeed, Coonrod has been intimately involved in efforts to curb the independence of stations in the noncommercial Pacifica network, which is now the object of an admirable strike by Pacifica Network News reporters.

The awful congressional action came as the consequence of a deal between Republican Michael Oxley and Democrat John Dingell, whereby the FCC will be forced to revert to the old three-frequency separation requirement, which would mean no more than 70 low-watt stations nationwide, all of them in the boonies. The FCC's two-frequency separation requirement of January would have allowed for about 1,000 low-watt stations. The bill piously calls for new studies by the FCC but is emphatic that the commission can never change separation requirements without congressional authority.

2000

The Hunt for the Smoking Gun

Alexander Cockburn

A S LONG AS I'VE LIVED IN AMERICA I'VE ENJOYED THE COMIC ritual known as the "hunt for the smoking gun," a process by which our official press tries to inoculate itself and its readers against political and economic realities.

The big smoking gun question back in 1973 and 1974 concerned Richard Nixon. Back and forth the ponderous debate raged in editorial columns and news stories: Was this or that disclosure a "smoking gun?" Fairly early in the game, it was clear to about 95 per cent of the population that Nixon was a liar, a crook, and guilty as charged. But the committee rooms on Capitol Hill and the Sunday talk shows were still filled with people holding up guns with smoke pouring from the barrel telling one another solemnly that no, the appearance of smoke and stench of recently detonated cordite notwithstanding, this was not yet the absolute, definitive smoking gun.

So it became clear that the great smoking gun hunt was really about timing, about gauging the correct temperature of the political waters. Then suddenly, in the late summer of 1974, that impalpable entity known as "elite sentiment" sensed that the scandal was becoming subversive of public order, that it was time to throw Nixon overboard and move on. A "new" tape—though hundreds of others had already made Nixon's guilt plain—was swiftly identified as "the smoking gun" and presto! Nixon was on the next plane to California.

In the mid-1970s post-Watergate euphoria, smoking guns were in fashion. In the Church Intelligence Committee hearings they actually held up a gun to demonstrate the profuse, well-documented efforts of the CIA to assassinate Fidel Castro. In other hearing rooms witnesses testified that multinational corporations offered bribes to win business.

Appropriately enough, it was a newspaper publisher who stepped forward in the late fall of 1974 to announce that the smoking gun show was now officially closed. At the annual meeting of the Magazine Publishers Association, Katharine Graham, boss of the Washington Post Company, sternly cautioned her fellow czars of the communication industry (many of them bribed to endorse Nixon in 1972 by his gift of the monopoly license to print money, known as Joint Operating Agreements).

"The press these days," Mrs. Graham declared, "should...be rather careful about its role. We may have acquired some tendencies about over-involvement that we had better overcome. We had better not yield to the temptation to go on refighting the next [sic] war and see conspiracy and cover-up where they do not exist."

By 1975 smoking guns were a thing of the past. The *coup de grâce* was PBS' *MacNeil/Lehrer Report*, which started in October 1975, dedicated to the proposition that there are two sides to every question, and reality is not an exciting affair of smoking guns, crooked businessmen and lying politicians but a dull continuum in which all involved are struggling disinterestedly for the public weal. In this new, prudent post-Watergate era, which has stretched through to the present day, there were no smoking guns. It wasn't long before those documented attempts to assassinate Castro became "alleged attempts" or, the final fate of many a smoking gun, "an old story."

CIA involvement in opium smuggling in Southeast Asia? There were smoking guns aplenty. In a 1987 *Frontline* documentary, Tony Po gave an on-camera interview confirming that in his capacity as a CIA officer he had given the mercenary general Vang Pao an airplane with which to transport heroin, because Vang Pao's use of the CIA air fleet was proving embarrassing. "We painted it nice and fancy," Po reminisced jovially. These days, the

CIA's complicity in shuttling heroin that came home to America in body bags from Vietnam has retreated to the decorous status of being an "allegation" and, simultaneously, "an old story."

Iran-Contra, cocaine-for-arms shuttles supervised by the CIA? More smoking guns in every filing cabinet, and all over Oliver North's diary. Ten years later Gary Webb of the *San Jose Mercury News* fished out further smoking guns and was rewarded by having his career destroyed by the *Washington Post*, *New York Times* and *Los Angeles Times*. When the hubbub died down, the CIA's inspector general admitted in his reports that yes, there were smoking guns, but the press only read the CIA's press releases, which strenuously maintained the opposite.

I think it was in the Reagan era that the smoking-gun lobby got decisively routed. Month after month the official press would write respectfully about Reagan's press conferences as though the president was a competent captain of the national ship instead of a fogged-up fantasist.

Another *coup de grâce* came in Clinton time, when the hunt for smoking guns became either incomprehensible (Jeff Gerth's stories on Whitewater) or tacky (Clinton's physical interactions with Monica Lewinsky). Special Prosecutor Ken Starr cried out that Yes, he had the smoking gun. The people looked at the stained dress he proudly flourished and said, If that's a smoking gun, we're not interested.

There are enough smoking guns in the Iraq saga to stock a whole new national museum. It's what makes the current 2005 muttering in the official press about the Downing Street memo so comical, with all the huff and puff about the "blogosphere" and how yes this is an old story, and an "uncorroborated" one (like all those stories from detainees about desecration of the Koran).

What's striking to me is how querulous and old-fashioned those "old story" put-downs about the Downing Street memo by Todd Purdum and others in the *New York Times*, or Howard Kurtz and Dana Milbank in the *Washington Post*, sound rather like very old uncles wagging their fingers at naughty little children and admonishing them to stay quiet until all the facts are in.

But the facts are in, and the naughty children have the public megaphones. The rules of the game are changing. History is one big smoking gun and the function of the official press is to say this isn't so. So what happens when fewer and fewer people take the official press seriously, or even read it?

2005

A Smoking Gun That Actually Smoked

Alexander Cockburn and Jeffrey St. Clair

JUST UNDER TWO YEARS AGO, IN LATE 1996, JOHN DEUTCH, at that time director of the CIA, traveled to a town meeting in South Central Los Angeles to confront a community outraged by charges that the Agency had been complicit in the importing of cocaine into California in the 1980s. Amid heated exchanges, Deutch publicly pledged an internal investigation by the CIA's inspector general that would leave no stone unturned.

It is now possible to review, albeit in substantially censored form, the results of that probe. At the start of 1998 the inspector general, Fred Hitz, released a volume specifically addressing charges made in 1996 in the *San Jose Mercury News*. Then, a few months later, Hitz finally made available for public scrutiny a second report addressing broader allegations about drug running by Nicaraguan Contras.

That first volume released ten months ago was replete with damaging admissions. The report describes a cable from the CIA's Directorate of Operations dated October 22, 1982, describing a prospective meeting between Contra leaders in Costa Rica for "an exchange in [U.S.] of narcotics for arms." But the CIA's Director of Operations instructed the Agency's field office not to look into this imminent arms-for-drugs transaction in light of the apparent involvement of U.S. persons throughout." In other words, the CIA knew that Contra leaders were scheduling an arms-for-drugs exchange, and the Agency was prepared to let the deal proceed.

In 1984, the inspector general discloses, the CIA intervened with the U.S. Justice Department to seek the return from police custody of $36,800 in cash that had been confiscated from Nicaraguan drug-smuggling gang in the Bay Area whose leader, Norwin Meneses, was a prominent Contra fund-raiser. The money had been taken during what was at the time the largest seizure of cocaine in the history of California.

The CIA's inspector general said the Agency took action to have the money returned in order "to protect an operational equity, i.e., a Contra support group in which it [CIA] had an operational interest." Hitz also unearthed a CIA memo from that time revealing that the Agency understood the need to keep this whole affair under wraps because, according to the memo (written by the CIA's assistant general counsel), "there are sufficient factual details which would cause certain damage to our image and program in Central America."

The 146-page first volume is full of admissions of this nature but these two disclosures alone—allowing a Contra drug deal to go forward, and taking extraordinary action to recoup the proceeds of a drug deal gone awry—should have been greeted as smoking guns, confirming charges made since 1985 about the Agency's role.

The report issued by Hitz a few weeks ago is even richer in devastating disclosures. The inspector general sets forth a sequence of CIA cable traffic showing that as early as the summer of 1981, the Agency knew that the Contra leadership "had decided to engage in drug trafficking to the United States to raise funds for its activities."

The leader of the group whose plans a CIA officer was thus describing was Enriqué Bermudez, a man hand-picked by the Agency to run the military operations of the main Contra organization. It was Bermudez who told Contra fund-raisers and drug traffickers Norwin Meneses and Danilo Blandon (as the latter subsequently testified for the government to a federal grand jury,) that the end justified the means and they should raise revenue in this way.

One of Bermudez' associates in those early days was Justiniano Perez, who headed up sabotage operations for the Contra group. Perez, presumably one of the men Reagan was referring to when he called the Contra leaders the "moral equivalent of our founding fathers," aggressively pursued a plan of bombings of civilian centers in Nicaragua and assassinations. He also developed a Contra fundraising scheme that, according to CIA memos, relied on "kidnapping, extortion and robbery." In late 1981, Perez quit the main Contra unit because he didn't feel it was ruthless enough. The CIA desperately wanted to bring him back. A 1982 CIA memo asked if Perez "could be influenced to employ tactics other than those used by terrorists." The answer the Agency apparently wanted to hear was "no." By 1984, Perez was viewed as "the only person in the entire FDN with the leadership charisma and military tactical ability to make the movement go forward in the manner CIA would like."

The CIA was uneasily aware that its failure to advise the Contras to stop drug trafficking might land it in difficulties. Hitz documents that the Agency knew that at that time it was obligated to report Contra plans to run drugs to the Justice Department and other agencies such as FBI, DEA, and Customs. Nonetheless the CIA kept quiet, and in 1982 got a waiver from the Justice Department giving a legal basis for its inaction.

Hitz enumerates the Contra leaders ("several dozen") the CIA knew to be involved in drug trafficking, along with another two dozen involved in Contra supply missions and fund raising. He confirms that the CIA knew that Ilopango air base in El Salvador was an arms-for-drugs Contra transshipment point, and discloses a memo in which a CIA officer orders the DEA "not to make any inquiries to anyone re Hangar No. 4 at Ilopango."

Thus, the CIA's own inspector general shows that from the very start of the U.S. war on Nicaragua the CIA knew the Contra were planning to bring cocaine into the U.S.A. It did nothing to stop the traffic and, when other government agencies began to probe, the CIA impeded their investigations. When Contra money raisers were arrested, the Agency came to their aid and retrieved their drug money from the police.

So, was the Agency complicit in drug trafficking into Los Angeles and other cities? It is impossible to read Hitz's report and not conclude that this was the case.

CIA: We Knew All Along

The *New York Times* has taken the first step in what should by rights be one of the steepest climb-downs in journalistic history. We allude to a story by James Risen, which appeared on page five of the *NYT*, on October 10, 1998. The story, headed "CIA Said to Ignore Charges of Contra Drug Dealing in '80s," must have been an unappetizing one for Risen to write, since it forced him to eat rib-sticking amounts of crow.

The CIA, Risen wrote, "repeatedly ignored or failed to investigate allegations of drug trafficking by the anti-Sandinista rebels in the 1980s." Risen went on to report that, according to the long-awaited second volume of CIA Inspector General Fred Hitz's investigation, the CIA had concealed both from Congress and other government agencies its knowledge that the Contras had from the very beginning decided to smuggle drugs to support its operations.

Probably out of embarrassment Risen postponed till his fourteenth paragraph the information from Hitz's explosive report that should rightly have been the lead to the story, which itself should rightly have been on the front page: "In September 1981, as a small group of rebels was being formed from former soldiers in the National Guard of the deposed Nicaraguan dictator, Anastasio Somoza Debayle, a CIA informant reported that the leadership of the fledgling group had decided to smuggle drugs to the United States to support its operation."

Thus does Risen put the lie to all past reports on this topic in the *New York Times* and his own previous story in the *Los Angeles*

Times parroting CIA and Justice Department press releases to the effect that vigorous internal investigation had entirely exonerated the Agency. In that single paragraph just noted we have four momentous confessions by the CIA's own inspector general. One: the Contras were involved in drug running from the very start. Two: the CIA knew the Contras were smuggling drugs into the U.S. in order to raise money. Three: this was a decision not made by profiteers on the fringe of the Contras, but by the leadership. Four: the CIA, even before it got a waiver from the Justice Department, was concealing its knowledge from the Congress and from other U.S. government agencies such as the DEA and the FBI. Remember also that the Contra leadership, was handpicked by the CIA, both in the form of its civilian head, Adolfo Calero, and of its military director, Enriqué Bermudez. The fact that the *New York Times* chose to run this story on the Saturday of a three-day holiday, on an inside page, suggests considerable embarrassment on the part of a newspaper that has had a long history of attacks on those who have charged CIA complicity in Contra drug smuggling, from Senator John Kerry, to Gary Webb, to the present writers in our book *Whiteout: The CIA, Drugs and the Press*.

From 1986 to 1988, Senator John Kerry of Massachusetts probed allegations about Contra drug running and CIA complicity in same, and issued a 1,000-page report. Even while the hearings were under way, the *New York Times* belittled his investigation in a three-part series by its reporter Keith Schneider, who attacked Kerry for relying on the testimony of pilots, many of them in prison. Some months after this series was published, Schneider was asked by the weekly paper *In These Times* why he had taken that approach. Schneider replied that the charges were so explosive that they could "shatter the Republic. I think it's so damaging the implications are so extraordinary, that for us to run the story, it had better be based on the most solid evidence we could amass." In other words, it should be based on a written confession by the Director of Central Intelligence.

And now, over a decade later, we have a written confession from the CIA's inspector general about the "explosive" and the "extraordinary" charges, and the story ends up on an inside page on an inconspicuous Saturday.

Two weeks earlier, the *NYT Book Review* featured an article on our book, *Whiteout: The CIA, Drugs and the Press*, and Webb's book *Dark Alliance*. The author was James Adams, a Washington-based hack who used to eke out a twilit existence as correspondent for the Murdoch-owned London *Sunday Times* before transferring from that lowly billet to the ignominious function of relaying Agency handouts and news droppings from Congressional intelligence committees for UPI.

Adams leveled two charges against *Whiteout*, to the effect that there was no evidence that any Contras were running drugs, and that our book could not be taken seriously because we had not solicited a confession of guilt from the Agency. In fact, as long ago as 1985, reporters accumulated and published evidence of Contra drug running. Among these reporters were Bob Parry and Brian Barger of Associated Press and Leslie Cockburn in documentaries for CBS. So far as Agency confessions are concerned, *Whiteout*, completed in late June 1998 and published at the start of September, contained precisely the main thrust of the inspector general's conclusions in the second volume, now discussed by Risen. Hitz anticipated this written report in his verbal testimony to Congress in May 1998 where he acknowledged the Agency's knowledge of Contra drug links and also disclosed that in 1982 CIA director William Casey had gotten a waiver from Reagan's attorney general, William French Smith, allowing the CIA to keep secret from other government agencies its knowledge of drug trafficking by its assets, contractors and other Contra figures.

Unlike the *Washington Post*, the *New York Times* never reported Hitz's sensational March 1998 testimony, and in his October 10 story Risen disingenuously fails to mention the 1982 waiver Hitz disclosed at that time. The omission has the effect of implying that the Agency was somehow acting in a "rogue" capacity, whereas the 1982 waiver shows clearly that the Reagan presidency was foursquare behind the whole strategy of concealment of what the Agency was up to. As we have written on the opening page of *Whiteout*, "Whether it was Truman's meddling in China, which created Burmese opium kings; or the Kennedy brothers' obsession with killing Fidel Castro; or Nixon's command for 'more assassinations' in Vietnam, the CIA has always been the obedient executor of the will of the U.S. government, starting with the White House."

For readers of the *New York Times* in its home port the newspaper's climb-down was not nearly as drastic as in the edition distributed in the Washington, D.C. area. The edition available in New York City did not have the fourteenth paragraph (quoted above) nor indeed five other concluding paragraphs. Why? A *Times* editor simply chopped them off to allow space for a large Bloomingdale's ad for a drug sale, thus confirming the truth of A.J. Leibling's observation years ago that the news diet of New Yorkers depends entirely on a bunch of dry goods merchants. The full story was also available on the *New York Times'* website, but not on the Lexis-Nexis database, where it ends at the thirteenth paragraph, plus a bland and uninformative final three-line resumé of the missing material. The Nexis database is where most people looking for Risen's story would go.

1998

What Happened to O'Reilly's Loofa? A Philological Inquiry

Alexander Cockburn

HANKSGIVING 2005 BROUGHT US THE ONE-MONTH ANNI-
versary of Bill O'Reilly's disclosure on his show that "to
protect my family" he had settled with Ms Andrea Mackris
and her lawyer Benedict Morelli, thus cutting off what millions of
O'Reilly haters had hoped would be a protracted season of public
humiliation for Fox's apex bully.

The settlement established that all parties agreed there had
been no wrong doing and as an offering of good faith O'Reilly
(if you believe the New York *Daily News*) has paid anywhere from
$2 million to $10 million to Mackris, nice money if true, though
not as nice as the $60 million Morelli had originally suggested to
O'Reilly as a satisfactory figure.

But there remains the mystery of the transmuted loofa, about
which I had been hoping for some pleasing courtroom exchanges. Let's pick up the thread in the court document lodged in
Nassau county, N.J., by Morelli on behalf of Ms. Mackris.

11.06 PM SEPTEMBER 1, 2004. O'Reilly calls Mackris, a 33 year-
old innocent from the Show Me State, working as a producer on
The O'Reilly Factor. She, poor lamb, says she thought it was about
business and told him she'd call him right back. At this point, we
surmise Ms Mackris may have activated a recording device and
with the tape rolling, dialed the boss, who promptly got down to
business, launching into what the complaint harshly stigmatizes
as "a lewd and lascivious, unsolicited, and disturbing sexually
graphic talk," about how he imagines he would handle personal
relations with Ms Mackris if they were in the West Indies.

First he'd get two wines into Ms. Mackris, "maybe intravenously." Then, "You would basically be in the shower and then I would come in and I'd join you and you would have your back to me and I would take the little loofa thing..."

A loofa! This is no Motel 6, though it's not the Ritz either, where loofas would scarcely be "little," though admittedly size doesn't come up in the description of loofa offered by *The American Heritage® Dictionary of the English Language: Fourth Edition. 2000.*

> SYLLABICATION:
> loo·fa
>
> VARIANT FORMS:
> or loo·fah also luf·fa
>
> NOUN:
> **1.** Any of several Old World tropical vines of the genus *Luffa*, having cylindrical fruit with a fibrous, spongelike interior. **2.** The dried, fibrous part of the loofa fruit, used as a washing sponge or as a filter. Also called *dishcloth gourd, vegetable sponge.*
>
> ETYMOLOGY:
> Arabic *loof* singulative form of *loofa*.

And what is O'Reilly, so strong, so masterful, planning to do with this... thing of Arab origin? "...I would take the little loofa thing and kinda' soap your back... and rub it all over you, get you to relax, hot water...and um... You know, you'd feel the tension drain out of you and um you still would be with your back to me then I would kinda' put my arms—it's one of those mitts, those loofa mitts you know, so I got my hands in it... and I would put it around front, kinda' rub your tummy with it and then with my other hand I would start to massage your boobs, get your nipples really hard... 'cuz I like that and you have really spectacular boobs...."

At this point, in the document filed at the court house in Nassau County, which would indeed appear to be a transcript right down to the ums, there's an ellipse.

"So anyway I'd be rubbing your big boobs and getting your nipples really hard, kinda kissing your neck from behind... and then the other hand with the falafel thing..."

NOUN:
1. Ground spiced chickpeas shaped into balls and fried. **2.** A sandwich filled with such a mixture.

What happened to the loofa?

Maybe Abe Foxman called him on the other line to warn about "going Arab on us."

And what is O'Reilly planning to do with the falafel?

"...I would take the other hand with the falafel thing [*sic*] and I'd put it on your pussy, but you'd have to do it really light, just kind of a tease business."

According to the courtroom document available for inspection on Smoking Gun (http://www.thesmokinggun.com/archive/1013043mackris1.html) the quality of the conversation goes down hill from there on in. It may be that O'Reilly's tour of Arab commodities was proleptic, as he began to shift gears through the vowel sounds. For an interesting discussion of the processes involved I recommend Sebastiano Timpanaro's philological investigation, published in translation years ago by Verso, entitled *The Freudian Slip*. From loofa to falafel, to what? Let Ms Mackris and her lawyer tell it their way. O'Reilly "suggested he would perform oral sex" on Ms Mackris and she would "perform fellatio on his 'big cock' but not complete the act," maybe to conserve his energies for further deployment of the little loofa or the falafel, though the lifespan of a falafel in a shower is surely limited in duration. After the exciting fa-fel-fell monologue and what to Ms Mackris' "repulsed" ear sounded like the hum of a vibrator and acoustic intimations of satisfactory climax O'Reilly launched into a discussion concerning how good he was during a recent appearance on *The Today Show*.

Mind you, though O'Reilly may have thought he was on safe political ground with presumptively Israeli falafel, the word—and indeed the snack—is also of Arab origin.

> ETYMOLOGY:
> Arabic *falfil*, pl. of *filfil*, pepper, probably from Sanskrit pippal. See pepper.

Thanks ever so much, Ms Mackris. It must have been just horrible for you, but it was in a good cause. You gave us a bright moment in a dark year.

2005

End It: Hunter Thompson
and Gary Webb

Alexander Cockburn

GUESS I CAN CALL MYSELF ONE OF THE DYLAN GENERATION SINCE, at 63, I'm the same age as him but the prose stylists that allured an Anglo-Irish lad hopelessly strapped into the corsets of Latinate gentility were always those of American rough-housers: first, in the mid-Fifties Jack Kerouac, then Edward Abbey, then Hunter Thompson.

Thank God I never tried to imitate any of them. Thompson probably spawned more bad prose than anyone since Hemingway, but they all taught me that at its most rapturous, its most outraged, its most exultant, American prose can let go and teach you to let go, to embrace the vastness, the richness, the beauty, and the grotesqueries of America in all its thousand landscapes.

I tried to re-read Kerouac's *On the Road* a few years ago and put it down soon enough. That's a book for excited teenagers. Abbey at full stretch remains a great writer and he'll stay in the pantheon for all time. Lately sitting in motels along the highway I've been dipping into his diaries, *Confessions of a Barbarian*, and laughing every couple of pages. "Writing for the *National Geographic*," Abbey grumbled, "is like trying to masturbate in ski mitts."

Could Thompson have written that? Probably not. When it came to sex and stimulation of the synapses by agents other than drugs or booze or violent imagery Thompson was silent, unlike Abbey who loved women. Thompson wrote for the guys, at a pitch so frenzied, so over-the-top in its hyperbolic momentum that often enough it reminded me of the squeakier variant of the same style developed by his *Herald-Trib* stable mate and exponent of the "New Journalism," Tom Wolf. In their respective stylistic uniforms they always seemed hysterically frightened of normalcy, particularly in the shape of girls, so keenly appreciated by Abbey.

Thompson's best writing was always in the form of flourishes, of pell-mell bluster wrenched from himself for the anxious editors waiting well past deadline at *Scanlans* or *Rolling Stone*, and in his later years often put together from his jottings by the writers and editors aware that a new "Fear and Loathing" on the masthead was a sure-fire multiplier of newsstand sales. Overall, Thompson's political perceptions weren't that interesting except for occasional bitter flashes, as in this sour and prescient paragraph written in 1972:

> How many more of these goddam elections are we going to have to write off as lame but "regrettably necessary" holding actions? And how many more of these stinking double-downer sideshows will we have to go through before we can get ourselves straight enough to put together some kind of national election that will give me, and the at least 20 million people I tend to agree with, a chance to vote for something, instead of always being faced with that old familiar choice between the lesser of two evils? I understand, along with a lot of other people, that the big thing, this year, is Beating Nixon. But that was also the big thing, as I recall, twelve years ago in 1960—and as far as I can tell, we've gone from bad to worse to rotten since then, and the outlook is for more of the same.

There's nothing much to the notion of "gonzo" beyond the delighted projections of Thompson's readers. The introduction of the reporter as roistering first-person narrator? Mark Twain surely did that, albeit sedately, and less sedately we had Henry Miller, another man who loved women, pushing the envelope far further than Thompson. (Which of the road books will last longest between Miller's *Air-Conditioned Nightmare*, *On the Road*, and *Fear and Loathing in Las Vegas*? Kerouac and then Thompson drove faster but they didn't write better.) Norman Mailer took the form to the level of genius in *Advertisements for Myself*, with political perceptions acuter and writing sharper by far than any-thing Thompson ever produced.

"Gonzo" was an act, defined by its beholders: the thought that here was one of Us, fried on drugs, hanging onto the cliff edge of reality only by his fingernails, doing hyperbolic battle with the pomposities and corruptions of Politics as Usual. And no man was ever a more willing captive of the Gonzo myth he created, decked out in its increasingly frayed bunting of *Fear and Loathing*..., "The Strange and Terrible...," decorated with Ralph Stedman's graphic counterpoints.

Like Evel Knievel, Thompson's stunts demanded that he arc higher and further with each successive sentence's outrage to propriety, most memorably in his obit for Richard Nixon:

> If the right people had been in charge of Nixon's funeral, his casket would have been launched into one of those open-sewage canals that empty into the ocean just south of Los Angeles. He was a swine of a man and a jabbering dupe of a president. Nixon was so crooked that he needed servants to help him screw his pants on every morning. Even his funeral was illegal. He was queer in the deepest way. His body should have been burned in a trash bin.

Kerouac ended sadly at 47. As Abbey nastily put it, "Jack Kerouac, like a sick refrigerator, worked too hard at keeping cool and died on his mama's lap from alcohol and infantilism." Abbey himself passed gloriously at 62, carried from the hospital by his pals to die at his own pace without tubes dripping brief reprieves into his veins, then buried in the desert without the sanction of the state.

How about Thompson? His Boston lawyer George Tobia Jr. told the *Globe* the 67-year-old author sat in his kitchen Sunday afternoon in his home in Woody Creek, Colo., stuck a .45-caliber handgun in his mouth, and killed himself while his wife listened to the shot on the phone and his son and daughter-in-law were in another room of his house. His wife had no idea what had happened until she returned home later.

Seems creepy to me, same way Gary Webb blowing his brains out a while back with a handgun was creepy. Why give the loved ones that finale as a souvenir? I suppose Thompson's message was: "We were together at the end." Webb was truly alone. He lifted the curtain on one little sideshow of the American Empire, and could never quite fathom that when you do that The Man doesn't forget or forgive. Thompson engaged the Empire on his own terms and quit the battlefield on his own terms too, which I guess is what Gonzo is all about.

2005

Index

AK Press

ORDERING INFORMATION

AK Press
674-A 23rd Street
Oakland, CA 94612-1163
U.S.A
(510) 208-1700
www.akpress.org
akpress@akpress.org

AK Press
PO Box 12766
Edinburgh, EH8 9YE
Scotland
(0131) 555-5165
www.akuk.com
ak@akedin.demon.co.uk

The addresses above would be delighted to provide you with the latest complete AK catalog, featuring several thousand books, pamphlets, zines, audio products, video products, and stylish apparel published & distributed by AK Press. Alternatively, check out our websites for the complete catalog, latest news and updates, events, and secure ordering.

Also Available from AK Press

The first audio collection from Alexander Cockburn on compact disc.

Beating the Devil

Alexander Cockburn, ISBN: 1 902593 49 9 • CD • $14.98

In this collection of recent talks, maverick commentator Alexander Cockburn defiles subjects ranging from Colombia to the American presidency to the Missile Defense System. Whether he's skewering the fallacies of the war on drugs or illuminating the dark crevices of secret government, his erudite and extemporaneous style warms the hearts of even the stodgiest cynics of the left.

Available from CounterPunch/AK Press

The Case Against Israel
by Michael Neumann

Wielding a buzzsaw of logic, Professor Neumann dismantles plank-by-plank the Zionist rationale for Israel as religious state entitled to trample upon the basic human rights of non-Jews. Along the way, Neumann also offers a passionate amicus brief for the plight of the Palestinian people.

Other Lands Have Dreams: From Baghdad to Pekin Prison
by Kathy Kelly

At a moment when so many despairing peace activists have thrown in the towel, Kathy Kelly, a witness to some of history's worst crimes, never relinquishes hope. Other Lands Have Dreams is literary testimony of the highest order, vividly recording the secret casualties of our era, from the hundreds of thousands of Iraqi children inhumanely denied basic medical care, clean water and food by the U.S. overlords to young mothers sealed inside the sterile dungeons of American prisons in the name of the merciless war on drugs.

Dime's Worth of Difference: Beyond the Lesser of Two Evils
Edited by Alexander Cockburn and Jeffrey St. Clair

Everything you wanted to know about one-party rule in America.

Whiteout: the CIA, Drugs and the Press
by Alexander Cockburn and Jeffrey St. Clair, Verso.

The involvement of the CIA with drug traffickers is a story that has slouched into the limelight every decade or so since the creation of the Agency. In Whiteout, here at last is the full saga.

Been Brown So Long It Looked Like Green to Me: the Politics of Nature
by Jeffrey St. Clair, Common Courage Press.

Covering everything from toxics to electric power plays, St. Clair draws a savage profile of how money and power determine the state of our environment, gives a vivid account of where the environment stands today and what to do about it.

Imperial Crusades: Iraq, Afghanistan and Yugoslavia
by Alexander Cockburn and Jeffrey St. Clair, Verso.

A chronicle of the lies that are now returning each and every day to haunt the deceivers in Washington and London, the secret agendas and the under-reported carnage of these wars. We were right and they were wrong, and this book proves the case. Never leave home without it.

Why We Publish CounterPunch
By Alexander Cockburn and Jeffrey St. Clair

TEN YEARS AGO WE FELT UNHAPPY ABOUT THE STATE OF RADICAL journalism. It didn't have much edge. It didn't have many facts. It was politically timid. It was dull. *CounterPunch* was founded. We wanted it to be the best muckraking newsletter in the country. We wanted it to take aim at the consensus of received wisdom about what can and cannot be reported. We wanted to give our readers a political roadmap they could trust.

A decade later we stand firm on these same beliefs and hopes. We think we've restored honor to muckraking journalism in the tradition of our favorite radical pamphleteers: Edward Abbey, Peter Maurin and Ammon Hennacy, Appeal to Reason, Jacques René Hébert, Tom Paine and John Lilburne.

Every two weeks *CounterPunch* gives you jaw-dropping exposés on: Congress and lobbyists; the environment; labor; the National Security State.

"*CounterPunch* kicks through the floorboards of lies and gets to the foundation of what is really going on in this country", says Michael Ratner, attorney at the Center for Constitutional Rights. "At our house, we fight over who gets to read *CounterPunch* first. Each issue is like spring after a cold, dark winter."

YOU CANNOT MISS ANOTHER ISSUE

A Bush & Botox World

By Saul Landau

Gore Vidal on Saul Landau: "Landau has opened many windows for the rest of us: parts of the world, where we are not usually allowed to know about except to be told how wretched they are."

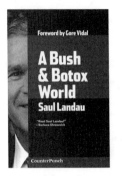

Bush & Botox World provides insight into the culture under which the Bush White House operates. It uses Botox as a metaphor for both the rapid technological change of the globalized world and its superficiality. Landau syncopates visits to modern Vietnam with analysis of the bizarre world of anti-Castro terrorists. He brings readers into the homes of corporate executives and into the street lives of African American kids on east Oakland's streets.

Between the prose pieces, Landau inserts pithy poems on aging, computers and a concert in Istanbul. He takes readers back to the horrors of the 1976 assassination of his friends and colleagues, Orlando Letelier and Ronni Moffitt on Washington, DC's Embassy Row and into the blood-filled streets of Falluja. The allegorical essays on Hearst's Castle and the Salton Sea stand as both insights into the contemporary world and warnings for the next generation.

Available from CounterPunch.org and AK Press
Call 1-800-840-3683
$15.00

The Secret Language of the Crossroads
How the Irish Invented Slang

By Daniel Cassidy

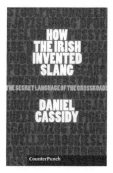

In *How the Irish Invented Slang: The Secret Language of the Crossroad*, Daniel Cassidy co-director and founder of the Irish Studies Program at New College of California cuts through two hundred years worth of Anglo academic "baloney" and reveals the massive, hidden influence of the Irish language on the American language.

Irish words and phrases are scattered all across the American language, regional and class dialects, colloquialism, slang, and specialized jargons like gambling, in the same way Irish-Americans have been scattered across the crossroads of North America for five hundred years.

In a series of essays, including: "Decoding the Gangs of New York," "How the Irish Invented Poker and American Gambling Slang," "The Sanas (Etymology) of Jazz," "Boliver of Brooklyn," and in a *First Dictionary of Irish-American Vernacular*, Cassidy provides the hidden histories and etymologies of hundreds of so-called slang words that have defined the American language and culture like *dude, sucker, swell, poker, faro, cop, scab, fink, moolah, fluke, knack, ballyhoo, baloney*, as well as the hottest word of the 20th century, *jazz*.